The Ignorance of Certainty

By Montagu and Darling

THE PREVALENCE OF NONSENSE

THE IGNORANCE
OF CERTAINTY

Ashley Montagu
and
Edward Darling

HARPER & ROW, PUBLISHERS
New York, Evanston, and London

1817

To William E. Spaulding, Gent.

LIBRARY OF CONGRESS CATALOG CARD NUMBER: 78–123955

Although symbols that have satisfied for centuries may appear temporarily devoid of significance, it is quite often precisely those concepts apparently most lacking in the power to move us that, without warning, can possess the greatest of import when rediscovered at crucial moments or presented in fresh garb. With equal astonishment, we find, conversely, that attainments long considered mythical are, of a sudden, looked upon as having been accomplished by an historical figure, as was the case, for example, with Alexander the Great, almost within his lifetime.

Dorothy Norman, *The Hero: Myth/Image/Symbol*

Who cares what the fact was, when we have made a constellation of it to hang in heaven, an immortal sign?

Ralph Waldo Emerson

Contents

Acknowledgments

Material which cannot be found in print can sometimes be supplied by an authority with practical experience in the field; and many complete strangers into whose lives we have intruded with questions have been extremely generous in supplying information. In some cases our investigations might have come to a halt, or been forced to a simmering condition on a rear burner, without the personal assistance for which we herewith express thanks.

Particularly we owe gratitude to the following: the Reverend Arthur H. Birtles, Church of the Messiah, Birmingham, England, and the writer of "Mercian" in the *Birmingham Post,* for help in tracking down the Lady Godiva story and the publication of the Coventry Corporation, *Godiva of Coventry,* by Joan C. Lancaster.

The Reverend John Nicholls Booth of Long Beach, California, author, lecturer, world traveler, and internationally known magician, for leads on the Indian Rope Trick and refinements of details.

Mr. Richard W. Edgerton of Marineland of Florida in Saint Augustine, for critical information on dolphins including the famous coast-to-coast conversation between Splash in Florida and Speedy on the Pacific coast over 2,500 miles of telephone lines.

Mr. John Hastings of Hastings Laboratories, Bass River, Massachusetts, inventor and developer of special surgical instruments, for sharing an analysis of human sweat made for him by a research associate at Children's Medical Center, Boston, and demonstrating that instead of being a fairly simple product, it often contains at least a score of chemicals in measurable amounts.

Dr. and Mrs. P. K. Hatay of Schaffhausen, Switzerland, for

fascinating details of ions, their sources and euphoric effects.

Dr. Jan Koch-Weser, pharmacologist at Massachusetts General Hospital, Boston, for critical support of the contention that nobody has discovered a true aphrodisiac.

Mr. William D. London of the New York legal firm of Davis, Gilbert, Levine, and Schwartz, for expert opinion on libel and on the statute of limitations.

Dr. J. L. McHugh for a release from the Fish and Wildlife Service of the U.S. Department of the Interior, in which he exposes the r month as a myth in connection with eating oysters.

Mr. Thomas S. O'Bannon of Ferguson, Missouri, for convincing confirmation of the folk legend that the head of a decapitated turtle continues to snap for many hours after severance.

Professor Houston Peterson for the Munchausen lead.

Mr. Nathanial Pulsifer of Listening, Inc., Arlington, Massachusetts, researcher and developer of instruments such as the MDT-5, Man to Dolphin Translator—who kept a dolphin in his own back-yard pool during the summer of 1969—for up-to-the-minute information on dolphins.

Mr. Leo Rosten (*The Joys of Yiddish,* etc.) for his letter giving final clarification of the Voltaire exposé.

Mr. Worth Rowley, attorney, of Washington, D.C., for supplying the actual texts of laws about free speech in public conveyances—especially airplanes—when the subject of conversation is bombs or hijacking.

Mr. John H. Ryther of Woods Hole Oceanographic Institute, for clearing up the misunderstanding about r months and oysters and the poisonous *Gonyaulax*.

Hon. Edward O. Weant, Jr., Associate Judge, Fifth Judicial Circuit of Maryland, Westminster, for permitting us to see his twelve-page opinion in a blasphemy trial, and for brilliantly summarizing the subject of blasphemy and the law over the last two thousand years.

Mr. Frederick C. Wilbour, Jr., Director, Division of Marine Fisheries, Department of Natural Resources, Commonwealth of Massachusetts, for more oyster support.

Preface:
The Road to Canterbury

This book is about beliefs, myths that we believe to be untrue which are in fact true, a kind of magic-lantern show with a sound track. We flash on a picture of some well-known myth, some widely familiar story or allegory or parable that everybody recognizes as part of our cultural heritage, but which, of course, is not "true" in the practical workaday world we live in. Then the authors run along on the sound track, slyly suggesting that no legend exists without a reason, and inviting the reader to consider possible hidden meanings or subtleties of intention behind the fancy. The purpose of the sound track is not to make converts: the reader need not undertake the gargantuan labor of changing his mind if he prefers not to. We merely want to point out some of the rich associations that surround any myth, just because they make fascinating stories in themselves and because they open the most amazing vistas to the speculative mind.

For example, your hand accidentally knocks over a salt shaker at a dinner party. Some salt spills onto the linen. Before your neighbor can say "God bless you!" you have picked up a few grains and thrown them over your left shoulder. Everybody laughs, and the incident is forgotten. But you have reacted almost by reflex signal to a complicated ancient myth whose teaching you do not believe, except as you may harbor some unexplained uneasiness about anything associated with "bad luck," which can take so many forms. Perhaps in today's super sophisticated urban society you would not even bother to toss the salt over your left shoulder. Possibly you would not even think of it. Would you murmur "Gesundheit!" to a friend's sneeze?

In either case you would be crossing the Devil; your purpose is to prevent evil (that is, in the earliest use of "prevent"—get there first to defend the place: "Prevent us, O Lord, in all our doings!"). We take our salt for granted—it's about six cents a pound, thoroughly cleaned and packaged, in an inflated market—and we forget how precious it used to be, especially in communities far from the sea or from natural salt deposits and in cultures where meat and vegetables were boiled instead of roasted, thus losing more of any natural salt in the food itself. (In Biafra, salt was reported at forty dollars per pound, January 1970.)

Nor was it merely a matter of taste: salt is *necessary* to maintain the body's water balance and osmotic pressure; and if there is extensive loss of blood—as among fighting peoples—or very heavy sweating—as among agricultural peoples in hot climates—the sodium in the salt must be replaced. Of course, we get salt from milk, cheese, whites of eggs, meat, and from some vegetables—but what a luxury to have it at hand, in a container as a seasoner. Wasting such a commodity would be accounted a crime against the community. In former days, of course, the salt was in an open dish, not in a salt cellar; so that tipping it over might mean spilling a lot of it.

Hence, nobody in his right mind would tip over the salt on purpose. Therefore the Devil, or some evil spirit, caused the mishap.

Now, evil spirits—and particularly the Devil—peer over one's left shoulder by preference. One just *might* get the rascal in the eye by throwing the salt over the left shoulder. (*Left*, as we know, has pejorative associations, just as *right* suggests virtuous attributes: Latin *sinister*, left hand; *dexter*, right hand.)

These matters were not even in your consciousness when you spilled the salt, in all probability; but it was in the traditions of the culture.

And it was there for a reason, or for a whole congeries of reasons.

Once, perhaps, in less complicated days, we accepted our myths as representations of objective truth; they were part of our religion, helping to explain man's relationship to unknown forces, providing a remedy for ills, a satisfaction for needs, and the hope of survival. Vestiges of the ancient fears are still powerful in many of us, especially where the irrational is concerned, as with the thirteenth floor, breaking a mirror, walking under a ladder. . . . But as our sophistication grew and we became literate people able to read the record of the past, we relegated most of the myths to the nursery: they were fit only for women and children. (At the same time, we clung tenaciously to bits of false knowledge equally irrational and used them as guideposts for behavior.)

In feudal days when the noble knight received a serious wound, he knew there was one fairly certain way of guaranteeing that infection would not follow: searing the wound with a red-hot iron. It was a fearful cure, to be sure. But he would not have submitted himself to the indignity of having moldy cheese spread on the gash, as the peasant from the buttery did. Such a "cure" was nothing but fable. Yet it was fable with a base of reason: there is penicillin in that mold, as we know today.

But in addition to the folklore and superstition which—despite our uneasy laughter—may have a sound base in truth, there is the deeper field of myth where the psychoanalysts have staked out certain claims, especially since Freud (did it ever occur to you that the story of Jack and the Beanstalk is actually a masturbatory reverie?). Here, in the dark backward and abysm of the unconscious, we may find yet other raw materials for the construction of myth. Whether we regard a myth as a simple story for children, or whether we see in it an unconscious symbol of man's relationship to the Great Unknown and perhaps of his aspirations to immortality, myths shadow and color our path at every turn.

So in the end it does not matter whether Little Red Riding Hood is really a dawn maiden, whether the story is actually a copulation drama representing women who hate sex (as Erich Fromm has suggested), or whether the tale is simply that of a deceived child who is revenged on her deceiver. Whatever the story "really means," it is so firmly woven into the tapestry of our culture that not one of us is untouched by it.

In the pages that follow, we hope to show that some of the familiar myths are a good deal more than cherished deceptions whose main purpose is to bribe a child into his crib. And we intend sturdily to eschew the methods of Euhemerus, the Greek historian who flourished about 300 B.C. and whose *Hiera Anagraphe* (*Sacred History*) analyzed all mythology "into the history of human kings, heroes and adventurers. . . . Zeus, for instance, his kinsfolk and children, he represented as in reality an ancient family of Cretan kings. . . ."[1] Some myths, of course, did grow out of human lives; but those are not our concern here: our business is with propositions usually held to be untrue, and thus myths, but which are, in fact, true or based on truth. For example, the ancient harmless lunacy about men and animals talking together—is it wholly imaginary? Not any more. Men and dolphins are able to communicate at a fairly sophisticated level, as the reader will see in the last entry of Chapter II if he gets so far. Chimps and men, dogs and men— there has never been a time since the domestication of animals that there was any question about *communicating* one with the other; but in the ancient Greek tales at which we smile, they actually *talked*. Conversed. Not about the square root of the hy- potenuse, to be sure; but in concrete terms—"Help me by chasing in that school of fish for my nets." And perhaps, after a lapse of two thousand years, we are doing it again. There are those who claim that we are, and the writing—fiction and nonfiction—on the subject of the dolphin now crowds a good-size shelf.

The ignorance of certainty is that lack of information which makes us bold to assert that we see the truth, pretty much the whole truth, and discard anything which is not the truth. It appears to be a human trait that our certainty is inversely proportional to our knowledge—that is, the thinner our information is, the surer we are we're right and the more viciously will we defend our position and the more fiercely liquidate deviationists of every color,

1. Oskar Seyffert, *A Dictionary of Classical Antiquities* (New York: Meridian, 1956).

preferably (at the low ebb of wisdom where the barrens of complete ignorance begin) with suitable torture. The heretic must die in agony.

We have our warning, therefore: if we are dead sure of a proposition—that pickles and milk at the same meal will produce a bellyache, for instance—so sure that we forbid the children to try it and see, then we have clearly reached the point where we should open our minds to the *possibility* that we are wrong. And that is what the deeply ignorant cannot do. They don't "know enough" to open the mind and therefore they lack the free will. But let's say we have just a little knowledge—the information that the contents of the stomach *must* be sour, as the phrase goes; that there is no such thing as a "sweet" stomach; that digestion requires acidity. If we have no more knowledge than that, we can be saved, if we will.

In preliterate days, the myth was the treasury of human wisdom. Man's fears, aspirations, despairs, his interpretation of the world and his place in it, were expressed in fable, myth, legend, fairy story, proverb, or apothegm: this was his way of being articulate. It is no wonder that we find it difficult to shake off the power of the myth in our own time. And before we become too lofty in our scorn of any particular myth, it might be well, as Harry Levin reminds us, to understand the almost universal trait of rejecting one myth as false because we have another, rival myth of our own that conflicts with it.[2] As the carved motto says over Jake Wirth's famous bar in Boston, *"Suum cuique,"* to each his own.

One of our own myths has been that science would solve everything. Anything that was scientific had to be good. But we are beginning to see that while science can put men on the moon and perhaps even manufacture robots more intelligent than any one man, science cannot seem to remove greed and cruelty from the human heart, because of which stunted children starve, in very large numbers.

What we will be doing in the pages that follow is examining

2. Henry A. Murray, ed., *Myth and Mythmaking* (New York: George Braziller, 1960), p. 14.

lore which is felt to be simply myth and testing it to see what truth underlies it. In this light, a fairy story is not a chronicle of events which are imagined to have happened in time, but carries what Alan W. Watts calls "The tremendous dignity of myth, which is 'once upon a time' in the sense that it is behind all time."[3]

We read in *The Larousse World Mythology* that "myth is far from foreign to our daily thought, and, what is more, far from opposed in essence to scientific thought."[4] If the present book can be helpful to one reader in making the intelligent progression from cocksure ignorance to thoughtful probability, your correspondents will feel rewarded. Not amply rewarded, perhaps. But rewarded.

3. *Myth and Ritual in Christianity* (Boston: Beacon Press, 1968), p. 2.
4. Pierre Grimal, ed., *The Larousse World Mythology* (New York: G. P. Putnam, 1965), p. 9.

Myths from the Bible Laced with Truth

The Heavenly Manna

Moses was told to stretch forth his hand again over the Red Sea when the Israelites had safely passed through; and the waters closed over the chariots of the pursuing Egyptians. And then Moses and the children of Israel sang a victory song, and Miriam the prophetess led a dance with the refrain "Sing ye to the Lord, for he hath triumphed gloriously; the horse and his rider hath he thrown into the sea."

Thereafter the Israelites went into the wilderness of Shur, and for three days they had no water that was not brackish. Then they arrived at Elim, where there were seventy palm trees and twelve springs. But in late May or early June, they entered the Sinai desert and the food gave out. ("Ye have brought us forth into this wilderness, to kill this whole assembly with hunger." Exodus 16:3.)

"Then said the Lord unto Moses, Behold, I will rain bread from heaven for you. . . ."

There are more than a dozen entries in the Old Testament and five in the New in which manna is mentioned, the first being Exodus. Here *The Jerusalem Bible* puts the matter charmingly in a new translation (1966):

When the coating of dew lifted, there on the surface of the desert was a thing delicate, powdery, as fine as hoarfrost on the ground.

When they saw this, the sons of Israel said to one another, "What is that," not knowing what it was. "That," said Moses to them, "is the bread Yahweh gives you to eat."[1]

Then Moses told them to collect "one omer a head," and warned against trying to hoard the stuff. It would rot and stink. An omer is about half a peck. They made the collections in the cool of the early morning, because when the sun got hot, the material dissolved. In Exodus we learn that the manna "was like coriander seed; it was white and its taste was like that of wafers made with honey." But in Numbers the word is that "the taste of it was as the taste of fresh oil."

Such an appealing idea could hardly fail to enter our literature. Wendell Phillips, the revolutionary Boston Brahmin, said in a famous speech on *Public Opinion:* "The manna of popular liberty must be gathered each day, or it is rotten. . . ." And of course Shakespeare used the idea: "Fair ladies, you drop manna in the way/ Of starved people." (*The Merchant of Venice,* V. i. 294-95)

But perhaps more impressive to the modern mind is the information that manna is "a concrete saccharine exudation obtained by making incisions on the trunk of the flowering or manna ash tree, *Fraxinus Ornus,*" which is tapped in July or August, and that its "chief constituent is . . . a hexatomic alcohol, $C_6H_8(OH)_6$."[2] That doesn't have the sound of myth, somehow. The writer adds, however, that the manna known today is not the same thing as the old-time material, and has been familiar only since the fifteenth century. He then names several kinds of manna, including that of the tamarisk tree—or at least that which is *found* on the tamarisk. It is at this point, apparently, that we can tie biblical manna in with objective, scientific fact. Many reports from travelers in the Sinai district—where Moses was leading the Israelites in the days we have read about—have mentioned a manna associated with the tamarisk thickets of the region, according to Marston Bates.

---

1. *The Jerusalem Bible* (Garden City, N.Y.: Doubleday & Co., 1966). Exodus 16:14, 15.
2. *Encyclopaedia Britannica,* 11th ed.

"This granular, sweet manna appears every year for a period of some weeks in June," he tells us, "though it varies greatly in abundance from year to year. It has generally been assumed to be a secretion of the tamarisk itself, but Dr. Bodenheimer [F. S. Bodenheimer, author of *Insects as Human Food*], who visited Sinai to study the manna, found that it was the product of two species of scale insects living on the tamarisk shrubs. His argument that this insect is the source of the biblical manna is, for me, convincing."[3]

The argument is that the timing is right, the territory is right, and various parallels between the biblical account and what is known from eyewitnesses are right. The Bible has the Israelites discovering manna on the fifteenth day of the second month after leaving Egypt; and Bodenheimer locates this time as being late May or early June—which is when the granular manna appears today, in the Sinai territory, the area through which the exodus passed. In both Exodus and Numbers it is stated that the manna fell at night; and the sweet secretion of the scale insects is also more likely to accumulate during the night, when ants are not carrying it off—although the insects produce the secretion constantly. The similarity between the manna and dew, Marston Bates points out, is carried over into English and other languages in such words and phrases as "honeydew" and "the dew of heaven."

Bedouin Arabs to this day collect the drops that are secreted in spring by the insects and that fall to the ground when the drops have dried, according to Michael Avi-Yonah.[4] He adds, "The *manna* is now understood to have been the sweet edible drops of fluid secreted by two kinds of tiny insects living on tamarisk trees. . . . The Arabs still call such dry pellets *man* or *man min sama* ('Manna from heaven')." Bodenheimer uses the phrase, *man-es-simma*, "manna from the skies," and reports that it is often

3. Marston Bates, *Gluttons and Libertines: Human Problems of Being Natural* (New York: Random House, 1967), p. 54.
4. Michael Avi-Yonah and Emil G. Kraeling, *Our Living Bible* (New York: Mc-Graw-Hill, 1962), p. 51.

mentioned in Persian and Arabic pharmacopoeias. His chemical analysis of it shows manna to consist "mostly of a rare disaccharide sugar called trehalose."[5] Collecting it for the market is not exactly big business, but the Iraqi authorities recently estimated that about sixty thousand pounds per year are sold in the Baghdad bazaars. It is used by the confectioners, usually mixed with eggs, almonds, and various essences.

All in all, it does not strain the imagination to comprehend why the Israelites might become thoroughly sated with manna as the main dish of the day, and complain, as they did, to Moses that the variety of foods in Egypt made the meals in captivity seem like feasts by comparison with what was being provided in the desert.

"We remember the fish, which we did eat in Egypt freely; the cucumbers, and the melons, and the leeks, and the onions, and the garlic: But now our soul is dried away: there is nothing at all, besides this manna, before our eyes." (Numbers 11:5)

One more thing about manna makes the myth-fact intriguing: the scholars are not fully agreed either about its source or the meaning of the word; and what we have given here is merely what seems to us (and to Marston Bates and some others) probable. *The Dartmouth Bible* calls manna still a mystery, and feels that the whitish resinous gum exuded by the tamarisk is at best a possibility; and the word is given the translation derived from Hebrew words meaning "What is it?"[6] Still others have believed it to be a lichen, *Lecanora esculenta,* which produces "pea-sized fruiting bodies that are prized as sweet delicacies. These fruiting bodies are light enough to be blown about, so that they could conceivably form a manna rain."[7]

At least we know that there is manna *today,* and that it has a market value; and this certainly makes the biblical manna more than a myth.

5. Bates, *Gluttons and Libertines,* p. 56.

6. Roy B. Chamberlin and Herman Feldman, *The Dartmouth Bible,* 2d ed., rev. and enl. (Boston: Houghton Mifflin Co., 1961), p. 114.

7. Bates, *Gluttons and Libertines,* p. 53; *Encyclopaedia Britannica,* vol. 14, 1970, p. 798.

The Old Testament Prophets: A Youth Movement

Among people to whom the flowing beard suggests age, wisdom, and judgment, it is easy to see why a prophet is visualized as a bearded man, and the bushier the better. Thus it is all but impossible to picture the great prophets of Israel, men like Amos, Hosea, Isaiah, Micah, Jeremiah, and Jonah, without also adorning their dark faces and chins with hirsute magnificence. Men of Islam, indeed, when swearing an oath, took Mohammed's beard as a witness that they meant what they said; and in medieval days, Englishmen were always swearing by the beard and various parts of the body of Christ, as Chaucer noted with apparent horror—and probably with his tongue in his cheek.

Because the beard is important, we feel that it has to be there. And because of a tradition that the oldest citizen is the wisest, prophets are almost never young men, as we habitually picture them. They are stern-faced, ancient, bearded, wise; and they are the true patriots of the nation, who understand, either from direct communication with Deity or from revelation by means of visions and dreams, the right way from the wrong. Such is the conventional picture of the prophet.

Is there any evidence that this picture is hazy on the edges?

The answer, of course, is yes. This picture shows only the retired prophets. If one examines the sixteen great men of the Hebrew prophetic tradition working in Palestine during a period of about half a millennium, who in their period of power developed the crude, primitive faith of Israel into something ethically mature and lasting, one finds such amazing parallels with our times that it is hair-raising.

In their own day they were regarded "as unpatriotic and subversive, and were often treated as traitors . . . atheists,"[8] and not as the spiritual geniuses who, as we now see, were generations ahead of their time in their visions of a higher kind of religion than their

8. Rolland Emerson Wolfe, *Men of Prophetic Fire* (Boston: Beacon Press, 1963), p. 3.

own age could imagine. Because they disturbed entrenched interests and fearlessly criticized kings and commoners, they were called the equivalent of "do-gooders" and meddlers, and sometimes the crowds turned on them, as they have done upon good men and women in our own day, in ignorance, not knowing that the just society for which the prophets called would automatically benefit the common people. We have seen recently, for example, that when the courageous—and fully informed—Ralph Nader exposed to public view the dangerous features of high-speed automobiles (*Unsafe at Any Speed*), the first reaction was to shut him up in any way possible. But if such an individual succeeds, and a whole industry is reformed as a result of his leadership, *then* he becomes a prophet. Of course, the prophets of old were not concerned with consumer protection; their aim was moral improvement. But the parallels remain.

Art and sculpture have portrayed the prophets as bearded, bald old men, as we have said. But actually they were in their twenties and thirties, for the most part. King Josiah, for instance, who struggled to stamp out idolatry and the Canaanite-Phoenician fertility cults involving sex-worship of Ashtoreth (which Solomon himself had supported) was "just eighteen years old" at the time.[9] Jeremiah was also in his teens when he began his work; and as for living to a ripe old age, "Persecution and martyrdom prevented most of them from enjoying a prolonged hearing."[10] Specific information on this subject is not found in the Old Testament. If the narratives originally carried records of the deaths of the prophets, the information was censored later. We have general statements, such as the words of Yahweh (Jeremiah 2:30): "Your sword devoured your prophets like a destructive lion," and many suggestions that more than a few met violent deaths. Readers will remember that Jesus wept over Jerusalem as a city accustomed to killing its own prophets. It appears to be a fact in all human societies that reformers, when they are seen as "bad for business," are often silenced very quickly and secretly. The prophets of Israel did their effective work

9. Webb Garrison, *Strange Facts About the Bible* (Nashville, Tenn., Abingdon Press, 1968), p. 96.
10. Wolfe, *Prophetic Fire,* p. 4.

largely as young men, and if a couple, like Isaiah and Jeremiah, were allowed to live past the age of forty, they seem to have been the exceptions.

Another popular delusion current about these men is that their first order of business was predicting the far-distant future. There are sects in our own day who firmly believe that everything that has occurred in the world since the age of the prophets, and everything that will happen was foretold by them. Actually the prophets were intent on criticizing and improving the religious and social conditions of their own time, of which they were keenly aware. The fact that we have some of the same kinds of problems cannot possibly mean that these men of long ago had us in mind. Problems of poverty, war, justice, brotherhood, against which they threw themselves, are still with us; and the advice given so long ago might well be put to practical application by ourselves—that much we can say. Their voices at least were not timid. And it is still true (Isaiah 6:10) that most people do not hear with their ears, see with their eyes, or understand with their hearts.

The final parallel between the age of the prophets in Israel and our own era of student revolt, youth rebellion, and resistance to the work of the fathers is that in both instances the old world—the establishment—is faced with a strong youth movement—a fact immediately lost to sight if one insists on long white beards, bald heads, and the weight of years in portraying the Old Testament prophets, the men who most influenced teaching in Israel for some five hundred years beginning with Amos about 760 B.C. He had been preceded by such influential men as Moses, Samuel, Nathan, Elijah, Elisha; but it was Amos who was the first to bring the prophetic tradition into flower, from the moment of his first public address in Samaria, when he warned that Yahweh would be revenged upon the Syrians for a brutal border incident in which Israelite captives had been murdered by the unspeakable method of having oxen draw iron-toothed harrows over them, bound on the ground. His threat of divine punishment to be visited upon the enemy undoubtedly called forth applause from this audience; but when he accused the rich in Israel of being guilty of equally barbarous crimes against Israel's own poor and promised the punishment of Yahweh against Israel itself, shouting that the time had now come, we get an idea of the sort of bombshell he was capable of handling.

These men were of a stamp different from anything which had been seen before—just as some of the campus movements of the late 1960s were different from any college or university behavior of the forties or fifties. And they spoke at a critical moment in history, a "turbulent era of intrigue, war and apostasy,"[11] when Israel was in great danger of becoming submerged in a barbarous, polytheistic culture. In fact, it is the superb *quality* of their message to civilized man that makes it so hard to think of them as predominantly young people. Professor Emil G. Kraeling of Union Theological Seminary states: "The influence of the Hebrew prophets on human history has been so vast that it is impossible for any individual to appraise it or describe it."[12]

However, there is a deep truth behind the belief that the prophets of old were ahead of their time and thus older in wisdom than their contemporaries; and with the foregoing footnotes to understanding, perhaps one should not disturb the legend. For we are referring to a period in the dark arcanum of time as deeply buried as the death of Solomon the King, six hundred years before Aristotle. . . . And we are speaking of men who, surrounded by barbaric savagery, dreamed of an ethical system of a quality not yet attained by our species. It is only natural to venerate and honor such men, and if thinking of them as patriarchs is helpful, surely there's no harm in it. The English word "prophet" is *nabi* in Hebrew and has the connotation of "message bearer." They were all of that.

Jonah and the Whale: Contemporary Evidence

Ever since the "Monkey Trial" at Dayton, Tennessee, in 1925, when the redheaded John Scopes was fined one hundred dollars for teaching evolution contrary to the public laws of Tennessee,

---

11. Louis Cassels, *Your Bible* (Garden City, N.Y.: Doubleday & Co., 1967), p. 184.
12. Quoted in Cassels, *Your Bible*, p. 186.

fundamentalism and the literal belief in the Bible as the infallible
word of God Himself has "no longer seriously contended for the
mind of America,"[13] although important spokesmen have maintained the doctrine of the plenary inspiration of Holy Scripture,
to the comfort of many thousands of followers. John Gresham
Machen of Princeton Theological Seminary stated in 1936 that the
spirit of God preserved writers of the Bible from error so that "the
Bible, is in all its parts the very Word of God, completely true
. . ."[14]—precisely the teaching of Pope Leo XIII in the 1893 encyc-
lical *Providentissimus Deus*. Orthodox Judaism holds the same view.
So do thousands of Bible Belt citizens; and it is of record that an
attempt by the Tennessee legislature to repeal the old prohibition
against teaching evolution was stopped in its tracks in the spring of
1967.[15] This was because science was understood to compete with
the Word of God as the vehicle for truth. Hence, while Gaustad
is probably right in the opinion that Scripture is no longer a serious
contender against science among enlightened citizens today, it is
important to bear in mind that a great many people still take the
Bible literally.

To them, there is no question that the prophet Jonah was cast into
the sea after the lots were drawn, that he was taken into the interior
of the "fish" (both the King James and the Revised Standard Version render the word "fish" in Jonah and "whale" in Matthew), and
that he remained "in the belly of the fish for three days and three
nights."

To the literalist, the scientific facts of life must be made to fit the
words, and thus we find C. I. Scofield explaining: "No other miracle
of Scripture has called forth so much unbelief. It has been claimed
that a whale could not swallow a man, yet types of whales have been
found that could easily do so. However, the word used here, like the
one in *Matthew 40* where the word is mistranslated, does not mean
whale but *sea monster,* possibly the whale shark or rhinodon, the

13. Edwin Scott Gaustad, *A Religious History of America* (New York: Harper &
Row, 1966), p. 260.
14. Ibid., p. 261.
15. *New York Times*, 13 April 1967; 5 May 1967.

largest of all fish, sometimes attaining a length of 70 feet."[16] We have not been successful in finding "rhinodon" in any lexicon; but it is composed obviously enough of *rhino,* nose, and *dont,* tooth, and sounds perfectly frightful.

Fortunately we can now announce positively that if it is any comfort to those for whom the Bible should be taken literally, a grown man can definitely traverse the gullet of a whale. The last experimenter we know of to make the trip reported that it was a messy business but by no means unbelievable.[17] Hence any of our readers who had dismissed the Jonah story as physically impossible—at least the entry and exit from the mouth of the whale or monster—may now make a mental correction.

Another interpretation of the story, current among the more inventive of the literary critics, has been a symbolic one, of course, borrowed from Jonah's own words addressed to the deity and referring to his stay inside the fish: ". . . Out of the belly of hell cried I, and thou heardest my voice." Hell is *sheol* in RSV. The adventure is seen as one of those journeys across the Styx or into the Land of the Dead such as Ulysses and other heroes took: a period of stress and torment, of trial and agony. (King Arthur is full of instances in the Grail sequences, and compare *Beowulf* and the Nordic sagas of Asgard.)

But to Neil, Chamberlin, and others it is entirely patent that such interpreters have missed the whole point. The story, they are sure, is a fable, a parable, devised to illustrate the truth that Yahweh through Israel wished to reach all of mankind with his love and that Jonah, in trying to keep the word from the outrageous Gentile (Nineveh being a well-known criterion for religious infamy), was making the same mistake that some ultraorthodox Jews appear to be making today in trying to keep the covenant with the Lord strictly to themselves. The Book of Jonah, in short, is not a story

---

16. C. I. Scofield, ed., *The New Scofield Reference Bible* (New York: Oxford University Press, 1967), p. 942.

17. *This Week,* 24 September, 1967. Mr. Eugene Geiling of Chicago was the investigator. He reported that the passage had been "pretty slimy," but that there was plenty of room.

about a whale at all; it is a story about a prophet who does not want to carry God's warning to the heathen for fear that they will hear it, accept it, repent, and be forgiven: to take their place among the chosen people. Jonah ships in an opposite direction from that in which he was commanded to go. The Lord raises the storm; the sailors draw lots; Jonah goes overboard; and three days later the whale vomits him up on the shore again and he has to start all over. (It is reliably reported that upon expelling Jonah the whale exclaimed, with some relief, "Small prophets and quick returns.") Attempting to avoid the will of Jehovah, in short, is a little futile, just as it is a little futile to think that any one can have all of God's love; and "applying the yardstick of zoological science . . . to a parable" is being on the naïve side,[18] even if one ends up proving that it *is* physically possible for an adult male to make the reportedly very slimy trip.

The Mandrake for Fertility: It Worked for Rachel

The story of Jacob meeting Rachel at the well, falling in love with her, agreeing with Laban, her father, to work for him seven years in payment for Rachel, and the trickery that was practiced upon the young man by passing off the unattractive elder sister, Leah, on the night of the wedding (girls wore veils over their faces until the marriage, and either it was quite dark in the tent or Jacob had celebrated so heartily that it never occurred to him to do any checking up)— that whole complicated family history certainly matches any shenanigans accomplished in the vicinity of Olympus by the legend-makers of Greece; but there is one point of particular interest which, to most readers, has seemed such an obvious case of supernatural intervention that it has been shrugged off as amusing but impossible.

One remembers that in the morning, when Jacob asked Laban

18. William Neil, *Harper's Bible Commentary* (New York: Harper & Row, 1962), p. 294; and Chamberlin and Feldman, *Dartmouth Bible* (Boston: Houghton Mifflin Co., 1961), p. 376.

what was the idea of palming off old Leah on him instead of giving him Rachel, as specifically agreed, Laban said, "It is not the custom in our country to give the younger before the elder. Finish this marriage week and I will give you the other one too in return for your working with me another seven years." (Genesis 29:27) We are allowed to believe that Jacob shrugged and agreed to the new schedule. But Leah had all the children—all sons, at that—and Rachel was barren. It made her frantic. She had the looks, the grace, the beauty —and Leah had the sons: Reuben, Simeon, Levi, and Judah. (They do not rush the action in these tales of the old days.)

Apparently Rachel thought it would bring her one step closer to her heart's desire if Jacob slept with Rachel's slave girl, Bilhah, and perhaps sired a child "so that she may give birth on my knees; through her, then, I too shall have children." Whereupon Jacob proceeded to have two sons by Bilhah, to Rachel's great delight. At this point Leah, who had stopped conceiving, took *her* slave girl to Jacob as a way of evening the score. Zilpah also had two sons, and Leah was beaming with joy. Close figuring would indicate that by this time, eight sons since the wedding, the oldest of Leah's boys was at least nine, and perhaps ten. This was Reuben.

He was a curious youngster and liked to watch the men at work; so he went out with the harvesters when they were cutting the wheat (King James: wheat; Jerusalem Bible: corn); and what did he find, as he nosed around in the fields, but a colony of mandrakes—plants that grow wild all through the eastern Mediterranean region.

There are very few plants to which more folklore has attached itself, some of it extremely contradictory, some of it full of dark dangers and lethal magic, and some of it bright and hopeful. Its supposed values were varied, and the traffic in mandrake plants and roots was so brisk that a whole side industry sprang up at one time, with salesmen getting good prices for fake mandrakes—usually bryony roots, sometimes carved a little to make them look more like human figures, as the mandrake so often did.

Not to wander from our story at this point, however, we see that one of the chief attributes of mandrake is "its power to affect conception."[19]

Reuben, like a well-trained child, delivered his mandrakes to his mother, and Rachel heard about it. She asked her sister for some of the plants and received the horse laugh in reply. The favored wife requests a favor from the unattractive wife? But Rachel deliberately lays down her ace: some mandrake for me, and Jacob goes to your tent tonight. Leah kept telling herself that she could make Jacob favor her over Rachel if only she could produce some more sons. So the deal was made: and as luck would have it, Leah became the mother of not one, but two more sons of Jacob's. Later she gave him a daughter, Dinah.

Meanwhile, Rachel followed the prescribed recipes and thereafter —one cannot say *because* of her use of mandrakes—she became the mother of Joseph. Later, on the journey to Canaan near Ephrath, she gave birth to Benjamin, and died in childbirth.

As we have said, they didn't hurry the action in these ancient tales. A week after Jacob married Leah, he took Rachel to wife also, at her father's suggestion. This tied Jacob down for another seven years. Now Rachel goes childless—and is very bitter about it—for a whole decade while ugly old Leah has four sons and the two maids have two apiece; yet still Jacob loves the childless one more, because she is beautiful. But in all this time it never occurs to her to use the mandrake prescription, which obviously she knows about. She merely waits until, by pure chance, young Reuben comes home with the plants. *Then* she goes into action immediately. She believes the mandrake medicine will help her to conceive. "And God remembered Rachel, and God harkened to her, and opened her womb. And she conceived, and bare a son: and said, God hath taken away my reproach: and she called his name 'Joseph.' "

Medicines cannot command Nature; the best they can do is make it easier for Nature to function. We should not permit the language to confuse the issue here. In King James English the translation

19. Maria Leach and Jerome Fried, eds., *Funk & Wagnalls Standard Dictionary of Folklore, Mythology and Legend*, 2 vols. (New York: Funk & Wagnalls, 1949–50).

"And God remembered Rachel" could be the equivalent of "the tranquilizing action of the mandrake relaxed Rachel so that Nature could take its course." There's no way to prove the fact; but "some physicians now administer modern tranquilizers to foster conception,"[20] and the legend could be entirely true. It makes sense.

It is impossible to leave this subject without a brief note about mandrake, a word related to the French *main-de-gloire* of infamous memory. A "hand of glory" was a charm made from the dried or pickled hand of a hanged criminal, and it conferred invisibility—just the thing for a thief robbing a house. In fact, it is never mentioned in connection with honest men, so far as we have seen. A mandrake root shaped like a human hand (usually they look more like a manikin) was *called* a "hand of glory" and was especially valued as a charm.[21] The mandrake plant (*Mandragora officinarum*), to be distinguished from the May apple or mandrake of America (*Podophyllum peltatum*), was supposed to utter a piercing shriek when it was pulled from the earth, and "living mortals, hearing them, run mad." (*Romeo and Juliet*, IV. iii. 48) So they used dogs to pull them. Circe is supposed to have used mandrakes to effect her spells on visiting sailors. Mandrake was used for anesthesia in surgery (Greece); it reveals the location of hidden treasure; it permits one to prophesy; it is aphrodisiac; it is narcotic, soporific, and is also known as "insane root." A handy thing to have around for all occasions.

Noah and the Ark: A New Design

It is no strain on the imagination to accept the prologue to the Flood story: "The earth also was corrupt before God, and the earth was filled with violence" (Genesis 6:11). But for the rest of the Flood narrative we enter a territory which has its misty contours, even to staunch believers in the literal truth of the version of the Bible they happen to espouse. The King James, for example, has well-known inconsistencies within a few lines of each other ("two of every sort shalt thou bring," and "Of every clean beast thou shalt take to thee

20. Garrison, *Strange Facts*, p. 22.
21. Joseph T. Shipley, *Dictionary of Early English* (Paterson, N.J., Littlefield, Adams & Co., 1963).

by sevens"; a forty-day rainfall and one of a hundred fifty days' duration, in Chapter 7). These and similar obvious contradictions, according to Neil, occur when "the editor of *Genesis* has combined the J tradition with the P tradition, interweaving their versions. . . ."[22] (The reference is to the four documents which make up the Pentateuch, the first five books: J being collected in Juda, the so-called Yahwistic document of the Southern Kingdom; E, from Ephraim, the Northern Kingdom; D, a separate document largely legal; and P, the priestly document.)[23]

Also there is the common-sense question about how one boat could have held everybody. This matter was a favorite for speculation in the days before scientific criticism of the Bible. We start with God's directions to Noah to make the boat 300 cubits long (450 feet), 50 cubits in breadth (75 feet), and 30 cubits in height (45 feet). No fuzziness there: the directions are specific; and Scofield holds that "the dimensions of the Ark are themselves an evidence of the accuracy of the Scriptures."[24] He compares the measurements given in the King James Version with the cuneiform representation of the Ark, shaped like a six-story cube of 262 feet with a mast and the pilothouse on top; and with the Greek legend which, according to Berosus, gave the length as 3,000 feet and the width as 1,200. It is clear to Scofield that the nonbiblical accounts represent irresponsible reporting. Artists and illustrators have offered all kinds of interpretations: fifteenth- and sixteenth-century woodcuts of the Age of Belief suggest everything from a houseboat with a slate roof and a birdhouse on top (in a German Bible printed by Heinrich Quentell at Cologne in 1478, artist unknown) to a three-story rectangular barn with a flat roof, which the animals entered by way of a gangplank leading to the third level (from a Vulgate printed by Guillaume Roville at Lyons in 1581, again by an unknown artist).[25] God ordered it made of gopher wood, which the *Britannica* identifies variously as cypress, pine, and cedar, but which Webster II calls the "un-

22. *Harper's Bible Commentary,* p. 32.
23. Chamberlin and Feldman, *Dartmouth Bible,* p. 8.
24. *Scofield Reference Bible,* p. 11.
25. Helen Slocum Estabrook, *Old Testament Stories in Woodcut* (Boston: Beacon Press, 1947), illustrations facing pp. 9, 10.

identified wood used in the construction of Noah's ark," which lets us off where we got on. At any rate, the first edition of the *Britannica* (1771) had the answer for those who questioned the capacity: "Buteo and Kircher have proved geometrically, that, taking the common cubit of a foot and a half, the ark was abundantly sufficient for all the animals supposed to be lodged in it. Snellius computes the ark to have been above half an acre in area . . . and Dr. Arbuthnot computes it to have been 81062 tuns [*sic*]. . . . If we come to a calculation, the number of species of animals will be found much less than is generally imagined, not amounting to a hundred species of quadrupeds nor to two hundreds of birds. . . . Zoologists usually reckon but an hundred and seventy species in all." The article was changed in the eighth edition to explain that the Flood affected only that one region of earth, not the whole globe, and therefore all that Noah had to preserve were the species in the vicinity of the Persian Gulf and the Tigris-Euphrates valley. This is an alluring explanation, because we know that Aristotle, who died in 322 B.C., listed 500 kinds of animals, and his pupil, Theophrastus, who was the most eminent botanist of ancient Greece, listed about the same number of plants. Either they discovered new species rather rapidly (the J document, the oldest of the Pentateuch, "was written about 850 B.C.")[26] or we had better accept the local-species-only theory, since by the year 1800 scientists had identified 70,000 different species; and by 1960 "more than 1.25 million different species, two-thirds animals and one-third plants, are known, and no biologist supposes that the count is complete."[27] To make matters worse, if Noah had been doing a really perfect job, he would have had to take into the Ark a pair of Indian elephants and *also* a pair of African elephants (because they are not the same species: they cannot breed with each other); and a pair of one-hump camels and a pair of Bactrians, for the same reason. The whole picture gets terribly confusing. One begins to wonder if the *Queen Mary* at the height of her fame could

26. Fred Gladstone Bratton, *History of the Bible* (Boston: Beacon Press, 1959), p. 108.
27. Isaac Asimov, *The New Intelligent Man's Guide to Science* (New York: Basic Books, 1965), pp. 684–85.

have been able to handle the load intended for the Ark—and she was a fifth of a mile from stem to stern (1,019 feet, 6 inches).[28]

Other doubts about the Flood story include the known parallels with similar stories in other cultures. There was such a tale in Phrygian circles, plus "an Indian deluge legend, a Zoroastrian myth, and it was also found in the folklore of Tibet, Australia, Polynesia and the Americas."[29] In fact, the story in the sixth chapter of Genesis "is the Hebrew version of a much older Babylonian myth which relates the adventures in similar terms and in almost exact parallel of one Utnapishtim . . . who is warned by the god Ea of an impending deluge, builds an ark, and is saved in the same manner as Noah."[30] This refers to the Gilgamesh Epic, which was found on a tablet by George Smith in 1872.

All these things being so, the Flood story did come to be thought of as a myth by educated people, except for those who were intransigent on the literal interpretation of the Bible. "It had no place among matters of fact; it was considered to be nothing more than an ancient legend."[31] It was classified among the myths of a "saving community" whose good works prevent total world destruction. Such a tradition runs from Shem, Enoch, and Seth up to Jesus Christ; and thereafter it continues through legends of the saints and heroes at least as far as Lincoln in America, and perhaps beyond.

Therefore, at least among intellectuals, the whole point of the Flood story is theological, and nobody wrestles any longer with the number of square feet allotted to the water buffalo in the Ark. "The significance of the story . . . lies in the realm of theology . . . the redemptive power of the Church in the midst of the world,"[32] and the judicious are permitted a knowing smile when they read news accounts of the discovery of some skeleton framework on some far-off Armenian mountain, believed to be part of Noah's Ark.

Yet research and fuller knowledge have a disconcerting way of

28. Lloyd's Register quoted in *The World Almanac,* 1967, p. 791.
29. G. S. Wegener, *6,000 Years of the Bible* (New York: Harper & Row, 1963), p. 11.
30. Neil, *Harper's Bible Commentary,* p. 31.
31. Wegener, *6,000 Years,* p. 11.
32. Neil, *Harper's Bible Commentary,* pp. 30–31.

raising fresh questions about many events previously accepted as myths. For nobody seriously questions the *fact* of a devastating pre-biblical flood in Mesopotamia—at least not since 1929, when Leonard Woolley sent home the famous wire "WE HAVE FOUND THE FLOOD," and his findings at Ur were confirmed by Dr. Stephen Langdon at Kish soon thereafter. Woolley was leading a joint archaeological expedition sponsored by the British Museum and the University of Pennsylvania. Diggers were at work at Tell Muqayyar, near the Persian Gulf, believed to be the site of Ur of the Chaldees, birthplace of the patriarch Abraham. They had found the royal cemetery, and after six years of excavating, had hit apparently the lowest depth, dating back to about 2800 B.C. Then they struck a pure clay, clean of rubbish. It could only have come there by the power of water.

Scholars differ a little about the source of the water. Bratton believes it resulted from "a great inundation from the Euphrates . . . covering a territory approximately 400 miles long and 100 miles wide."[33] Wegener holds that "It could not have been the river Euphrates because the layer was too high above the ground, and besides it was too thick."[34] (It was eight to ten feet in depth.) The digging continued, and suddenly the clay ended as abruptly as it had begun —and beneath it Woolley found debris belonging "unmistakably to the Stone Age. . . . The Flood was a legend no longer. . . . It was established history."[35]

So *that* part of the myth was true.

Still in question was the Ark, a central part of the drama. The Ark gives every indication of remaining a matter for speculation; but at least one scholar with sound credentials believes he has the answer: he is Meir Ben-Uri, an Israeli, who, after exhaustive and complicated reckoning, completed a model of the Ark totally unlike anything shown so far. It was displayed in Jerusalem's Hechal Shlomo (Palace of Solomon) in February, 1968. Ben-Uri concluded that the Ark had to be a "prismatic rhomboid," a floating longhouse with a diamond-shaped cross section, the same height and thickness

33. Bratton, *History of the Bible*, pp. 38–45.
34. Wegener, *6,000 Years*, pp. 14–16.
35. Ibid.

from one end to the other, something like a dozen or more honey boxes stuck together and fastened into a single structure which supposedly floated on one corner, the opposite corner being the roof. According to Ben-Uri, this design "could easily accommodate three decks and provide a capacity of some 5,500 tons, enough for at least 1,000 pairs of animals."[36] This scholar has no doubts. He asserted: " 'I believe that the Bible is a true account of what actually happened. It is up to us to unravel its secrets.' "

The Tower of Babel: A Lot of Talk

In nine short verses the entire story of this famous episode is set down in language whose terse and simple perfection—even in translation—could be a model for the most laconic. (1) All men spoke one tongue. (2) There was a migration from the east into Shinar (southern Mesopotamia). (3) They made bricks and used slime for mortar (no rocks of any kind in this alluvial soil). (4) With the bricks they built a city and a tower to make a name for themselves. There is the background, there are the persons of the drama, and such is the action undertaken. In the next five verses we see the problem the previous action raised, and the denouement. (5) The Lord came to earth and saw the tower. (It was impressive.) (6) So the Lord said that from now on, there was no telling *what* these people would do; and (7) they should be stopped right away by having their language confounded. (8) He did this, and they stopped building and were scattered. (9) Hence the place is now called Babel (this involves a play on words: "Babel" is compared with *balal*, Hebrew for "confusion," and the same Hebrew characters that render "Babel" also give "Babylon." *Bab-ilu* in the Accadian means "gate of god." The Hebrew never gave the word "Babylon," but only "Babel"; but the Greek mode of spelling the latter was "Babylon").

The question, of course, becomes an inquiry into what exactly is behind such a legend. Is it merely a myth, a parable to illuminate a theological doctrine? Or was there such a tower? Michael Avi-Yonah suggests that "the whole account seems to be a legendary

36. *Time*, 23 February 1968.

echo of the penetrations of the Sumerians (coming from the east) into the marshlands of Babylonia. In their former land they had built with stones and mortar, but now they had to learn to use the different building materials available in rockless Mesopotamia."[37]

To the orthodox, however, there is no doubt that these things happened; and again the sinfulness of man is at the center. In judgment upon sinful man's first attempt to establish a world state in opposition to the divine rule, God struck at the very thing which binds men together, namely a common language."[38] But even the most sedulous reading of the nine verses that contain the story reveals no "opposition to divine rule." The men want to produce a magnificent city with a superb tower in order to make a name for themselves; one could say they wanted to celebrate human achievement. What's wrong with *that*? According to the King James Version, this is to be a tower "whose top may reach unto heaven." Are we to understand that mankind intends to invade heaven and the throne of God? RSV retains this suggestion: "with its top in the heavens." But elsewhere the metaphor is used to mean "very high," as in Deuteronomy 1:28, where the "cities are great and walled up to heaven." *The Anchor Bible* gives the redaction "with its top in the sky," and the new (1962) translation of *The Torah* by the Jewish Publication Society of America also says "with its top in the sky." Yahweh, as quoted, does not indicate that he anticipates any threat of an invasion of heaven from sun's planet number three, so perhaps we are justified in believing that those ancient enthusiasts were thinking of a skyscraper rather than a literal road to heaven. One learned commentator cheerfully suggests that many huge ziggurats were constructed in Mesopotamia both for the purpose of drawing men closer to the gods, and "to offer the gods a ladder down which they could climb to earth,"[39] which is a warm and hospitable gesture.

The sinfulness of man is an idea so attractive, however, that it

37. Avi-Yonah and Kraeling, *Our Living Bible*, p. 25. Avi-Yonah handled the OT section.

38. *Scofield Reference Bible*, p. 17.

39. Luc. H. Grollenberg, *Shorter Atlas of the Bible* (London: Thomas Nelson & Sons, 1959), p. 31.

persists. Webster III states without equivocation that the Tower "was erected for the purpose of reaching heaven and incurred the wrath of God, who as punishment made the builders' speech mutually unintelligible." One can only say that this idea is not expressed in any of the translations of the Bible in English, so far as we can discover. *The Anchor Bible* holds that Yahweh is punishing man's folly and presumption.[40]

What Yahweh *says,* according to the text we have, is one or another variation on this: "Behold, the people are one, and they have all one language; and this they begin to do: and now nothing will be restrained from them, which they have imagined to do." (*Jerusalem Bible:* "This is but the start of their undertakings! There will be nothing too hard for them to do. Come, let us go down and confuse their language. . . .")

Others who reject the interpretation of sin on man's part—since they cannot discern anything approaching sin in the construction described—take the story to be a simple folk tale to explain the many languages and how they arose, cognate with dozens of other such tales, which tell how the chipmunk got his stripes and why the sea is salt. There were plenty of languages even in the old days in Shinar: "In the south there were Sumerians and Elamites, in the north Akkadians and Assyrians, semitic Babylonians and Aramaeans, Indo-Iranian Hurrians and Mitanni, Indo-European Medes and Hittites, nomadic Ammonites, Edomites and Moabites. . . ."[41]

An explanation of language origins would be all the more welcome today, when "nearly four thousand languages are spoken by mankind on this planet."[42] We have had a plethora of theories to tell how they happened, but nothing as good as the Tower of Babel. The bow-wow theory, the ding-dong theory, the yo-heave-ho theory, the pooh-pooh theory, the ta-ta or wig-wag theory—Noah Jonathan Jacobs summarizes them all in a book which should be famous but

40. E. A. Speiser, trans. and annotator, "Genesis" in *The Anchor Bible* (Garden City, N.Y.: Doubleday & Co., 1964), p. 76.
41. Herbert Wendt, *It Began in Babel* (Boston: Houghton Mifflin Co., 1962), p. 80.
42. Lincoln Barnett, *The Treasure of Our Tongue* (New York: Alfred A. Knopf, 1964), p. 5.

tends to be forgotten, *Naming Day in Eden*. And then a scholar like Holger Pedersen comes along and assures us that the true story is "the conception of a series of coordinated languages which descend from one and the same language no longer existent. . . ."[43]

A final interpretation—and perhaps it makes the most sense of all —is that the parable of Babel as a story is actually a teaching device, almost in a class with visual aids, which illuminates a theological point and has nothing to do with science or the growth of languages or anything else. It shows how the divine plan unfolds: God will now choose one group out of the peoples of mankind, and "out of this group one tribe, out of this tribe one man, and Abraham the son of Terah will be chosen as the foundation member of a community which God will make his own" to be an agent of purification to all nations. The city we have seen, built primarily for the glory of man rather than the glory of God, with its violence and vice, must go down. We must start over again with a Chosen People that can lead mankind to spiritual values. . . . The idea is not unheard of in the last third of the twentieth century.

But in the days when it originated, the story "had a demonstrable source in cuneiform literature."[44] It went back before the Jewish manuscripts, to the writings before the tenth century B.C. But the tower was real enough, for about the year 458 B.C., Herodotus beheld this wonder of the world with his own eyes. These are his words: "In the middle of the precinct there was a tower of solid masonry, a furlong in length and breadth, upon which was raised a second tower, and on that a third, and so on up to eight. The ascent to the upper towers is made on the outside, round all the towers. When one is about half-way up, one finds a resting-place and seats, where persons are wont to sit some time on their way to the summit. On the topmost tower there is a spacious temple. . . ." and in it stood the bed of the King of the Gods, Marduk himself.[45]

43. *The Discovery of Language* (Bloomington, Ill., Indiana University Press, 1962), p. 7.
44. Neil, *Harper's Bible Commentary*, p. 38.
45. Herodotus, *The History of Herodotus of Halicarnassus*, G. Rawlinson, trans. and rev. and annotated A. W. Lawrence (London: Nonesuch Press, 1935), pp. 115–16.

The Tower was known to the Babylonians as E-temen-an-ki. Each side measured 288 feet in length and the height was also 288 feet. "The walls of the temple were plated with gold, and decorated with enameled brickwork of a bluish hue, which glittered in the sun, greeting the traveler's eye from afar.[46]

Obviously the Tower of Babel is not entirely without foundation, both historical *and* rhetorical. How much meaning it has for our own day may depend in part on how intelligent we are. In short, the chipmunk persistently retains his stripes, generation after generation.

Samson and That Haircut

Human hair as a woman's crowning glory has moved poets in all ages to some of their most extravagant lyrical outbursts. "And beauty draws us with a single hair," sang Pope, to say nothing of the effusions of Burton, Dryden, Carew, Howell, Bland, and others. Swinburne, we always thought, carried the idea about as far as one could hope to, within the bounds of serious poetry: "Kissing her hair, I sat against her feet," he murmured, scarcely able to contain himself; he even imagined it to be a perfect death, if life should end for him in that posture. Kipling, of course, as is well known, tried to break the image—and the hearts—of the Victorians by characterizing a certain woman as "a rag and a bone and a hank of hair," but only in the mood of bitterest disillusion does anybody read "The Vampire" any more. (In every large herd there is bound to be one maverick.)

We say "human hair"—which the reader perhaps took for an instance of supererogation or redundancy in style—deliberately to date our essay to the period of mankind's history prior to the take-over, if it should come, by the Union Carbide people in their attempt to substitute Dynel modacrylic "wigs, wiglets, perukes, shimmery falls, evening braids and chignons" for the traditional strands the poets celebrated. "THEY ARE NOT FAKE ANYTHING," the full-page ad

46. C. W. Ceram, *Gods, Graves, and Scholars,* 2d ed. (New York: Alfred A. Knopf, 1967), pp. 288–89.

cries. "THEY ARE REAL DYNEL. Just be sure you insist on that little phrase."[47]

"Porphyria's yellow Dynel wound thrice about her throat. . . ." No, we seem to resist it. We'll stick to human hair. In which connection a contemporary wit has affirmed that not since the days of the Indians' scalp-gatherings have so many people been going around with hair that is not their own.

Hair has been a symbol not only of beauty but also of strength, status, social position, age, marriageability, and other things. It has taken its place in the field of communication as part of that vast "silent language" that speaks without saying anything. We look back at some of the elaborate hairdos in elegant ballrooms of the past and see engenderments that took hours to arrange and were as complicated as a charade, perhaps with a ship in full sail riding the waves of tresses. That would be the one-of-a-kind creation so dear to woman, something that sets her apart from every other female— apart and above. The justices on the bench show their status by their wigs. In *New Faces of 1952* there was a lovely song, extremely poignant, announcing Nanty's seventeenth birthday, the day when a maiden lets down her skirt and puts up her hair. Greek children used to let their hair grow until they were eighteen; but when one became an ephebus, it was time for a haircut. There are those among us today who appear to have reversed this usage: they cut their hair until the teens, and then let it grow unhampered. Which merely supports the view that hair is an extremely important adjunct to being human. People have perfumed and colored their hair, have adorned it with jewels throughout the course of history.

Hair being considered so vital, it is no wonder that legend and fable have taken account of it—from the princess Rapunzel, in her high, inaccessible tower ("Rapunzel, Rapunzel, let down your long hair!") to the horror of the Gorgon Medusa, with snakes instead of hair, the very sight of whom turned a man to stone.

Among the male of the species also the ownership of thick and abundant long hair has been important. There was not only Samson, who was a Nazarite and therefore bound by a vow never to cut his

47. *New York Times Magazine,* 24 November 1968.

hair, but such various characters as Absalom, third son of David the king and supposedly the handsomest man in the kingdom, who gloried in his long hair and died because of it (he was caught up by the hair in the thick, low "boughs of a great oak" as he rode a mule under the tree, and was killed as a traitor as he hung there, by Joab and his ten armor bearers. II Samuel 18:9–15); Colonel George Armstrong Custer, of the Little Bighorn; and the famous western hero Wild Bill Hickok, who sported his blond hair supposedly as a challenge to any redskin who might dare to come and try to get it. The limit appears to have been attained by Swami Pandarasannadhi, head man of the Thiruvadu Thurai monastery, who grew hair to the length of twenty-six feet.[48]

We're getting closer to Samson every minute. Anticipating the tragedy following the loss of his hair—although it was clearly his own foolish misjudgment that allowed it—one would like to trace the idea of shame, evil, bad luck, grief which among so many peoples has accompanied the cutting of hair. We know that among the Germanic tribes, and with the Franks and the Celts, long hair was a sign of status and honor and short hair signalized submission —a symbolism that probably derived from the custom that conquering Roman legions had of shearing the hair of tribesmen for the Roman slave market. They paid for that later. In Central Europe and elsewhere, a woman, once she was safely married, was expected to conceal her hair, presumably to indicate that she was no longer available. This was taken as a sign of submission to her husband. She didn't cut the hair off, but bound it all up in a coif.

Short hair meant servitude to army recruits at Exeter, England, as recently as 1968: the lads, in fact, were so ashamed of their short service haircuts that when they went into town they wore wigs, according to Cecil Bagwell, who was taking orders for the wigs personally.[49] ("The girls ignore them and the local boys taunt them," he said). And of course we are aware that bald-headed men take a lot of good-natured kidding, and that some of them are deeply

48. *Guinness Book of World Records* (New York: Sterling Publishing Co., 1966), p. 17.
49. Boston *Globe,* 19 September 1968.

troubled about their loss of hair, despite an outer bonhomie. If the hair loss did not really bother them, then the more than ten thousand males who have been patched by the new hair grafts (taken largely from their own necks and other hairy areas in small sections of skin containing about thirty tufts) would not have gone through the agony.[50]

There may be some tie-in between the idea of evil in cutting the hair and the custom of tearing the hair out by handfuls in spasms of grief—trying to do evil to oneself to placate the spirit of the dead person. No single pattern appears, however—long hair in some cultures has been regarded as frivolous, foppish, effeminate, and altogether unmanly and, by extension, untrustworthy (compare the Roundheads of Cromwell and the Cavaliers of King Charles). There was a law against long hair for men in the English colonies in 1634; and the overseers of Harvard College forbade the wearing of curls or powdered hair; the institution was supposed to be training ministers, which was—and is—serious work. On the other hand, Jonathan Edwards and his son-in-law, Samuel Stoddard, both preached, on the basis of scriptural and rational authority, that it is blasphemous and wicked for men to cut their hair.

At any rate, the Samson story illustrates the point of view that long hair in men is honorable, a sign of strength, and even more than that: the container and habitation of that strength. Samson is called the last of the great judges. He was a judge for twenty years: not in the sense of a peruked official presiding at courts of law, but more as a champion of his people, who were settling down in the land of milk and honey, giving up their nomadic ways, and trying to coexist with the Philistines, a more urbane and sophisticated people, who had come into Canaan from the sea. Naturally there were conflicts, just as there were intermarriages; and Samson, as we know, was seldom in the mood to take any nonsense from the Philistines. He was thus a folk hero—a "judge." But there was more to it than that: he was the son of Manoah and his previously

---

50. *Ladies' Home Journal*, June 1967. The technique was pioneered by Dr. Norman Orentreich of New York, and according to Dr. D. Bluford Stough III, University of Arkansas, it is "no longer experimental."

barren wife; his birth was foretold by an angel, who warned the mother-to-be (she is not named) to become a teetotaler because she was going to give birth to a son who would be consecrated to the Lord all his life—a Nazarite, eating no grapes, drinking no wine, letting the hair grow, and never touching a dead body. In fact, regarding *any* man who gave himself to the Lord as a priest, "there shall no razor come upon his head." (Numbers 6:5)

Some commentators have wondered whether to take Samson seriously, suggesting that this saga is a later interpolation among the histories of the hero-judges and that Samson himself is more like the antic and exaggerated characters such as Tyll Eulenspiegel or Paul Bunyan—completely uninhibited, of limitless strength, and almost entirely irrational. But his heroic death and the fact that he is the archetypal victim of treacherous love command our profound compassion, and his story has enormous vitality. He *must* be taken seriously, even if certain exploits, such as carrying off the gigantic city gates of Gaza to the top of the mountain at Hebron (forty miles away and three thousand feet above sea level)[51] cannot be accepted without some effort.

Many scholars have suggested that the whole Samson legend is a solar myth (the *Britannica* compares the name with the Hebrew *shemesh,* "sun"; and *The Oxford Dictionary of the Christian Church* finds a parallel in Hebrew *shimshom,* "solar"). The story has been placed in parallel with the Gilgamesh epic from Babylon, the Horu-Ra legend from Egypt, and the Hercules story from Greece and Rome. The appeal of the Samson narrative as a subject for the local troubadour, jongleur, or minnesinger celebrating the invincible folk hero was in any case irresistible. Whether or not the spirit of the Lord works mightily within him, Samson performs titanic operations impossible for little people to do and appears to apply a sort of wry humor to it all—if humor is the word we're fumbling for. There is, for example, the riddle about the lion and the bees, supposedly propounded in innocent good spirits to the thirty young men who have come to keep Samson company during the seven days of his wedding feast. The guests can't solve the

51. Chamberlin and Feldman, *Dartmouth Bible,* p. 210.

riddle, so they threaten the bride and her parents with death by burning if she doesn't worm the answer out of Samson. Apparently this is something any female can do if she puts half her mind to it; so she tells the young men—and Samson has to pay the forfeit of thirty linen garments and thirty festal garments. He does this by walking into Ashkelon and killing thirty men of the town, whose garments he then turns over to the guests. Samson is a real card. Like the time he caught the three hundred foxes and tied them tail to tail, with a "torch between each pair of tails," and sent them into the standing grain.

But it's basically the hair thing that concerns us. Sir James G. Frazer has given us many parallel folk tales in which a man's soul or his strength is bound up with his hair (the phrase is Sir James's) so that when he loses his hair he loses his life or grows weak. "The maleficent powers of witches and wizards resided in their hair," it was believed, and no torture "could make any impression on the miscreants so long as they kept their hair on."[52] He cites instances from the natives of Amboyna to the Aztecs of Mexico, indicating that the belief is worldwide.

As the Samson saga became crystallized in print and accepted into the Old Testament canon (Judges 13:1–16), we are told that Israel had again fallen into error in the sight of the Lord, and "the Lord gave them into the hand of the Philistines for forty years," but all this time Yahweh was "seeking an occasion against the Philistines," for he intended Israel to conquer. Samson, when "the Spirit of the Lord came mightily upon him"—that is, in his unbuckled manic moods—would undertake such matters as slaying up to a thousand Philistines with whatever weapon happened to be lying around—such as the jawbone of an ass, the sort of thing one found underfoot in those days, apparently. Now, if Samson was fully aware of the fact—if he really was convinced—that the spirit of the Lord was with him as long as he met the required conditions (no liquor, no unclean food, no touching the dead, and no haircuts), then he also believed that the spirit of the Lord would be removed from him if the conditions were *not* met. Therefore,

52. *The Golden Bough*, 1-vol. abr. ed. (New York: Macmillan Co., 1958), p. 789.

if his hair were to be cut, he truly *would* become weak, because he would believe that the Lord had departed from him and that there was no sense fighting it. Frazer cites case after case of witches and wizards on trial who never budged an inch under torture but who folded up immediately if they were shaved. And we know that voodoo killing results in a death as real as could be accomplished by a beheading, principally because the victim believes in the efficacy of the curse. If that is magic, let us make the most of it. The best proof that Samson did lose his strength when his hair was cut is that the Philistines put out his eyes—a gesture Samson would have been inclined to resist under ordinary conditions, one assumes. That his soul was that of a child—as with other folk heroes of enormous physical prowess—is indicated by his telling Delilah of Sorek the fatal secret, knowing her to be a Philistine herself. True, she vexed his soul to death (RSV) and was probably a skillful woman; and he was in love with her. Men in love sometimes act upon impulse, we understand. This particular impulse was the death of him. The reader and the ordinary graduate of American schools and colleges "knows" that a haircut does not cause him to lose his strength, and therefore, by extension, denies that it would have any ill effect upon Samson—and he writes off the story as pure myth. With Samson, as with the witches and voodoo victims, there was truth in it.

Incidentally, the seven locks of Samson's hair that the Philistine barber removed from the Israelite's head consisted of different hair from that with which Samson had grown up. It was not the same hair he had worn at the age of sixteen, for instance. And lest we be accused of propounding riddles ourselves, the answer is that the hair on the head of man is shed and replaced over a period of about four years.[53] That there really was strength in Samson's hair is indicated by the fact that a single hair can hold a weight of something like two or three ounces; that the total number of hairs on the head of a dark-haired twenty-four-year-old individual is about 110,000; that there are about 625 hairs to each square centimeter

53. William Montagna and Richard L. Dobson, eds., *Hair Growth* (New York: Pergamon Press, 1969).

on the head and forehead, and that therefore a whole head of hair has strength enough to lift from 3,600 to 5,400 pounds.[54]

With a sigh, we conclude here; but it is difficult to do so, because our days are more filled with talk about hair than has been the case in any previous decade of this century, and perhaps of any century prior to the seventeenth. Irresistible is the temptation to mention the musical comedy *Hair,* written by Gerome Ragni and James Rado, two actors in their twenties, with music by Galt Mac-Dermot, which burst upon the scene in 1967. Leonard Bernstein is reputed to have walked out of the theater halfway through the show; and Richard Rodgers damned the "love-rock musical" as being without melody; but a year later it was still playing to full houses in New York, Stockholm, London, Munich, Copenhagen, and Los Angeles. The show celebrates hippie hair, "long, beautiful, shining, gleaming, steaming, flaxen, waxen, long, straight, curly, fuzzy, snaggy, shaggy, ratty, matty, oily, greasy, fleecy, down-to-there hair."[55]

In a way, we have come full circle: young rock musicians have testified that they have been ruined by required haircuts, more or less as Samson was.

54. A. F. Savill, *The Hair and Scalp* (Baltimore: Williams & Wilkins, 1945).
55. Elenore Lester, notes on the RCA Victor Dynagroove album *Hair.*

II

Myths from Nature More True than Fiction

Never Duel After Breakfast

How long is it since one has had any advice about dueling? Alas, the elder exquisite customs droop, from inattention; people in our age are more interested in going to the theater to observe nakedness than they are in knowing whether the Reproof Valiant precedes or follows the Countercheck Quarrelsome—a point which might have involved life and death with your courtly lover of old.

Matters of this ilk came flooding back to us as we idled through some year-old issues of JAMA (the *Journal of the American Medical Association*), paying especial attention to that feature which reprints materials first published seventy-five years earlier, now reassembled for their amusement value more than anything else. It appears that on 14 October 1893, Dr. Bernays was explaining to Surgeon General Sternberg the proposition that a man "shot in the abdomen shortly after eating a hearty meal" is in much greater danger than his tentmate who went without lunch that day. An immediate operation is called for with the first man, but the identical wound inflicted on the hungry man can be treated without an operation. Hence the best time for a battle, as far as abdominal wounds are concerned, is before breakfast. No doubt the good doctors were able to enjoy some excellent fresh-from-the-lab professional laughter over this proposition; and one hopes that they did not forget that each of them owed a cock to Aesculapius for keeping them at the medical convention and thus off the battlefield.

The medical editors advance the theory a little further by calling attention to the fact that practically always it is the hours before breakfast that are chosen for any duels that may be scheduled, and no doubt for the same reason. "From time immemorial, the early morning hour has been the chosen time for the duello, for the 'settlement' of private quarrels. It is a logical arrangement, and moreover the appetite for breakfast is not sharp until after the quarrel has been appeased."[1] Folklore has long acknowledged what every experienced married couple has discovered, that "fighting and arguing make one ravenous."

It is almost strange that Dr. Bernays did not refer the surgeon general, in the context of his argument, to the example of Alexander Hamilton and the events of the early morning of 11 July 1804, on the dueling ground at Weehawken. Here, opposite today's Forty-Second Street, was a small ledge some twenty feet above the river. Persons on the ledge were hidden from above and from below; and there, as the mists rose from the Hudson, Aaron Burr had his final "interview" (the actual confrontation, weapon in hand, was frequently called that) with Alexander Hamilton and the scripture was fulfilled as written by Burr shortly before: "Nothing now is possible except the simple Message which I shall now have the honor to deliver."[2] The message was a slug from a twelve-inch pistol with a flint lock and the trademark "J. Twiggs, London." The ball produced just the sort of abdominal wound Dr. Bernays had mentioned to the surgeon general: it struck Hamilton in the right side, hit the "second and third rib, fractured it about in the middle, passed through the liver and diaphragm, and seemingly lodged in the first and second vertebrae, which splintered."[3] These facts, of course, were not known when Dr. Hosack was ordering Hamilton to be removed from the field; but "he had no pulse and no respiration," and it was obvious that the wound, if not mortal,

---

1. *Journal of the American Medical Association* 206, no. 3 (14 October 1968): 485.
2. Herbert S. Parmet and Marie B. Hecht, *Aaron Burr, Portrait of an Ambitious Man* (New York: Macmillan Co., 1967), p. 206.
3. Ibid., p. 212.

was very serious. If Dr. Bernays is right, it would have been more serious if the duel had occurred after breakfast. At the autopsy, "about a pint of clotted blood was present in the belly cavity, probably effused from the divided vessels of the liver." Nothing could have saved Hamilton. The French consul even had surgeons from French ships in the harbor—men accustomed to gunshot wounds— look at the dying man. . . .

Most readers of American history tend to see Burr as pretty black in soul, purpose, principles, and methods; and Hamilton as the son of morning. They were both human beings, both trapped by a foolish custom. There is no doubt that the Albany *Register,* 24 April 1804, carried quotations from letters of Charles Cooper to a friend explaining that Hamilton considered Burr untrustworthy and had said so in public. Burr had to demand a retraction; Hamilton had to refuse it. And the world was watching.

Hamilton found the only way out, for him: he wrote the night before the encounter that he intended to "receive and throw away his first fire"—hoping that Burr would "pause and reflect." But Aaron Burr was not of that mettle. He took a quick but careful aim, fired, and saw Hamilton fall. Even the eyewitnesses did not agree on exactly what happened; Hamilton supporters believe their hero did throw away his first fire; those on the other side thought Burr shot first, hit Hamilton, and caused him to twirl and shoot into the trees. The agreed facts are that both pistols were discharged within seconds of each other and Burr's shot took effect. After all, they were only ten paces apart and firing miniature cannon. Also, in the context in which we were raising this American example, it is probable that the wound, being an abdominal injury, would have been fatal more quickly if it had been inflicted after breakfast, as Burr had wanted it: he was not in favor of these early-morning encounters and would have met between seven o'clock and noon if he'd been able to have his own way.[4] Actually, by the period of the Burr-Hamilton duel, thoughtful people no longer accepted the *principle* of the duel as a technique for maintaining one's honor, keeping the peace, or determining guilt. Hamilton

4. Ibid., p. 207.

strongly disapproved of dueling; and Burr had been required to fight a duel and win it before he could go ahead with the "interview" with Hamilton. This is a little-known fact and still much shaded with secrecy. But one Samuel Broadhurst, who admired Hamilton, and who was related by marriage to Burr, heard about the impending duel. Although it was none of his business, he took it upon himself to insist on a chat with Burr at Richmond Hill, where he tried to persuade Burr to give up the fight. Instead, he was forced to give satisfaction himself, at Weehawken, where Burr gave the peacemaker a slash in the shoulder with a sword, thus winning the debate and leaving Burr free to go on with the Hamilton affair. But Aaron Burr should have remembered the time (in 1797) when Hamilton had challenged James Monroe. On *that* occasion, Burr was the peacemaker.

Politics was a rough-and-tumble game in our earlier days; and but for lucky accidents the pages of our history would be stained with considerably more blood: Clay and Randolph, for example: they had a duel, but even at the distances given they both missed —or was it on purpose?[5] Morison suggests in another place that it is possible that the "Cavaliers" of the American South were quick to pick a fight and quick to demand the satisfaction of their honor because they could not bear to be thought fearful. One of their governors (John L. Wilson of South Carolina) even wrote a textbook on dueling in 1838.[6]

Once in a while, even today, one reads of men with wounded feelings meeting in the morning mists to gain satisfaction, even if it's against the law. Representatives Conrado Rodriguez and José Luis Martínez of the Cuban House of Representatives shot at each other on a couple of occasions in 1955, missing each time, of course. "There was no reconciliation," says the report, "but the duelists . . . withdrew the personal descriptions of each other that had provoked the duel."[7]

5. Samuel Eliot Morison, *The Oxford History of the American People* (New York: Oxford University Press, 1965), p. 417.
6. Ibid., p. 503.
7. *New York Times*, 16 March 1955.

Readers with sharp eyes will be able to update the documentation on this subject with a new instance almost every month or so, if it seems worthwhile to them to do so—and it should, for we ought to retain some of our childhood wonder and not permit ourselves to become ancient, bored, satiated. Fourteen years after the Cuban duel, for instance, we find a United Press International wire story from Reykjavik. It pointed out that dueling in Iceland had been illegal since A.D. 1000, but that a Dr. Skuli Thoroddsen had nevertheless defied law and convention far enough to offer to duel to the death with any champion Queen Elizabeth of the British Isles might nominate. If he won, Britain would agree to remove the NATO troops then maneuvering in Iceland. If he was slain, all the British had to do was to pay for his funeral—nothing more.[8] But you really couldn't call this an affair of honor: this was, instead, the old tradition of the champion v. the champion—David v. Goliath, Sohrab v. Rustum—an excellent and most civilized way of settling a war, ten thousand times superior to dropping bombs and napalm and all that. Much too sensible a solution to be harbored by any contemporary ruler with the morale of the military-industrial complex on his—or, as it turned out, her—mind.

The formal ritualistic dueling as practiced today in West Germany by the Deutsche Burschenschaft, intended to create attitudes of manly courage, is something else again. This is not dueling for revenge or for any gain except to one's personal reputation for unflinching physical bravery in the face of probable bloodletting on a nonlethal scale. The Burschenschaft, Germany's oldest fraternal organization devoted to dueling, voted down a motion the other day to stop requiring members to fight at least one match with unbuttoned rapiers. These matches customarily draw blood, because the ritual demands that the participants must not flinch and may not move the feet to avoid a cut. The fraternities are supported, according to the special wire to the *Times* from David Binder, by "subsidies of rich former members" who enjoy seeing the old-fashioned virtue of male hardihood maintained.[9]

8. *New York Times*, 27 May 1969.
9. *New York Times*, 9 June 1969.

Blue Blood in a New Light

Quite properly scoffing at the notion that aristocrats have bluer blood than the rest of us, we once maintained that "no human being has blood with the faintest tinge of blue in it; all human blood is pure red, from vermilion to alizarin . . ."[10] and therefore the Spanish *sangre azul* is nonsense, and the pride in having "pure Castilian, uncontaminated with Jewish or Moorish blood," like the heroine of Maria Edgeworth's novel *Helen,* is an idiot arrogance.

The persistence of the idea was easier to understand when cultural notions of beauty involved very white skin, untouched by the sun, as they did before the suntan years. As our skin thickens in protection against direct rays of the sun on a beach or tennis court, naturally the veins do not show "blue" through the epidermis as they did when inactivity and a precious delicacy approaching downright bad health marked the beautiful heiress. Perhaps the phrase "blue blood" will gradually go out of usage if we continue to worship the sun. Even in the white-beauty days there were those who saw through the fantasy of blue blood, however. In *Euphues and His England* (1580) John Lyly said, "You talke of your birth, when I knowe there is no difference of blouds in a basen."

But is there, indeed, no such thing as blue blood, as previously claimed with such confidence?

In Rhoda Truax's *The Doctors Warren of Boston,* there is an eyewitness account of an open-heart surgical operation, in which she reports:

It is impossible to keep from shuddering when the retractors pull open the gaping wound to reveal the body's most vital organs. One can almost appreciate the ancient cry of "Sacrilege!" as hands reach in, a lung is thrust aside, and the throbbing heart, itself the size of the surgeon's fist, is grasped. Then, to one's secret relief, it becomes impossible to see exactly what is being done. Instruments are used, incisions are drawn, a cannula introduced, a catheter slipped into a blood vessel, tapes are ap-

10. Ashley Montagu and Edward Darling, *The Prevalence of Nonsense* (New York: Harper & Row, 1967), p. 83.

plied, hook-ups are completed—and the heart pumps blood no longer, it has become a useless organ. Outside the body a machine has taken over, drawing in blue blood, turning it red, and pumping it back into the body again.[11]

True, the blue blood doesn't *stay* blue; but it raises questions. Fortunately the inquiries are readily answered. The red cells in the blood of man are heavily loaded with the respiratory pigment hemoglobin, a protein that makes up over 30 percent of their weight. In the circuit from lungs to tissues and back—a tour of duty requiring something like forty-five seconds—the blood is not idle; and therefore, while its composition is kept nearly uniform by various regulatory mechanisms, it does change as it works. (Incidentally, "each red cell travels some 700 miles in its lifetime" and something like 1 percent of our red cells wear out daily—all of them being renewed within a period of about four months.)[12]

It is the job of the hemoglobin molecule to load and unload oxygen with all possible efficiency, and do much of the work of transporting carbon dioxide. "Each hemoglobin molecule is made up of four subunits. A subunit consists of a colorless protein portion (globin) and a flat red iron protoporphyrin molecule (heme). The iron forms a weak bond with the O_2 molecule and is thus directly responsible for the O_2 transporting property. This bond forms about a thousand times as fast as it breaks. The oxygenated molecule, called oxyhemoglobin, *is red in color; non-oxygenated hemoglobin is purple.*" [Italics added.][13]

Unless we are being very technical and perhaps speaking in actual wavelengths, purple and blue are close enough to be interchangeable, in a rough way. Thus what seemed blue to Mrs. Truax could have seemed purple to another observer. At least we do have respectable evidence that there does exist such a thing as more or less blue blood; also that in the same person, the blood may vary in color—

11. *The Doctors Warren of Boston: First Family of Surgery* (Boston: Houghton Mifflin Co., 1968), pp. 326–27.

12. James R. Newman, ed., *The Harper Encyclopedia of Science*, rev. ed. (New York: Harper & Row, 1967), p. 164.

13. Ibid., p. 871.

bluer just before picking up oxygen in the lungs, more crimson as it returns through the arteries.

In cyanosis, a condition in which the skin becomes blue, excessive amounts of deoxygenated blood enter the skin capillaries. Deoxygenated blood is intensely dark blue in color. It is the quantity of deoxygenated hemoglobin in the arterial blood that determines the degree of cyanosis. Since the red color of oxygenated blood is weak in comparison with the dark blue of deoxygenated blood, when the two are mixed the dark blue of the deoxygenated blood has the dominant coloring effect. When one turns "blue with cold," the effect is due to the slowdown of the blood flow in the skin capillaries with resulting deoxygenation and cyanosis.[14]

All we now ask is that if anybody finds himself bleeding blue after a cut or a scratch, please let us know. This one we'd like to see.

The Wasps of Skid Row

When Reginald Heber (1783–1826) wrote, in his "Missionary Hymn," "Though every prospect pleases,/ And only man is vile," he was reflecting a doctrine which the first Englishmen on these shores sternly inculcated into their children: in the words of the Bay Psalm Book, "In Adam's fall/ We sinn'd all." Man by comparison with the sweetness of the rest of nature is thoroughly depraved. An angry God will dangle him over the pit of hell as a boy roasts a spider (to employ Jonathan Edwards' cheerful simile, which had women screaming and fainting in the aisles at Enfield, Massachusetts, 8 July 1741).

So it is no surprise to encounter the myth of Man the Only Drunkard. Man, after all, is the only animal, according to many authorities, who makes war on his own species; who batters his own offspring— sometimes to death; who misuses the female of his species; who fouls his own environment with pollution and poison. No beast of the field or forest would behave so badly. Man is vile, thieving, lech-

14. Arthur C. Guyton, *Textbook of Medical Physiology*, 3d ed. (Philadelphia, W. B. Saunders, 1966), p. 612.

erous, depraved, and sodden. No other creature drinks itself into a stupor and then returns for more of the same. So goes the myth.

In terms of strict fact, man is not the only drunkard. Perhaps he does more harm than any other creature when he is drunk; but he is not the only creature to seek the solace of alcohol.

"Mr. Lawson Tait, the well-known English surgeon, says that sugar in certain fruits becomes changed into alcohol during the process of decay, and the wasps sometimes get very drunk thereon. On grapes and certain plums he says, 'You will see them get very drunk, crawl away in a semi-somnolent condition, and repose in the grass for some time till they get over the "bout," and then they will go at it again.' "[15] The English surgeon added that their sting was considerably worse when they were drunk, "both in the virulent nature of the stroke and in the utterly unprovoked assaults of which they are guilty." The good doctor ought to have known: he was himself bitten by a drunken wasp, and was poisoned for several days.

There seems to be no evidence to indicate that the act of the wasp is not completely deliberate. Perhaps he forgets, when he recovers from a spree, that it was the rotting grape or plum or apple or pear that sent him reeling; perhaps in his simple, direct mind, there is no connection between the fruit and the merry dizziness; or perhaps, manlike, he goes back for more with the determination that this time he won't take too much. The point is, he does go back. Whether he enjoys the "wild anarchy" of drink, as Ben Jonson put it, or the scent is so alluring that he cannot resist and says, with Stephano, "Tell not me! When the butt is out, we will drink water; not a drop before: therefore bear up and board 'em,"[16] we cannot know. It is tempting to think of him throwing back his regal shoulders, as it were, with a gesture and announcing the royal determination: "Today it is our pleasure to be drunk;/ And this our queen shall be as drunk as we."[17]

Any viniculturist is aware that fermentation begins about six hours after the pressing of the grapes, and the alcohol content in-

---

15. *Journal of the American Medical Association,* 206, no. 11 (9 December 1968): 2413, in the column "75 Years Ago," a reprint feature.
16. *The Tempest,* III. ii.
17. Henry Fielding, *Tom Thumb the Great,* I: 2.

creases steadily for something like forty days. (Ten centuries before Christ it was a law that "new wine had to be at least 40 days old before it could be offered as a drink offering" among the ancient Jews.)[18] Thus there is plenty of opportunity for the wasp to backslide, since rotting fruit lasts much longer than six hours.

Possibly it is true with insects, as it is with men, that heavy drinking will appeal to some and not to others. Perhaps the wasps who get drunk and go back for more are the problem drinkers among their kind. The old Hebrews were thankful to God for "wine that maketh glad the heart of man" (Psalms 104: 15) and even for the reinforced stronger drink that resulted from mixing certain spices with the wine—the combination produced "a very intoxicating concoction"[19]—as expressed in Proverbs (31: 6-7): "Give strong drink unto him that is ready to perish, and wine unto those that be of heavy hearts. Let him drink, and forget his poverty . . ." But they strongly condemned the abuse of liquor, and pointed to several black sheep as illustrations—Noah, Lot, Nabal, Benhadad, Ahasuerus, Holofernes, etc. And its use was forbidden to those administering the law—even to kings during judgment. There is a Talmudic story about Noah and the Devil which has Satan helping Noah to plant the first vine. Over the plant Satan successively sacrifices a lamb, a lion, a pig, and a monkey, thus warning Noah that one drink makes a lamb of you; two drinks make you a lion; three, a pig; and four, a monkey.

In the latter connection, an ancient tradition has it that monkeys are "drunken beasts." But there is no truth in this whatever. Certainly monkeys and apes are capable of becoming inebriated, but they do not do so under natural conditions, only when they are forced to by misguided men. As Ramona and Desmond Morris point out, it is the monkey's behavior, rather than its supposed love of alcohol, that led it to be described as drunken.[20] Inebriated men carry on in much the same wild and uncontrolled manner as monkeys normally do. Hence, by analogy, monkeys must be drunken.

18. Walter Duckat, *Beggar to King: All the Occupations in the Bible* (Garden City: Doubleday & Co., 1968), p. 266.
19. Ibid., p. 267.
20. *Men and Apes* (New York: McGraw-Hill, 1966), pp. 41-42.

The analogy is murky, its quality is not strained. It has no more of a leg to stand upon than a drunken soldier.

Yet there is truth in the "man the only drunkard" myth, if it is properly interpreted. If we read it to mean that man is the only animal to whom liquor is available and who has a mind capable of understanding what too much liquor will do to him, but still goes ahead, very much to his own hurt and the hurt of those close to him —and very likely to the hurt of the complete stranger in the car with which the drunkard collides—then the myth is the deadly truth. And very probably the man is sick. If not dead.

Hagridden by Hiccups

Probably the reader numbers himself among the thousands of sophisticates who scoff at most of the standard folk cures for colds and coughs, sneezes, belches, and hiccups. And why not, indeed, since so many folk remedies are patently silly—such as placing a sharp ax beneath the bed with the edge up to cut the pains of childbirth.

However, with hiccups it can be different, and one should scoff only with the most penetrating discrimination. Some of the tricks work.

The first thing to do is discriminate between coughs, belches, and sneezes on the one hand and hiccups on the other: the first three are reactions that protect the organism—a regular part of the body's apparatus for defense. One clears the throat; one eases the flatulent stomach; one opens the stuffed nostril. But the hiccup is a useless spasm that does nobody any good: it is nothing but a reflex—impulse to receptor to muscle—caused by an abnormal stimulation of the phrenic and the vagus nerves, which control the diaphragm and the glottis (the mouth of the windpipe). Hiccups often follow a surgical operation, or any one of a host of diseases.[21] Unless they are interrupted, they can be fatal, and it's a miserable way to go.

John Byron's best advice to himself was "To take what passes in good part/And keep the hiccups from the heart." Of course Plato mentions them—as what does he not? One recalls that Aristophanes

21. Berton Rouché, "Annals of Medicine," *The New Yorker*, 5 April 1969.

could not take his part in a dialogue because he had the hiccups, from either eating or drinking too much, and Eryxmachus advised him to try holding his breath. If that didn't work, he was to gargle with water. And if the hiccups continued, he should make himself sneeze by tickling his nose with a feather. It was the latter that worked, and this was also the method most approved by the famous Hippocrates. Even in those days it was known that once a series of hiccups is interrupted, the siege may be, and probably is, over.

Other routine folk remedies were to scare the patient unexpectedly; put a cold pack on the back of the neck; give the tongue a sharp tug—if one could hold onto it; and to drink a tumbler of cold water slowly. Today a doctor trying to cure a persistent hiccup might "wash out the stomach," use sedatives or narcotics or enemas and oil, or, as a last resort, operate upon the phrenic nerve itself to short-circuit the impulse causing the reflex.[22]

Roueché favors, among the empirical cures, having the patient breathe "for two or three minutes into a paper bag." This, of course, builds up the carbon dioxide—first, in the bag; second, in the lungs; and third, in the blood. That causes an emergency to which the respiratory centers in the brain respond in defensive action. "They move to eliminate the dangerous concentration of carbon dioxide by quickening and deepening the contractions of the diaphragm, and the hiccup spasms are tripped and broken."[23]

It is not always that simple, since hiccups can be caused by an allergy—possibly an allergy to some drug the doctor may already be giving to fight infection, as with a "strep throat"—or by a chronic but not serious illness such as irritation of the prostate gland; or perhaps it may have a psychological origin, which makes the symptom no less painful; or sheer age with its inevitable arteriosclerosis. In the case of Eliot Warren, which Roueché describes with such detailed fascination, cures for hiccups were accomplished, at least temporarily, by the use of digitalis, aluminum hydroxide, tolbutamide, an antihistamine, a diuretic, a choleretic, and sulfamethizole.

22. Morris Fishbein, ed., *Modern Home Medical Adviser* (Garden City, N.Y.: Doubleday & Co., 1949), pp. 35-37.
23. *New Yorker*, p. 108.

In the end it turned out that the last-named was a kind of drug the patient could not tolerate, and hence the hiccups continued and became so powerfully installed that for four weeks the patient could not be relieved of his distress: four tortured weeks of unbroken hiccups, constant jerking, sleepless nights, almost foodless meals until poor Warren was nearer dead than alive. Since in this case they were unable to interrupt the spasms—which is usually enough with most people—and could not find drugs to stop them, there remained no answer this side of surgery unless some mysterious allergy was at work. With the discovery that sulfamethizole activated the allergy, it was only a matter of substituting some other antibiotic, and the patient was cured permanently.

So we come back to the medical folklore of cures for hiccups—which, as many a physiologist will patiently explain, are merely a modified form of respiration[24] and are different from coughs and sneezes only in the fact that, as with the common mosquito, they appear to serve no useful purpose of any kind—and we find that, after all, most of them are true for *somebody*. The strangling singultus in young Jane, caused by a distention of the stomach, causes a sudden contraction in the diaphragm which is quickly cut off by the closing of the glottis; we say, "Poor Janie's got the hiccups," and we put her over our shoulder and gently burp the child. Very effective. Holding the breath works with Peter. A long cold drink does the job for you; a sneeze does it for me; and Uncle Henry, a tougher citizen than the rest, stops the hiccups by breathing into a paper bag. The sudden presentation of a new car as a gift will do it for almost any but the Eliot Warrens among us. Apparently the element of surprise combined with a sudden distraction will often cause that hesitation in the repeating reflex which returns us to normal.

We have waited until the end of this entry to give the reader something which we have steadily warned against—an absolute, infallible answer. In doing so we recognize that the swanlike necks of your correspondents are extended very prettily for anyone qualified to play the headsman. We just don't believe that any such person is

24. Edwin B. Steen and Ashley Montagu, *Anatomy and Physiology* (New York: Barnes & Noble, 1959), 2: 51.

ıg to show up; and that faith is based on thirty years of testing and experiment. The first reader to confute us gets a free ax.

Fritz Warndorf, the colorful founder of the Wiener Werkstadt movement in Austria in the 1880s, was the first to reveal the secret; and he had it from a young Viennese actress, which is as far back as we can trace it. After three decades of testing, it was written up in a report for the medical fraternity.[25] Here, then, is an infallible cure for hiccups:

Run water into a glass tumbler—it doesn't have to be full. Thrust into the glass of water a metal knife, fork, or spoon, with the handle sticking out. Place that handle against the right or left temple (of course, one must lift the glass to keep the metal submerged in water). Hold it in that position and sip the water slowly from the glass. Very slowly, with dainty swallows! *Little* sips, not great gulps.

It works in a few seconds. We don't know why it should—but it does.

The Severed Head That Lives On

Just as no field of human inquiry has been richer in supplying us with some of the most absurd imbecilities—nonsense at its aphelion, one might say—than the area of natural history, so we must concede that no field has been richer in providing things that have been *accepted* as myths but are based on truth. Perhaps a sort of transitional area can be called the proper home of the myth of the decapitated turtle.

The myth is that the turtle, in common with the snake, will not die until sundown, no matter what you do to him during the working day. Cut off the turtle's head—the body will wriggle around aimlessly for hours, and the eyes will follow your finger and the mouth snap at it, an act apparently of the severed head thinking for itself.

We said rather flatly in another place[26] that this attribution of supernatural powers to the turtle might reflect a "fear of the reptile

25. Ashley Montagu, "An Infallible Cure for Hiccups," *Journal of the American Medical Association*, vol. 196 (1966): 106.

26. Ashley Montagu and Edward Darling, *The Prevalence of Nonsense* (New York: Harper & Row, 1967), p. 263. (Also available as a Delta paperback, 1969.)

as a class" native to man—or rather early learned in man's primitive culture—and then we added, with something like a sublime smugness, "Certain it is that any vertebrate whose head has been removed is dead. Muscle spasms may occur after the removal of the head; but the snake *as a snake,* or the turtle *as a turtle,* is dead."

In the former book we invited readers, as we do here, to let us know where they find us in error. It's the only way: he who shows you your mistake is no enemy—he helps you to improve your case! Suitably enough, it was a man from Missouri (Ferguson, Missouri, to be exact) who wrote to us on this statement. He was forthright.

" 'Tain't true," he said. "I have witnessed the very occurrence of which you speak. The turtle in question was a small snapping turtle which my sister and I had caught on a fishing line intended for perch. Since we could not retrieve our hook from the turtle's mouth while it was alive, my father chopped its head off. However, it refused to die. The body wandered aimlessly around—which will surprise no one who has ever killed a chicken. The head, with the hook still in its mouth, continued to show every sign of life. By life I mean conscious awareness. The eyes continued to follow our movements and when we tried to get our fishhook from its mouth it snapped at us, as it also snapped at anything we put near it. Whether the setting of the sun had anything to do with its eventual demise I am not prepared to say. It was still alive at dusk when we went inside. It was dead next morning when we went out to look."

Subject to further confirmation we believe that story. It involves a final decision on the definition of death. It also raises the compelling moral question whether there is more than one definition of death. Or of life. The issues involve birth control and religion; human transplants of "spare parts"; and many extremely troublesome questions, on the subject of which mankind from priest to layman to medical specialist has been badgered. . . .

The most experienced heart-transplant surgeon, Dr. Denton Cooley of Saint Luke's Hospital, Texas Medical Center, Houston, has a definition which Harvard Medical School and others have endorsed. To him, the human heart is not the "seat of the soul, the source of courage," but a pump, "a servant of the brain. Once the brain is gone, the heart becomes unemployed. Then we must find it other employment."[27] But the man, *as a man,* is dead when the brain ceases to function. Still the heart, the liver, many other parts, may be life-giving to the patient who needs them. When the Dominican father Damien Boulogne received a new heart at Hôpital Broussais–La Charité in Paris, 1968, he asserted that the donor had not made any "sacrifice," as some kept saying. "He has already been in a closed circuit (the heart-lung machine) for days, and is therefore already dead. . . ."[28]

There may be useful life in the heart, the kidneys, and other organs, but when the brain ceases to function, the man is dead. That is the contemporary medical definition that seems to be establishing itself.

But what about the "conscious awareness" in the letter from Missouri? We cannot answer it. The eyes followed human movements from the severed head. The central nervous system was disconnected. But the beak still snapped. Was this conscious awareness, and is conscious awareness life? There is more in the myth of the turtle, in short, than meets the eye. Who has some better answer for the man from Missouri?

June Night and Moonlight: The Only Negative Things Are the Ions

The poetry of love makes it clear that the gentle passion is given additional tremulous courage under special conditions, such as the magic of moonlight or the mystery of a corner table illuminated only by tapers. Other favorable settings include the flickering hearthfire touched with the captivating incense of burning logs. Or, in a more active mood, the clear air of mountaintops—hills of high adventure from which the workaday world is a wonderful hazy blur. And, of course, Hollywood's favorite of all myths, the walk into the gorgeous flaming sunset where a promise is a holy thing.

27. Joseph Fletcher, "Our Shameful Waste of Human Tissue," in *The Religious Situation 1969,* ed. Donald R. Cutler (Boston: Beacon Press, 1969), p. 242.
28. Ibid., p. 242.

In fact, one of the things that makes June (American pronunciation: "Joon") the perfect stop for a line of poetry is that it rhymes appropriately with moon, as do practically all other rhymes in that family with the exception of "coon," "goon," "loon," and "prune," which are inappropriate and irrelevant.

This leads the inquiring mind to speculate on the possibility that if indeed there is some magic in moonlight and the other phenomena just named, whether there be not a cause, and what the nature of this cause might be. In a mood of generous chivalry, we could be tempted to say the magic resided in the lovely companion who shared the witchery. In that, dear reader, we would be wrong. That she heightened the magic cannot be denied; but the magic has its own existence apart from all human manipulation. In fact, we are again face to face with legend solidly supported by scientific research and established truth. Being reasonably certain that our brief recital cannot possibly harm the effectiveness of the enchantment itself, let us venture to draw the curtain aside.

With this warning: our simple explanation must not be looked upon as the sole and complete analysis of a situation as complicated as two lovers in the moonlight. We merely add an important factual decoration: but it *is* important, and perhaps it will be new to some readers.

The air we breathe is teeming with electrically charged particles called gaseous ions. In our generation, as is becoming more and more obvious, it is also full of many other things, products of industry and war, but of those we do not speak at the moment. These gaseous ions are generated by the billions through the operation of such natural processes as cosmic rays and ultraviolet radiation, as well as by radioactive elements in the soil, the friction caused by dust or sand blowing, storms, waterfalls, and winds.

Moreover, we can make these ions artificially by using radioactive isotopes, highly charged electric wires or coils, and by ultraviolet high-energy radiation. If there is an excess of positive ions—which of course we are breathing into the lungs and thus distributing into the bloodstream—then those of us with asthma begin to suffer; we all feel depressed and heavy; tempers flare; the crime rate rises;

domestic warfare increases; people with rheumatic joints feel an uncomfortable tingling in the bones; and the ants go into their holes and pull the covers over them. Positive ions are likely to be in excess during the blowing of any hot, dry wind, like the Alpine foehn flowing over southern Europe, or the Rocky Mountain chinook in America that drives the cattle half mad. And, of course, the famous dusty sirocco which blows northward from the deserts of Africa and Arabia is notorious for its effects upon behavior. It brings hot dry weather to Turkey, Greece, and Italy. "In Turkey," Ellsworth Huntington tells us, he "knew a missionary, a most noble character, who secluded himself as far as possible when the hot, dry sirocco blew. He feared that he would lose his temper and say something disagreeable."[29] Also a deep drop in barometric pressure causes an excess of positive ions. Blood pressure increases and people feel tentatively worried; those with sinus troubles find themselves with increased irritation and inflammation. Life is more work than it should be—harder to enjoy. Clarence A. Mills[30] tells of a man who could not continue to live in Cincinnati, an "extremely stormy" city, because he suffered so from sinusitis, which the climate exacerbated. Both the hot winds and the falling pressure appear to pull the positive ions from the soil and everybody feels lousy, except the young fry, who seem to be adaptable to almost anything. Much the same effects were found among people who work in air-conditioned buildings; but engineers have been trying to correct that and it should not prove a permanent disadvantage.

Quite the opposite effect is caused when there is an excess of negative ions in the air we breathe: we feel refreshed, alert, full of energy and euphoria. This has been demonstrated by machines in the laboratory, but it needs no learned physician with mask, gauntlets, and stethoscope to inform us whether we are breathing positive or negative ions. In the first case it's like being in a room full of stale hot air; in the second, it's like being on a mountaintop at dawn. When a thunderstorm approaches and the air is full of electricity which is building up to the corona point (point of discharge), there are

29. *Mainsprings of Civilization* (New York: John Wiley, 1945), p. 296.
30. *Climate Makes the Man* (New York: Harper & Brothers, 1942), p. 111.

clouds of negative ions in the atmosphere—and those breathing the
air feel as frisky as young colts. The same is true when the air is
clear and the barometer high or rising—which is usually the situation when lovers are out under a full moon that shines down with
that old silver magic. Part of the magic is negative ions. Which de-
tracts no whit from the delight of the occasion. Candles and open
fireplaces give off negative ions—and with them a feeling of well-
being.

Nobody is claiming that negative ions will *cure* anything; but
while one is breathing them, they improve one's attitude toward
life. More than that, patients rushed to hospitals with severe burns
have been treated with air containing five thousand to seven thousand negative ions per cubic centimeter and the pain has disappeared within minutes; and hay fever sufferers have found relief in
the same way.

Psychologists and others attempting to relate climate and weather
to human behavior have come up with a theory from time to time
to explain—or illuminate—trends which seem to match. For instance, Dr. Raymond Holder Wheeler of the University of Kansas
was convinced that warm, dry periods such as the decade 1920–30
tend to produce fanaticism, neurotic behavior, persecution of mi-
nority groups, and so forth, while colder periods bring religious re-
vivals and stimulate peace and travel.[31] If he is right, it ties in with
the ion theory, as does the unspoken prayer of head coach Earl
Blaik of Army the day before the 1946 Notre Dame game, the so-
called game of the century, when more than eighty thousand people
were expected to fill the stands. He was quoted by sportswriter Bill
Cunningham: "Given one wish at this point, I think we'd make it
for a dry, windless, but very cold day." That was because Army was
going to need stamina, and "the colder the day, the less exhausted
they'll get."[32]

If it were necessary to justify our talk about this subject by proving
that it has some practical application, one could do so easily enough.
No group of people takes themselves more seriously than the sales

31. Boston *Post,* 23 September 1945.
32. Boston *Herald,* 8 November 1946.

department, and they are always writing articles and how-to pieces on getting better results. "How Humidity Affects Sales" was the title of such a piece,[33] and the point was made that when people are physically uncomfortable, they spend a lot of money for health and comfort; thus "humidity's effect upon health and comfort is important for market analysis." The author goes on to show that now's the time to push those foot powders and lotions that fight fungus infections and keep the feet dry; and also to sell sandals to men; and air-conditioning and dehumidifiers and mildew removers and liquid cosmetics of many kinds, to say nothing of nonblistering paint and repair kits for cracked plaster in the house. . . . All these things come during high-humidity days—days when the positive ions are making you feel terrible anyhow. What happened to that moon?

The Worth of a Man: 87 Cents?

Though he be as great a teacher as Socrates, or music master to the gods, like Mozart, or a painter of the stature of Rembrandt, or an incredibly eloquent poet, like Shakespeare—as a man he is composed of hydrogen, oxygen, nitrogen, calcium, and so on, the total market value of which would not keep a chickadee in sunflower seeds for a month. There is some mocking devil in our makeup that reminds us of this from time to time. We hear Hamlet saying: "What a piece of work is a man! how noble in reason! how infinite in faculties! in form and moving how express and admirable! in action how like an angel! in apprehension how like a god!" (II. ii. 319–22) From Milton we hear that man is "a reasonable creature, God's image" (*Areopagitica*), and from Sir Thomas Browne that "Man is a noble animal, splendid in ashes and pompous in the grave" (*Urn Burial*) —and perhaps it gets to be a little too much, and for relief we turn to Pope, to learn that man is the "glory, jest, and riddle of the world" (*Essay on Man*), and we smile at the endless contradictions within this ape bereft of his tail and grown rusty at climbing. He can be heroic, he can be villainous, brilliant and stupid—and how

33. Paul H. Anderson, in *Printers' Ink* (28 January 1949). Author is Professor of Marketing, Loyola University of the South.

often, for all his wit, is he happy? There is an Oriental tale of a melancholy prince who sought to cure his sadness and was told that all he had to do was to wear the shirt of a perfectly happy man. So he sent out couriers according to the inescapable usage in these matters, and the messengers searched high and low and hither and yon until, on one dusty noon, one of them came in contact with a beggar who, like the famous miller, envied nobody and was entirely happy. "Great," said the envoy, much relieved. "I have sought you high and low and hither and yon. What'll you take for your shirt?" "It's not for sale," said the beggar, laughing more loudly than the messenger thought necessary. "Come on," he said, "no haggling. I'll pay whatever you ask—and I've got to have it!" "Very sorry," said the beggar. "I'd like to oblige. But you see, I don't *own* a shirt."

Hence, when the chemists tell us that a man—prince or pauper—is, intrinsically, worth very little in terms of raw materials, the fact satisfies some egalitarian longing to be as good as the next man and, with a flourish like putting whipped cream on the pudding, proves that none of us is worth much. We accept the myth.

And now, all of a sudden, the myth is outdated. It is no longer true. As Joseph Fletcher (author of *Morals and Medicine*) put it in a recent essay: "Not very long ago we found a measure of gallows humor in saying that a dead body or cadaver was worth about 87 cents—for its residual chemicals. But now a body has become very valuable—indeed, supremely precious—in terms of its lifesaving values."[34]

He is referring, of course, to spare parts no longer needed by the dead which can be used in modern surgery for transplants. Gruesome it may sound to the layman, not aware of how much medical lag he is suffering from; but when one realizes that in New York City alone there are always scores of kidney disease victims whose blood has to be periodically cleansed by running it through a machine outside the body for lack of a new kidney—which might be available to them from patients who had died in a city hospital (something like 80 percent of our people die in hospitals and not

---

34. "Our Shameful Waste of Human Tissue" in *The Religious Situation 1969*, ed. Donald R. Cutler (Boston: Beacon Press, 1969), p. 223.

at home)—the stark reality of the situation presents a bleak challenge to religious taboos of the dark ages in which we still live emotionally. Fletcher drives hard on this point:

"In cases of renal failure alone, 7,644 patients died in the United States in 1963. In the same year there were 10,600 kidneys available from patients dying of subarachnoid hemorrhage, a fairly abrupt death which leaves the kidneys in a normal condition."[35] In short, there were plenty of kidneys available. Patients who were slaves to chronic dialysis could all have been freed to useful living in society; and most of those who died could have been saved.

Not a great deal is said openly about this subject. Perhaps the reader was mildly shocked when we referred to "spare parts" a few lines above. People, sir, are not automobiles! They are not machines!

And yet a person dying from brain damage is really not going to be needing that liver of his, or those kidneys, once he is gone. In 1963, 4,000 livers were needed; and 5,300 persons died in hospitals of brain hemorrhage—more than enough to supply the need; yet the liver sufferers went on to death while the families cremated the victims of brain damage. Thus these cremated remains, instead of being worth a new life for some patient, were reduced to their intrinsic 87 cents' worth of residual chemicals—and nobody even thought of trying to cash in on that. So the whole operation was waste.

Which, indeed, makes the myth true, after all. It will be true that a man, intrinsically, no matter who he is or what genius he gave to the world while he was living, is worth essentially 87 cents in residual chemicals—uncollectible—until the time comes when we are ready, emotionally, to accept the enormous value he represents in terms—excuse it, please—of spare parts.

The Helpful—and Garrulous—Dolphin

Newspaper and magazine readers who saw the photograph of the interview which actor Jim Thorne had with the TV star Flipper could hardly help smiling. Thorne's grin was wide and his enjoy-

35. Ibid., p. 225.

ment was plain; but Flipper, who is a dolphin, had a smile which literally divided his head, opening it from eye to eye and displaying more teeth than anybody had seen in one gathering since one's own drawings in the golden nursery days. In the photo, Flipper is having a true belly laugh, there's no doubt about it. He is guffawing. And the teeth seem sprinkled all over the mouth. They do not look dangerous, and the merry glint in the dolphin's eye is utterly convincing of genial intention. There is none of that basilisk quality one sees in the eyes of a tiger who is displaying his teeth, for instance—and perhaps part of this depends upon there being no canine rippers in the dolphin jaw: all the teeth are the same size. "The mouth," says the *Britannica,* "is armed with sharp, slightly curved teeth, of uniform size, varying in number from forty to fifty on each side of both jaws." In short, the photograph may be showing as many as two hundred teeth in Flipper's jaws; there are fewer in Thorne's, but he looks equally happy.[36]

The reason for the photograph and the interview was the recent publication of Jim Thorne's book *The Underwater World* (New York: Thomas Y. Crowell, 1969), in which the author discussed some of the recent experiments of scientists and Navy men attempting to establish communications between men and *Tursiops truncatus,* the bottle-nosed dolphin—with a view, of course, to the former's controlling the latter and getting certain jobs done more easily. The dolphin should have a private word with the farm horse before he commits himself too far—that is, if he can find any farm horses. (They don't crowd to the pasture bars the way they used to: of the 17,912,944,000 total horsepower of all prime movers in this country in 1968, only 1,460,000 was produced by work animals.)[37]

Two years before the Thorne-Flipper interview, the Hudson Laboratories at Dobbs Ferry, New York, operated for the Navy by Columbia University, announced through its director, Dr. Alan Berman, that "Dolphins have been trained to attach wires to tor-

36. *Publishers' Weekly,* 19 May 1969.
37. *Statistical Abstract of the United States,* 1969, p. 509.

pedoes and missiles lying on the ocean floor, thus greatly simplifying undersea recovery operations." Other things that get lost in the sea are sunken submarines, occasional lost hydrogen bombs, and things like airliners that crashed on the water. "One of the most effective recovery tools," said Dr. Berman, "is a trained porpoise." He meant the bottle-nosed dolphin, according to Walter Sullivan, the *New York Times* reporter who filed the story, and referred to work being done at the Navy's Marine Bioscience Facility at Point Mugu, California.[38]

Recovery techniques with dolphins have reached a high stage of sophistication; the animals will "home" on the signal of an acoustic beacon. "The dolphin has been so far domesticated that even though free in the open ocean, it swims back to its mother ship or base after completing its task," the Sullivan account said.

It is this sort of new interest in dolphins which in recent years has caused a reexamination of ancient myths and former knowledge of these curious animals. Mankind has always been fascinated with dolphins. Anyone who visits one of the pools where they live and disport themselves (the number of these is growing every year) can understand why, in the first ten seconds. The dolphins squeak and gork, they make a creaking-door sound, they appear to laugh, they are playful, powerful, graceful, and very, very curious. Our interest in them is more than five thousand years old, as indicated by a seal from Crete probably dating from 3500 B.C., with a dolphin as the central figure. Dolphins appeared in temples, on floors, in paintings, on vases from Cyprus, in Minoan art, in Corinth, Tiryns, and many places; and of course—then as now—they became part of the literature in both fiction and nonfiction. Without pressing this aspect too hard, one can point to the *New York Times Book Review* of 13 July 1969, where on one page appears an advertisement for *This Summer's Dolphin* by Maurice Shadbolt (Atheneum) and on another a review of Robert Merle's *The Day of the Dolphin* (Simon & Schuster) in which Nancy Wilson Ross (*The Left Hand Is the Dreamer*) says: "There is probably no mammal on the face of the earth or in the depths of the sea which has so captured the warm

38. "Dolphins Operate Sea Lost & Found," *New York Times,* 23 March 1967.

affection and the slightly mystified admiration of man as the dolphin. . . ."

In Greek days, dolphins were associated with Dionysus in a number of ways. The god of fertility and especially of the vine was supposed to be a native of Thebes, where he "was born to Zeus by Semele, the daughter of Cadmus. Semele was destroyed by the lightning of her lover, and the child was born after six months. Zeus accordingly sewed it up in his thigh till ripe for birth and then gave it over to Ino, the daughter of Semele. . . ."[39] (The Greeks liked their stories interestingly complicated.) The worship of Dionysus began to spread out to the wine-growing islands and flourished in particular at Naxos, where the god took Ariadne to wife. A tale from Naxos narrates that some Tyrrhenian pirates shanghaied Dionysus and took him in chains to their ship. But as soon as they got the wind in their sails, the chains fell off the prisoner, the sails and masts became covered with vines and ivy, Dionysus himself turned into a lion, and all the sailors jumped overboard —and became dolphins.

In another version, Dionysus, like other nature gods, disappeared or perished in the winter (precisely like Persephone) and returned to life in the spring—brought back by dolphins.

Just as in the literature of today, much that was written about dolphins in the old days was purest fantasy; but much of it was true. The whole body of literature and belief about dolphins was, until quite recently, largely rejected as entirely mythological. But it is now beginning to be seen as true, at least in part. That is the point of this essay. It is also the main thesis of a little book published in 1963.[40]

In this study of *The Dolphin in History*, it is maintained that stories and facts which had been known for thousands of years to earlier people, especially inhabitants of the Mediterranean world, suffered "a virtually complete loss of knowledge" and disbelief, particularly in the sophisticated circles of the western world. Scholars

39. Oskar Seyffert, *A Dictionary of Classical Antiquities* (New York: Macmillan Co., 1906).
40. Ashley Montagu and John C. Lilly, *The Dolphin in History* (Los Angeles: Clark Memorial Library, University of California, 1963).

"dismissed as myths the tales told about dolphins in classical antiquity."[41]

However, our present book is concerned with alleged myths that are true; and we will hold that any wholesale dismissal of the classical library on this subject is folly—as is being more clearly demonstrated every day we live. Some of today's narratives about dolphins are clearly fiction; some of yesterday's were also fiction, it is equally clear. When we read that Icadius was saved from drowning by a dolphin who swam the hero over to Parnassus, where he founded a temple to Apollo, his father, thus setting up the cult of Apollo Delphinus (from which Delphi gets its name), and that in consequence Apollo held the dolphin a most sacred animal from then on, we are entitled to a smile—but one no broader than that occasioned by the personality changes engendered in humans by a dolphin whose cave the bipeds invaded, as described in a 1969 novel, *Destiny and the Dolphins,* by Roy Meyers!

Pliny the Elder wrote that dolphins love to play around ships in the harbor, that they will eat out of one's hand, gambol with swimmers, and give piggyback rides to children; and in a more practical mood, help fishermen by driving schools of fish into the nets. The *Britannica* says that their playfulness "and apparent relish for human society have attracted the attention of mariners in all ages" and that running into a school of dolphins at sea "was regarded as a good omen."[42]

An Associated Press dispatch in 1969 told of divers in Galway Bay who were trying to lay the foundations for a new lighthouse. They soon noticed that a dolphin was watching closely everything they did. Soon he began diving up and down with the workers, clearly under the impression that they wanted to play. As a starter, he "knocked over bags of cement from pontoons with his snout,"[43] and managed to tangle up the lines mooring the boats of the divers. As he danced away, waiting for one of his human playmates to make a countergesture, observers guessed his weight at about a ton, and his

41. Ibid., p. 6.
42. *Encyclopaedia Britannica,* 11th ed.
43. *New York Times,* 16 September 1969.

speed in the water at about fourteen miles per hour—at which rate
he could knock the breath out of a diver pretty thoroughly. The only
thing the local humans could think of to do was to scare the dolphin away with an underwater explosion or something of the sort.
It was impossible to explain to him that this was not a game and
that while they loved his frolicsome spirit, they had to get the damn
stones in place within a certain time span. It seems a great pity; but
when our communications systems have advanced further, perhaps
a better solution will be found.

At any rate, the playfulness recorded among the classical Greeks
is obviously a trait which is still being exhibited by these charming
creatures; and in the same way, the tales of help given to Greek fishermen, who would attract schools of fish with torches and then call
out a signal to the local dolphins, whereupon they would gather
and chase the fish into the nets, are echoed in our own day by stories
from New Zealand, Queensland, the Florida and Carolina coasts,
and elsewhere—some areas will produce fishermen who claim that a
gifted person among them can call the dolphins by name, although
this may cause a cocking of heads among the skeptics.

Visitors to dolphin tanks have seen for themselves that the animals can be taught to walk on their tails upon command; jump
eight feet out of the water to take a cigarette from the mouth of the
trainer or twist through a hoop; throw a basketball through a goal
ring, and do all sorts of tricks.[44]

In short, we have an extremely interesting animal under consideration, and he has been fascinating us for thousands of years. We
can therefore forgive an occasional fantasy, such as Poseidon's woo-
ing of Amphitrite—which could not have prospered unless a dolphin
had revealed to the god the hiding place of the nymph. Poseidon,
in gratitude, set the dolphin among the stars in the constellation
bearing its name even today. Not all the tales of dolphins saving
swimmers from drowning are fiction, whether related by Herodotus or by a modern wire service. The Greek historian cited the instance of Arion of Methymna, the world's foremost artist on the

44. Photographs in *New York Times,* 7 August 1969; Cape Cod *News,* 11 September 1969, etc.

lyre and supposed inventor of dithyrambic poetry, who was saved from robbers when he jumped overboard and was carried to Taenarum on a dolphin's back. More recently, there has been reported the adventure of E. J. Lemaire, the captain of a shrimp boat out of Port Lavaca, Texas, who fell overboard into the Gulf of Mexico, five miles from land, in shark-infested waters. A school of dolphins surrounded him shortly after he started swimming, he said, and pushed and nudged him along—at the same time keeping the sharks away. Lemaire said he never in the world would have made it without the dolphins' help.[45]

In short, the friendliness of dolphins toward mankind is not only a matter of tradition; it is, in its way, a somewhat pitiful modern truth—pitiful because even when the dolphin is tied up helplessly and subjected to scientific experimentation (including having electrodes hammered into the skull and whatnot) he won't fight the scientist. "Dolphins, even if painfully treated, do not attack human beings. . . . They will attack sharks. . . . They are quite capable of tearing or biting an arm or a leg off a man or of damaging him internally by ramming, but there is no record of these animals ever having damaged a human, even when the human has mistreated them."[46]

And so it goes: as one reconstructs the old-time proverbs, legends, myths, and beliefs about dolphins and compares them with today's laboratory discoveries and news reports, it is amazing how many items check out as verifiable. It is also delightful to note how many fanciful stories have sprung from mankind's interest in the animal— but one could point to the dog, for example, or to the domesticated (if that ever really happens) cat as similar sources of amazing fact and amazing fantasy. As a sample of the middle ground, dolphins were said to feed on trees—by Lycophron, Ovid, and Nonnus Panopolitanus, among others. Fact: the diet of dolphins—with one exception—is fish. The one exception: *Sotalia teuszii,* which inhabits

45. *New York Times,* 9 July 1969.
46. John C. Lilly, *The Mind of the Dolphin* (Garden City, N.Y.: Doubleday & Co., 1967), p. 61.

the Cameroon River, does eat vegetable matter and may feed on it exclusively—but how in the world would such news reach Ovid and the rest? Perhaps it never did—we have to accept that possibility. Those authors could have "just made up" the story. We can put it down as a wonderful coincidence and let it go at that.

But what about the numerous stories of children—and adults, too —riding on a dolphin's back to safety? In our day there has been plentiful evidence of the truth of this picture. Not that a child has mounted a dolphin as the animal's master and director, as with a pony or a horse—although the illustrations suggest this relationship; but that the human has at least partly ridden the dolphin at the dolphin's invitation and has indeed been steered into safe waters. It would be a pretty piece of balancing on a slippery surface to ride a dolphin in the manner of Marlowe's Tamburlaine ("Is it not passing great to be a King . . . And ride in triumph through Persepolis?"). Nevertheless, the idea of riding to safety is no myth. "The boy riding on the back of a dolphin is now removed from the realm of fancy and placed squarely in the realm of fact. It has been corroborated and sustained."[47] One of the most endearing corroborations came in 1955 from Opononi, on the western side of North Island, New Zealand, where Opononi, a female dolphin, used to enjoy coming into the shallow water at the beach and playing around the wading children. Opononi liked Jill Baker especially—probably because she was gentle and did not rush at the animal with cries and splashings. Opononi liked to be stroked and patted and was a real playmate for Jill, who wrote the experience in her own words.[48]

In fact it is a remarkable commentary on the arrogance and ignorance of the certainty of the learned that man's centuries-old understanding of the dolphin was simply cast aside, forgotten, derided by the academicians and scientists of the western world after the dawn of the Age of Science. The typical attitude was expressed by Norman Douglas in his criticism of the Greek Anthology: "The dolphin cares no more about us than cares the haddock. What is the origin of this

47. Montagu and Lilly, *Dolphin in History,* p. 16.
48. Antony Alpers, *Dolphins,* 2d ed. (London: John Murray, 1963), pp. 206–21.

belief? . . . Mankind, loving the merry gambols . . . were pleased to invest it with feelings akin to their own. . . ."[49]

Now we have the answer, according to Dr. Lilly—one of the founders, in May 1959, of the Inter-Species Communications Research Institute. It's a matter of brain size and complication: the number of neurons and the interconnections between them. Humans have something like 13 billion neurons in the brain prior to birth; before we can speak, the brain must weigh 800 to 1,000 grams and have 10^{10} (10 billion) neurons and connections. "No interspecies communication has been achieved," says Dr. Lilly, "with primates having smaller brains than man's."[50] He means *inter*-communication, of course: messages passing both ways. That dolphins can communicate with each other has long been established. T. G. Lang and H. A. P. Smith of the U.S. Ordnance Test Station in Pasadena reported a series of tests in which a male dolphin in one tank chatted with a female in another by means of hydrophones, despite the fact that each was invisible to the other. The vocabulary consisted largely of whistles and clicks, but the investigators were convinced that a conversation was in progress. Dolphins also make creaking-door noises, barks, grunts, rasping sounds, and so on.[51]

"In 1957," Dr. Lilly says, "I discovered their ability to produce sounds similar to our speech sounds. . . . They quickly discover that they can obtain various kinds of rewards by making what we now call 'humanoid emissions' . . . When they make a sound . . . similar to a human syllable or word, we express our pleasure by rewarding the animals in various ways."[52]

Thus we have reached the point where not only is the language of the dolphins being decoded, as it were, but we are learning their speech and they are learning ours, and so, as Elisabeth Mann Borgese puts it: "Mankind has turned full circle, and mythical past and

---

49. *Birds and Beasts of the Greek Anthology* (London: Chapman & Hall, 1928), p. 161; cited in Montagu and Lilly, *Dolphin in History*, pp. 13–14.
50. *Mind of the Dolphin*, p. 20.
51. "Two Dolphins 'Chat' on Hydrophones," *New York Times*, 31 December 1965.
52. *Mind of the Dolphin*, p. 44.

scientific future, dream and reality, meet once more."[53] And Jacques Graven adds: "The question is settled: there can be, in the mind of an animal, a certain association between human language on the one hand and objects of actions on the other."[54]

In a human being about five feet nine in height, the brain averages two and three-quarters pounds; in *Tursiops truncatus,* the dolphin on which we have been focusing, the animal can be eight feet long and the brain can weigh three and three-quarters pounds. (Compare the chimpanzee, whose brain weighs three-quarters of a pound; and the gorilla, about one pound.) The dolphins learn very fast: in a case where it was necessary to flip a switch in order to obtain a reward, "the first successful trial was all he needed to learn the trick."[55] In another case, a baby dolphin was being nursed artificially in a tank, having lost its mother. Seeking comfort, the baby gave the dolphin distress whistle. Humans did not respond; nobody came to the baby. So he tried thumping his flipper rhythmically against the tank. The hydrophone amplified the sound, and people came running. In one jump the baby had learned how to get attention. There is certainly no question about the intelligence of these fabulous creatures; nor does anyone who has observed them performing for a trainer they understand and like doubt for one second that they understand much of what is said to them and thoroughly enjoy applause.

It is not hard to understand why there was a suggestion in the Greek tales that dolphins had once been men. They have traits that strike us today as being human. Perhaps we need to be reminded that millions of years ago, whales and dolphins lived on land and walked on all fours. Their long, slender bodies and finlike flippers give them so fishlike an appearance that even today many people do not realize that they are true mammals. This fact was emphasized dramatically not long ago when a Florida dolphin, purchased by Christian Toft for his castle in Denmark as a tourist attraction, drowned when its snout got stuck in a drainpipe. The dolphin is not

53. *The Language Barrier: Beasts and Men* (New York: Holt, Rinehart & Winston, 1968), p. 3.
54. *Non-Human Thought* (New York: Stein & Day, 1967), p. 180.
55. Lilly, *Mind of the Dolphin,* p. 77.

a sea animal, basically.[56] Indeed, it is a matter of general knowledge that whales, which are simply large dolphins, do drown fairly often. "When ill or exhausted, they tend to roll over and take too much water through their spouts.[57]

Nothing the Greeks related in their wildest fiction, however, surpasses in fantasy the material being ground out by our own science fiction writers about dolphins, and we should recognize this as an important indication that the dolphin has always fascinated man: the glossy and graceful animal with the big grin is by no means a has-been. To cite only one author, Roy Meyers writes "original paperbacks" for Ballantine Books. These are volumes one finds in railway stations, at airports, in subways and large drugstores—in short, popular books with large sales and first printings of at least sixty thousand copies. Meyers first produced *The Dolphin Boy;* then *Daughters of the Dolphin;* and in 1969, *Destiny and Dolphins.* The central character of the most recent book is Sir John Averill. He goes Mowgli and Tarzan one better: he was brought up by dolphins, having been lost in the Caribbean as a child. He has a "peculiar lung construction" which permits him to survive; and he talks dolphinese and can swim with the same speed and dexterity as the dolphins themselves (Meyers says, "hurtling through the seas at nearly thirty knots,"[58] which seems a *little* speedy, even for these sleek characters). The sea also gives Sir John an apparent immortality. At least, he does not age in appearance in the course of a score of years. This makes marriage between him and any human "upper air" girl a problem, of course—but that's not our concern. It was our purpose to show that some of the early writings about dolphins were not myth, as supposed, but based on fact; but that there was—and is—a great deal being written on the subject which *is* fiction.

One further indication of the popularity of the animal is the number of meanings which the word "dolphin" can indicate. According to the *Oxford English Dictionary,* "dolphin" has been used to mean

56. *New York Times,* 7 August 1968.
57. Charlie Rice in *This Week,* 6 November 1966.
58. *Destiny and Dolphins* (New York: Ballantine Books, 1969), p. 10.

a black aphis; the handles on a medieval cannon; a northern constellation; a symbol of the sea; a French gold coin; an emblem of love; the popular name for a colorful fish (the dorado) which changes color rapidly when taken from the water; a strap of plaited cords around a mast to aid in supporting the yard; a mooring with a ring in it; even a mass of iron or lead to drop on an enemy ship. And, of course, the musical organ called the delphinus. None of which are mythical.

III

Myths from Bucolic and Folk Medicine: They Had a Reason

Oysters Unwholesome in Non-r Months?

Nobody knows how long the oral tradition of the folk has insisted that oysters are bad for one in months which have no *r* in their name; but in the *written* tradition, the tireless Burton Stevenson has traced the idea to 1577, when William Harrison mentions the proverb in his *Description of England*. The maxim itself appears in English in 1599 in Henry Buttes' *Dyets Drie Dinner:* "The Oyster . . . is vnseasonable and vnwholesome in all the monethes, that have not the letter R in their name."[1] Stevenson adds, editorially, that from May to August oysters "are not really unwholesome, but merely insipid because they are spawning." However, the idea of seasonal poison persisted, and later writers of proverbs continued to repeat the notion, even so superior a character as Lord Chesterfield writing in a letter that the town is dull in summer, so that "there is no domestic news of changes and chances in the political world, which like oysters, are only in season in the R months, when the Parliament sits."

Bergen Evans duly records the saying in his blithe volume on nonsense, but brushes it off as a popular error parallel to the notion that oysters are aphrodisiacs, as Casanova held. He quotes a U.S. Government handbook, *Consumer's Guide,* to the effect that modern

1. Burton Stevenson, *The Home Book of Proverbs, Maxims and Familiar Phrases* (New York: Macmillan Co., 1948), p. 1735.

methods of refrigerating and shucking make oysters edible in any month.[2]

Others have explained the origin of the forbidden months by saying this has been mankind's way of conserving the oyster beds: if people let them alone during the growth period, there'll always be plenty of oysters, but if they're taken during the spawning season, the supply will dwindle.

But that there is any truth in the prohibition is denied by those in the know. One of us ate oysters in his youth by the double handful in July and August along the banks of Bass River, off Nantucket Sound, and lives to tell it.

However, if applied to other shellfish—that is, mussels—the legend does have a basis in truth. Oysters prefer warm, shallow water and river estuaries where the saltiness is reduced somewhat by the inflow of fresh water. Mussels thrive in colder temperatures, like those of the Pacific coast. Here, in summer and early fall, the plankton is likely to be full of the dinoflagellate *Gonyaulax*. (The plankton, composed of millions and millions of plants, makes the sea water seem like mercury in the moonlight. The single-cell dinoflagellates whip their way through the water with their flagella, one working in a groove around the "waist" and the other driving them forward from behind: "They screw themselves through the water."[3] Amazing things, some of them both plant and animal at the same time.)

This particular dinoflagellate, the genus *Gonyaulax,* "contains a poison of strange and terrible virulence," and mussels feeding on the plankton accumulate the poisons of the Gonyaulax in their liver. "The toxins react on the human nervous system with an effect similar to that of strychnine. Because of these facts, it is generally understood along the Pacific coast that it is unwise to eat shellfish taken from coasts exposed to the open sea where *Gonyaulax* may be abundant, in summer or nearly fall."[4]

2. Bergen Evans, *The Natural History of Nonsense* (New York: Alfred A. Knopf, Vintage Paperback, 1958), p. 158.
3. Alister Hardy, *The Open Sea: The World of Plankton* (Boston: Houghton Mifflin Co., 1956), p. 47.
4. Rachel L. Carson, *The Sea Around Us* (New York: Oxford University Press, 1951), p. 33.

Symptoms of strychnine poisoning are horrible indeed—suffocation, convulsions, the face livid, the eyes staring, spasms in which the body is bent backward—enough to scare anybody away from shellfish in the non-*r* days, to be sure. And since Alister Hardy pulled *Gonyaulax* out of the English Channel,[5] one would expect to find more credence in England for the *r*-months warning than on the East Coast of the United States, where the seasonal visit of *Gonyaulax* does not seem to occur.

It may be, indeed, that Rachel Carson has turned up a bit of folk wisdom as old as anything England can boast: she points out that "for generations before the white men came, the Indians knew" about *Gonyaulax;* and "as soon as the red streaks appeared in the sea and the waves began to flicker at night with the mysterious blue-green fires, the tribal leaders forbade the taking of mussels until these warning signals should have passed. They even set guards at intervals along the beaches. . . ."[6]

Here we have been able to trace a supposed myth back to the scientific fact which makes the strange thing true—but only for mussels. Applied to the much-loved oyster, the maxim, we report happily, is clearly false: in support of which claim we can cite three sources resulting from personal correspondence.

The first is a mimeographed release from the national Fish and Wildlife Service (dated 29 March 1964, and entitled "Interior Exposes Oyster 'R-Month' as Myth"). Here we learn that oysters "are fatter and taste better in spring," specifically in May and June, than at any other time, because they are then beginning to store glycogen preparatory to spawning. Far from being dangerous months, May and June are the best months, despite the fact that the harvest is habitually undertaken in September and October. Reason: "The demand is seasonal and the prices are highest at that time." The statement then adds that the economic fact is probably based on the false myth! As for the origin of the myth itself, Dr. J. L. McHugh of the Bureau of Commercial Fisheries is quoted as blaming the spawning habits of the European oyster, which is unique in that the mother retains

5. *Open Sea,* p. 48.
6. *The Sea Around Us,* p. 33.

the young until small shells have developed—and these are gritty to the bite during the non-*r* months, so nobody wants to eat oysters at such a time.

The second is a confirmation from Mr. John H. Ryther of the Woods Hole Oceanographic Institution: "The poisonous dino-flagellate has never been reported from New England south, in the heart of the oyster country. . . . Spawned-out oysters are thin and watery during the summer months and therefore not particularly good." He corroborates the gritty shells in the " 'flat' or 'Belon' oyster of France."

The third is from the director of the Division of Marine Fisheries of Massachusetts, Mr. Frederick C. Wilbour, Jr. He states: "Mussels do have a toxic effect created by the dinoflagellate *Gonyaulax,* but our Division of Food and Drugs monitors this shellfish for this condition and as yet have found no traces of it in Massachusetts. I have never heard of this condition existing in oysters."

The defense rests.

Nine Months for Gestation—and Then What?

When the first baby is born to newlyweds and the matrons of the neighborhood make a careful count of their fingers, with level or raised eyebrows as the case may be, the number in everybody's mind is most certainly nine. The gestation period in humankind is nine months, and let's not fool around with *that*. It may be—and indeed is—sixty-three days for cats and dogs and 624 for the elephant; but for man it is 267. "The longest period of gestation in man that has ever been admitted in the law courts in Great Britain is 360 days," says Webster III. And that was stretching it into the realm of the incredible.

Morals aside, it really does depend on what one means by "gestation." The word comes from a root which has been so rich in its various proliferations that cousin can hardly recognize cousin. Consider, for instance, the fact—the undoubted fact, according to Eric Partridge—that "congeries" and "register," along with "gesture," "exaggerate," "suggest," "gesticulate," "jest," "digest," and rags and tatters of a score of others, are all branches or twigs from the basic Latin *gerere,* "to bear, to carry, to act, to perform."[7]

However, there is a "usual" meaning, and Webster is sharp on this point. "Gestation," whatever the roots and flowerings, is being used in contemporary American speech to mean the carrying of the young, usually in the uterus, from conception to delivery, and the parallel is "pregnancy."

Incidentally, it was not always so in our tongue. Elyot, in his sixteenth-century book on health, averred, "Gestation in a chariot or wagon hath in it a shaking of the body, but some vehement, and some more soft." The reference, presumably, was to the previous year's model as compared with the one just released. (But of course there were no annual models with built-in obsolescence in those dusty, honest, pre-macadam, forty-miles-a-day eras.) Health experts, however, were telling their readers that it was a good thing to shake up the body occasionally. And they used the word "gestation," in a meaning now obsolete, as "being carried in a coach, litter, upon horseback, or in a vessel on the water."[8]

The period of gestation for man, however, to get right down to cases, is not nine months, as stated. It's more like nineteen or twenty months. And to understand this, one must forget customary assumptions and take a deep plunge into evolution, where things don't happen overnight and may, to be sure, take a score of millions of years to find a statement which satisfies everybody. If that reminds one of the United Nations, one can only remark, with a smirk, *"Plus ça change, plus c'est la même chose."* Something awfully satisfactory in that remark, French or no.

As man began to lose his instincts and had to rely upon his intelligence for survival (possibly because of climatic changes in the African homeland) he developed an "extended dependency period" during which he learned survival techniques from the parent during a season of comparative physical helplessness; and also developed a "complicated storage-retrieval repository, that is, a brain large

7. *Origins* (London: Routledge & Kegan Paul, 1959).
8. Richard C. Trench, *Dictionary of Obsolete English* (New York: Philosophical Library paperback, 1958).

enough to house the many billions of cells and their circuits necessary to serve such an intelligence."[9]

At this point we begin to approach the mark of the difference that
lies between ourselves and our cousins of the fields and forests. In
doing so, we also make less valid any parallels that one might be
tempted to draw between the two in order to explain the behavior
of man: a piece of folly that many intelligent investigators have permitted to betray them. For we are different: we are human. The
mouse, after nineteen days in the littered womb, emerges temporarily blind but able shortly to run like mad and needing no instruction in feeding. A human offspring unattended for month after
month would die. Instinct will not teach him to survive. But what a
piece of work he is thirty years later when he steps down off the
platform with his Ph.D. . . . This is a point which Goddard em-
phasizes again and again—the glory of our species: the slow beginning and the immense potential.[10]

Thus when the human child is *born,* "it has completed only half
its gestation. That part which it has spent in development within its
mother's womb is called *uterogestation.* The other half of its gestation the human infant must complete outside the womb in the continuing symbiotic relationship with its mother. This second half of
its gestation is called *exterogestation.* . . ." And this lasts about ten
months, at which point the infant usually begins to crawl around
by itself.[11] Part of the infant's environment, then, is manmade—it
is cultural. An erect posture, a large brain, a loss of instinctual behavior, a gain in responsive problem-solving activity (intelligence);
birth in a still highly dependent state, a long, dependent infancy, and
above all the development of cooperative behavior—these constitute
the unique endowment of every normal human offspring. To make
glib parallels between this small beast and any other animal is to
walk a tightrope with greased soles. For here is a mind capable of

9. Ashley Montagu, "Brains, Genes, Culture, Immaturity, and Gestation," in *Culture: Man's Adaptive Dimension,* ed. Ashley Montagu (New York: Oxford University
Press, 1968), pp. 102–13.

10. Harold C. Goddard, *The Meaning of Shakespeare* (Chicago: University of
Chicago Press, 1951), p. 21 and passim.

11. Ashley Montagu, *Man: His First Two Million Years* (New York: Columbia
University Press, 1969), p. 51.

using complex symbols, of facing novelty, of solving problems without prior experience in them. Inarticulateness for the first time is banished and control of the environment gets its initial faltering beginnings.

Yet the original belief is true: gestation is completed—to a point —with delivery of the infant. He is now, properly speaking, born. But among humans, nothing comes of this pending the learning necessary in an equal amount of time in the outside world—and in this difference lies what is laughingly referred to as man's salvation.

An Apple a Day: and a Rest for Your Doctor

The old couplet assures us that an apple ingested diurnally will put the doctor on welfare—a prospect cheerful enough for the patient, perhaps, but hardly calculated to encourage young men to invest in those grinding years of medical school and internship and all that. However, since the young men continue to enter medical schools, we can perhaps assume that the old rhyme—so old that it is not even attributed to any known author—is actually nothing but an ancient saw reflecting the health values of eating fresh fruit and using as an example the abundant pome fruit of the genus *Malus,* occurring in wild and cultivated form all over western Europe and the New World. Its very name is practically unchanged, from the Crimean Gothic *apel* across to the Old Norse *apall;* and many are its legendary attributes and powers. But it is necessary to remember that the term *apple,* probably referring merely to the shape, is also used in English to mean the May apple, the love apple (tomato), and the oak, pine, balsam, and thorn apple. Our reference here is restricted to the pome fruit.

Marvelous things are told of it. Beginning prosaically with its simple powers as a home remedy (Eugene Field said, "The best of all physicians is apple pie and cheese"), the apple gets credit as an aid to fertility (Gna, the messenger of Frigga, dropped an apple to King Rerir, and when he ate it in company with his queen, she was able to conceive) and eventually as a specific for every human disorder (Prince Ahmed in the *Arabian Nights* found that it cured anything).

Love charms based on use of the apple are found in voodoo, and in Danish, German, and English folklore. In one Danish tradition, the fruit is a test of chastity—the apple will fade magically if the owner is unfaithful. Among the Kara-Kirghiz, according to Frazer, women who are barren can become fertile—not by *eating* apples, but by rolling on the ground under a solitary apple tree.[12]

In one of the glorious adventures in Scandinavian myth, Idhunn kept a basket of apples which she handed out to the famous warriors to keep them in a state of perpetual youth. And then there was the marvelous apple which the woman from the Land of the Living threw to Conle, son of Conn, which lasted him for food and drink for a whole month and never diminished a bit. But it cast a spell of love upon him.

Among the American Iroquois, the central tree of heaven is the apple; and there is a Wyandot myth in which an apple tree casts a welcome shade upon the lodge of the Great Ruler.

> Eat an apple going to bed,
> Make the doctor beg his bread,

an old rhyme urges quite heartlessly. The fame of this fruit is thousands of years old. In old Rome, instead of eating "a complete dinner from soup to nuts," the phrase used to be, "from eggs to apples"—or, as the lads about town put it, *Ab ovo usque ad mala.* No feast is complete without apples. For the apple is a means to immortality—as both Hercules and Eurystheus knew; and it's a useful thing to have around in any event, because besides being a symbol of fruitfulness, it can act as a distraction in contests of suitors, a cure, a love charm, a means of divination.[13]

With all these beliefs sponsoring the apple as a truly magical fruit, it seems too bad that we have to listen to a dissenting voice

12. Sir James G. Frazer, *The New Golden Bough,* ed. Theodor Gaster (New York: Criterion, 1959), p. 80.
13. *Funk & Wagnalls Standard Dictionary of Folklore, Mythology and Legend* is rich in this field.

from Scripture, carrying with it the vast authority of the Holy Book if not the dictated Word of God Himself. Milton thundered about:

> . . . the fruit
> Of that forbidden tree, whose mortal taste
> Brought death into the world, and all our woe . . .[14]

Meaning Eve and the apple, of course. Browning was considerably less somber about this incident than most writers. He had Eve saying:

> Adam so starved me I was fain accept
> The apple any serpent pushed my way.
> —*The Ring and the Book*

All the evidence, however, seems to point to the probability that, even if we take Genesis 3 literally ("Now the serpent was more subtil than any beast . . . which the Lord God had made"), the fruit that dewy-eyed Eve nibbled was not a pome of the genus *Malus*. It was not an apple as we know apples. Nor does the Bible say it *was*. "But of the tree of the knowledge of good and evil, thou shalt not eat of it," God said. Early illustrations showed this tree as a date palm. Some have held that it was a quince. Sir William Temple's *On Gardening* contains this illuminating comment: "After the conquest of Afric [*sic*], Greece, the lesser Asia, and Syria were brought into Italy all sorts of their Mala, which we interpret apples, and might specify no more at first; but were afterwards applied to many other foreign fruits." The Hebrew word used in the Old Testament is *tappuach,* which is given the English redaction "quince" or "apple."[15] The apples that do grow in Palestine are in the wrong sort of soil for the fruit we are used to—as Byron said, "Like to the apples on the Dead Sea's shore, All ashes to the taste." (*Childe Harold's Pilgrimage,* III. 34)

The *Dictionary of Folklore* is quite definite on this point: "The apple as such is not mentioned in the Bible in conjunction with Adam and Eve. Despite the popular conception of the story, the

14. John Milton, *Paradise Lost,* I. 1–3.
15. Robert Young, *Analytical Concordance to the Bible,* 22d Am. ed. (New York: Funk & Wagnalls, n.d.).

cause of the trouble was the 'fruit [unidentified] of the tree which is in the midst of the garden.'" This editor also believes that the apple in the Song of Solomon and the Book of Joel is the apricot.[16] *Smith's New Bible Dictionary* and many others will accept quince, orange, apricot—even pomegranate—but agree that the fruit was not what we know as an apple, all the poetry of the ages to the contrary. By the Middle Ages the apple was firmly established as the means by which all the evil in the world was brought into it, and the scholars had even constructed a typically ten-ton academic epigram to that effect: *"Mala mali malo mala contulit omnia mundo."* So, true or not, we might as well go along with the apple —we're surely not going to be able to make editorial changes in a legend so fascinating and so well established that the folk and the poets and artists through the ages have made it a household tale. We will content ourselves with the remark that there are no apples in the New Testament: not one.

Our original concern, however, is with the apple-a-day proverb which, to the scientific twentieth century, appears open to question, despite a long heritage of belief in the almost miraculous curative properties of this fruit. One curious proverb, indeed, dating back at least to the sixteenth century, makes the suggestion that a bachelor in particular has need of the apple:

> He that will not a wife wed
> Must eat an apple on going to bed.

There is an opportunity for the cocktail psychologists to let theoretical speculation run riot, to be sure!

The first writer to question the apple-a-day formula, as far as we have been able to trace it, was Alfred Barton Rendle, Keeper of the Department of Botany in the British Museum and apple specialist, writing in the eleventh edition of the *Britannica* (1910). "In their uncooked state," he states, "they are not very digestible, but when cooked they form a very safe and useful food, exercising

16. Maria Leach and Jerome Fried, eds., *Funk & Wagnalls Standard Dictionary of Folklore, Mythology and Legend,* 2 vols. (New York: Funk & Wagnalls, 1949–50), 1: 68.

a gentle laxative influence." He has nothing to say about legend or myth or folklore; but he does make it clear why we should not expect to find pome fruit in Palestine—because soil "of a hot sandy nature" makes the plant liable to canker.

It is true that doctors advise patients who have chronic indigestion to avoid most raw fruits, especially "coarse foods with fiber, skins, seeds or gristle" along with salads containing celery, cucumbers, tomatoes, and pineapples, raisins or berries.[17] On the other hand, Phyllis Howe's analysis of apples as food in her study of nutrition shows nothing that could scare anybody off raw apples. A 150-gram apple, about 2½ inches in diameter, is 85 percent water, contains a neglible trace of fat and protein, 18 grams of carbohydrate, 8 milligrams of calcium, 0.4 milligrams of iron, 50 international units of vitamin A, 0.04 milligrams of thiamine, 0.02 milligrams of riboflavin, 0.1 milligrams of niacin, and three milligrams of ascorbic acid. Dilute acids stimulate the flow of digestive juices and encourage peristalsis, so we have another vote here for the apple.[18]

However, Macbeth was not the first to learn that the oracle can equivocate so that opposites are true: Birnam Wood, indeed, did in part remove to Dunsinane—and every apple has seeds. Recent laboratory research has reported "the presence of cholesterol and progesterone in apple seeds."[19] The amounts are not large—perhaps 385 milligrams per 100 grams cholesterol and 50 milligrams per 100 grams of progesterone. Hardly enough, says our medical editor, "to upset the applecart of confidence, but apt to sow seeds of mistrust in the current atmosphere of cholesterol-phobia and contraception consciousness."

The same writer reminds us of the discovery in 1963 of the "cheese reaction" and adds, "Clearly, cheese has been anything but beneficial to individuals receiving monoamine oxidase inhibiting tranquilizers." Which would seem to question at least the second

17. Morris Fishbein, ed., *Modern Home Medical Adviser* (Garden City, N.Y.: Doubleday & Co., 1949), pp. 392–93.

18. Phyllis S. Howe, *Nutrition for Practical Nurses* (Philadelphia: W. B. Saunders, 1967), pp. 49, 205.

19. *Journal of the American Medical Association*, 206, no. 13 (23–30 December 1968): 2891. Editorial citing A. M. Gawienowski and C. C. Gibbs, "Identification of Cholesterol and Progesterone in Apple Seeds."

half of the Eugene Field dictum with which we began. But this was something suspected long, long ago. A proverb by John Ray in 1670 rhymed: "Cheese it is a peevish elf;/ It digests all things but itself."

However, at least one recent medical writer severely chides the alarmists in the battle of the fatty acids which raised such clouds of fear in the final third of the twentieth century, scaring people off eggs and bacon and so forth, and telling them they must control the blood cholesterol. He is Dr. A. T. W. Simeons, and he says that abstruse scientific papers, such as never catch the eye of the medical reporter, have already been published proving that "food, abnormally high blood cholesterol levels, and vascular diseases are after all not *causally* related [italics added] so that we may safely return to the delicious fresh butter and the eggs and bacon of our benighted forefathers, instead of hopefully drinking rather disgusting polyunsaturated oils."[20]

And then, of course, one could point out that it is entirely possible —indeed, to some rather more pleasant—to eat apples and eject, or spew out, the seeds, thus eliminating the argument about cholesterol before it can be mentioned.

Yes, on the whole we must endorse it: An apple a day keeps the doctor away. But he hates making house calls anyhow.

Hearing Aid for the Serpent

It used to be generally agreed among prescientific experts in natural history that the adder is deaf—intentionally. In order to frustrate the snake charmer, she presses one ear into the dust and closes her other ear with her tail. This superstition has been prevalent in the East from time immemorial,[21] and made its way into western culture as trade and travel increased. Indeed, one can cite Scripture for it: in Psalms 58: 4-5 (King James Version) the wicked are compared to "the deaf adder that stoppeth her ear;/ Which will

---

20. *Food: Facts, Foibles and Fables: The Origins of Human Nutrition* (New York: Funk & Wagnalls, 1968), p. 107.
21. William S. Walsh, *Handy-Book of Literary Curiosities* (Detroit: Dale Research Co., 1966), p. 16.

not hearken to the voice of charmers, charming never so wisely."
The new *Jerusalem Bible* (1966) adds some clarity by rendering
the passage: "They are as deaf as the adder that blocks its ears/
So as not to hear the magician's music/ And the clever snake-
charmer's spells."

Like many other items in the folklore of snakes—creatures which
have always had an intense fascination for humans, as the vast bulk
of proverbs, folk sayings, fables, and superstitions clearly indicates
—the deafness of the adder is not without some basis. Snakes have
no external ears. So if by "hearing" we mean taking in and interpreting sound waves by way of the complicated mechanism of auricle,
canal, eardrum, ossicles, bony labyrinth, eighth cranial nerve, and
brain—if that's what we mean by the ability to hear—then adders
are deaf indeed. They are deaf by definition. But that doesn't necessarily mean that they are insensitive to sound in other ways. And
whether man's observation that snakes have no external ears led
to the myth that adders are deaf, or whether the story got started
some other way, we cannot be sure. Our point here, as elsewhere
in this book, is that a truth underlies the myth: there is truth in
the legend, regardless of the question of causation.

For those interested to explore it, there is much curious—if not
particularly utilitarian—information connected with the subject of
adders, especially in the use of the word by the scholars of the King
James Version, by whom the redaction "adder" was given to many
Hebrew words which originally meant anything from a true adder
to a cockatrice. They are justified in the first place in that the translators were not writing a manual of natural history, but were teaching a moral lesson. In the second place, they were writing 142 years
before the publication of the systematic nomenclature of Linnaeus,
and nobody was particularly concerned with exact classification
of orders, families, genera, and species.[22] In the third place, Englishmen, scholars or yeomen, knew only three varieties of snakes, since
all the snakes in England were wiped out in the last glacial period,
12,000 to 15,000 years ago, and the only snakes native to Britain

22. The foundation work of systematic zoology is the *Systema Naturæ* of Linnaeus,
dated 1758. There are about 2,500 species of snakes known today.

came in while the island was still connected with the European mainland, which it was until 5000 B.C., according to James A. Oliver.[23] Of the three British snakes, only one is venomous—the adder. Ireland, as we know, has no snakes at all.

Thus "adder" in English was sort of a generalization for any serpent. In the Hebrew there were at least four different words thus translated. In Psalms 140:3, "adder's poison is under their lips," the Hebrew word was *akshub,* "adder." In "Thou shalt tread upon the lion and the adder" (Psalms 91: 13), the Hebrew was *pethen,* "asp." In the proverb about "the wine when it is red" ending, "At the last it . . . stingeth like an adder" (Proverbs 23: 32), the Hebrew is *tsiphoni,* "basilisk, cockatrice." In the prophecy "Dan shall be . . . an adder in the path" (Genesis 49: 17), the Hebrew is *shephiphon,* "viper."[24] Knowing these things will not earn you an increase in pay, in all probability, so perhaps it's useless knowledge and you should forget it as soon as possible, as Sherlock Holmes wanted to forget that the world is round when he learned it accidentally— presumably to leave more room for other things he really needed. But we are disciples of Bertrand Russell in his desire "to appreciate the delicious savor of 'useless' knowledge"—that curious learning that "not only makes unpleasant things less unpleasant, but also makes pleasant things more pleasant." (*In Praise of Idleness*)

For those who like a touch of etymology in their discourse, "adder" has a picturesque source. We can't be certain of this, but one highly educated hypothesis is that the word goes back to Latin *natare,* "to swim," and thus influenced the formation of *natrix,* "water snake," which became Old Norse *nathr* and Old English *naedre*[25] and was used by Chaucer as *nadder,* "an adder" in Middle English (*The Marchantes Tale,* I. 542): "Lyk to the nadder in bosom sly untrewe."

We don't mean to keep you from the playground, but this adder-in-the-bosom business goes all the way back to Aesop (c. 570 B.C.) with his story of "The Snake and the Rustic," in which a country-

23. *Snakes in Fact and Fiction* (New York: Anchor Books, 1963), p. 157.
24. Young, *Analytical Concordance,* s.v. "adder."
25. Partridge, *Origins,* s. v. "adder."

man takes mercy on a freezing snake and warms him in his bosom —an act of gentility which the snake repays by biting him. Which is part of the folklore of snakes: they are untrustworthy. On the other hand, if you eat one your youth will be renewed; this legend is as recent as Thomas Dekker, in whose *The Honest Whore* (Part II. i. 2) a character, complimented upon his youthful appearance, replies with typical Dekker ebullience, "I eat snakes, my lord, I eat snakes. My heart hath never a wrinkle in it." (The year was 1605.)

Adders may be rough on the ordinary citizen, but they are very good mothers. According to the old bestiaries, if danger is imminent the mother snake swallows the little ones, thus providing an unexampled refuge.[26]

It is very possible that mankind has invented tales of snakes because the snake itself is so mysterious, so quickly out of sight, so quietly slithering through the grass, so cold to the touch. What man can understand the ways of the snake? Lidless eyes; only one lung; moving swiftly without feet . . . There is fear behind the stories —fear and worship. And the stories are in all literature. Virgil warned the chaps to run because "a chill snake lurks in the grass" ("*Frigidus, o pueri, fugite hinc, latet anguis in herba*"); Dante said the same thing (*Inferno* VII. i. 84) and Shakespeare warned against the adder in *Julius Caesar*. One last word:

We don't hear much in *praise* of the snake, especially of the particular snake which deluded our mother Eve. Scripture tells us that the serpent was the most subtle of all animals. But nobody takes the time to remind us that in the story of the Fall, "the serpent himself ate of the Tree of Life and became immortal, by periodically casting his skin.[27] Deaf, maybe; stupid, no.

The Athletic Field: Cradle of Heroes?

In the days when the British Empire was expanding to the point where the sun was never to set on it, and the British Navy was the wonder of the world (albeit a living hell for common seamen),

---

26. T. H. White, *The Bestiary* (New York: G. P. Putnam's Sons, 1954), p. 248.
27. Weston LaBarre, *They Shall Take Up Serpents* (Minneapolis: University of Minnesota Press, 1962), p. 55.

the belief became current among gentlemen, addicts of romance, and other unconscious humorists that the intestinal fortitude required of troops who don't know when they are beaten (and are therefore invincible) was built into them in their schoolboy days when they acquired the proper spirit of bulldog tenacity on the athletic fields. Attributed to Arthur Wellesley, first Duke of Wellington (1769-1852), was the phrase "The Battle of Waterloo was won on the playing fields of Eton." Some have suggested that he might, with more magnanimity and more accuracy also, have said that the Battle of Waterloo was won when the Prussian forces joined the British, at which point—and not before—Napoleon was routed (18 June 1815). The most recent scholarship holds that Wellington never made the statement at all. Wellington personally hated Eton and was actually a dropout from that school.[28] However, we are talking about the proverb. Its supreme expression, perhaps, appears in Sir Henry Newbolt's poem "Vitai Lampada," from which this is a typical stanza:

> The sand of the desert is sodden red—
>   Red with the wreck of a square that broke—
> The gatling's jammed and the colonel dead,
>   And the regiment blind with the dust and smoke:
> The river of death has brimmed its banks,
>   And England's far, and honor a name.
> But the voice of a schoolboy rallies the ranks:
>   "Play up! play up! and play the game!"

It can be asserted seriously that there are intelligent, educated men who cannot, today, recite those lines without a breaking voice, such is the grip the poem exerts upon the old school emotions. And one hears echoes of the apothegm in all sorts of droll connections. A political candidate who in his youth was an indomitable halfback and who later had a brilliant war record in the Air Force is assumed to be a superior aspirant for the office of state representative, where none of his duties will in any way resemble any of his

---

28. Elizabeth Longford, *Wellington: The Years of the Sword* (New York: Harper & Row, 1970), pp. 16–17.

previous experiences: but his spirit is assumed to be heroic, and that's enough.

It is clear that there is no parallel at all between a hard afternoon on the gridiron, where perhaps a player will see one or two buddies carried off with sprains and even broken bones, and a battlefield where two armies clash in hand-to-hand combat and the soldier sees his companions in arms run red with blood or crumple up in violent death. They're simply different situations, and to that extent one can say that the adage is untrue: Britain's battles were not won on the playing field.

Having said that, it must be admitted that one can see a reason for the persistence of the saying. The officers were men who had attended the schools; in the schools they learned the principles of sportsmanship and the bulldog devotion which motivates an athlete to fight his hardest right up to the final whistle. Thus, when it comes time to command troops in wartime, some of the never-say-die spirit remains and holds the men together much better than could be done by a chap who acted as if he believed they had begun to lose the day. We probably have to say that the adage is deeply romantic but *essentially* true.

Menstruating Women Are Bad Luck?

Pretty generally viewed with a knowing smile in these years of scientific knowledge, sophistication, and the new sexual freedom are the primitive fears and taboos associated with menstruating women. The superstitions are ancient, worldwide, and of great variety in their application; but they have in common the solidly embedded conviction that during the period of her catamenial flow, a woman is dangerous and unclean beyond any power of her own to control.

In the south of France, her breath alone will prevent mayonnaise from thickening. Throughout wide areas of East Africa, she is not allowed to come anywhere near the dairy or have anything to do with milk. In parts of Italy, if she comes near a mare in foal, the animal will abort. In Poland, she must not attend church—one drop of menstrual fluid would contaminate the whole place. And, as is well known, intercourse with such a woman is forbidden in Leviticus because it might produce a child who is an idiot, a cripple, an epileptic, or scrofulous. In many parts of the world her very presence will spoil new wine, just as it is beginning to ferment; cause flowers to wilt; prevent dough from rising; and make violin strings break with a snap.[29]

Worse than that, garments and objects handled by menstruating women can sicken and otherwise seriously affect those to whom they belong, hence very generally women must be isolated from everyone at the time of their "sickness."[30]

But just as one may quote Scripture, famous proverbs, or Shakespeare to prove almost anything, so the most persistent myths may mean different things on different sides of the mountain—as indeed Ambrose Bierce happily pointed out in his *The Devil's Dictionary* (under "Moral"). Menstruating women may be sheer poison, but if you want to make a powerful love potion, nothing has quite the magical potential of menstrual blood. In Spain, France, and Germany, at least, "several drops introduced into the food or drink of a desired lover 'binds' him to the woman."[31]

(That much, at least, is purest myth; continuing research has turned up nothing but corroboration of the assertion that there is no such thing as a true aphrodisiac or love potion. We made that statement in another place[32] and subsequent mail indicated that the public is not entirely ready to accept it. One learned gentleman insisted that a pharmaceutical called Yohimbine HCl, derived from a tree bark in West Africa, is listed in the pharmacopoeias as a sexual activator. He reported the claim of the manufacturer that it was also useful to veterinarians in getting animals to mate. For a while we considered this drug—entirely new to us—as a serious threat to our position; but we are resting easy again after a con-

29. Leach and Fried, *Dictionary of Folklore,* 2: 706 ff.
30. It is thus referred to by Sir James Frazer. See *The Golden Bough,* vol. 3, *Taboo and the Perils of the Soul* (London and New York: Macmillan, 1935), pp. 145–47.
31. Leach and Fried, *Dictionary of Folklore,* 2: 706.
32. Ashley Montagu and Edward Darling, *The Prevalence of Nonsense* (New York: Harper & Row, 1967), p. 57.

firmation from Dr. Jan Koch-Weser of the Clinical Pharmacology Unit of Harvard Medical School, Massachusetts General Hospital, who writes: "I agree entirely with your statement that nobody has discovered a true aphrodisiac. . . . Yohimbine is an alkaloid derived from Yohimbehe, a tree found in West Africa. Chemically Yohimbine is closely related to the alkaloids of *Rauwolfia serpentina* which are used in the treatment of hypertension. . . . As is true of so many pharmacologic agents, Yohimbine has occasionally been advocated as an aphrodisiac. However, there is absolutely no scientific evidence that it has any such effect.")

The myths recounting the dangerous aspects of a menstruating woman are, as we have suggested, very old. Pliny tells us that seeds become sterile at her touch, that she causes plant grafts to wither and plants and flowers to dry up, that fruit falls from the tree under which she sits, that her look can dim the brightest mirror and blunt the edge of steel instruments, and that a swarm of bees will die if she so much as looks at it, and so forth.[33]

To this day, in the mushroom-producing sections of France, menstruating women are not allowed to pick mushrooms during their catamenial periods; and in the perfumeries, they cannot work with the others; nor may they tend silkworms or participate in the wine industry; nor work in the sugar refineries.

It is necessary to underscore the fact that rejection of menstruating women is not universal, although it is common. Among some American Indian tribes, menstruation was hailed as a great thing, especially the first time; and in Northwest Melanesia, according to Bronislaw Malinowski, "There is no pronounced masculine dislike or dread of menstruous blood. A man will not cohabit with his wife or sweetheart during her monthly period, but he will remain in the same hut and participate in the same food." Menstruating women daily bathe "in the same large waterhole from which the whole village draws its drinking water. . . ."[34]

In any event, most people today would brush aside as pure myth

33. *Natural History*, trans. H. Rackham (Cambridge: Harvard University Press, 1942), VII. xv. 64, p. 549.
34. *The Sexual Life of Savages in Northwest Melanesia* (New York: Harcourt, Brace, 1929), p. 169.

these superstitions about menstruating women causing flowers to wilt and all the rest. The truth, however, is that not only is it *not* myth; it is demonstrable fact. The only uncertain question is whether the myth was created to illuminate experience, or whether the myth arose out of an irrational explanation of something believed to be supernatural and perhaps controlled by the moon. It must have been something powerful—a myth so widespread could not lack a cause.

But the proposition which will most greatly surprise most of our readers is that there *is* fact underlying the belief; or at least parts of the belief.

Despite the fact that many of the changes which occur during menstruation are not fully understood, a gradually increasing body of clinical and experimentally controlled evidence has accumulated in recent years which makes it impossible to deny that some of the noxious effects attributed to women during the catamenial period are true. For instance, there is the fact that various kinds of freshly cut flowers will actually wilt within twenty minutes of being handled by certain women during the first two days of the catamenia. The Hungarian-American pediatrician Dr. Bela Schick, who first noticed this phenomenon about 1920, discovered further that the menstrual discharge itself has the same effect, and he postulated the excretion of a "menotoxin" during menstruation. Later he found that sweat from the armpit and blood from the general system during menstruation are more toxic to blossoms than is the case at other times; and the growth of yeast is retarded by them in the same way. Another German, M. Frank, confirmed Schick's findings and made a test of blossom-wilting by placing flowers in a solution of the milk of menstruous and nonmenstruous women—with the result that the first group wilted appreciably earlier. He noted also the various disturbances in infants suckling menstruous women—and received confirmation from the work of a number of other investigators.[35]

35. For a full discussion of this subject (and some sixty references) see Ashley Montagu, "Physiology and the Origins of the Menstrual Prohibitions," in the same author's *Anthropology and Human Nature* (Boston: Porter Sargent, 1957), pp. 194–202.

Admitting that some of the changes during menstruation are not fully understood, as we have said, other clinicians have been inclined to accept Dr. Schick's postulate of a menotoxin, pointing out that during menstruation every organ of the body can be disturbed and thus every existing abnormality or condition of disease sharpened. Single observers have recorded the slowing of a frog's heartbeat when exposed to the axillary sweat of menstruous women; and that to guinea pigs a serum from a menstruous woman is more toxic than ordinary serum; and that the growth of yeast may be retarded—or, in some cases, accelerated!—after being kneaded by menstruous women. These investigators believe the active agent in the menotoxin is choline, excreted in cyclic fluctuations in the sweat from fingertips. Others have guessed that the menotoxin is an oxycholesterol. Someday we will probably know for sure; but even now we know that many experimenters have found that "the blood serum, the blood corpuscles, saliva, sweat, tears and urine of menstruous women produce inhibition of fermentation by yeast; that the mere handling of yeast by a menstruous woman is sufficient to produce wholesale destruction of these microscopic plants," as well as producing "retardative and toxic effects in *Paramecia* and trypanosomes, causing withering of freshly cut flowers . . . and generally producing a depressant effect upon plant and animal tissues." These findings have been repeatedly confirmed.[36]

Even more spectacularly, the botanist W. Christiansen demonstrated the fact that something emanating from the menstrual discharge can both retard and also actually kill yeast cells *at a distance*. Dr. Christiansen suggests that the effect may be due to the action of mitogenetic rays; and Drs. O. Rahn and M. N. Barnes repeated and confirmed his work.

In short, even with our imperfect knowledge, we can state as a fact that menstruating women are capable of exercising a noxious effect upon a variety of living things with which they come in contact, whether the responsible agent is an alkylamine, possibly trimethylamine, as the latest theories strongly suggest, or something

36. Ibid., p. 199.

else. They may not dim mirrors and dull the edge of steel, as some extremists among the troubadours have said; but there are excellent reasons for believing in the truth behind the legend, even if we do not know the whole truth.

The Weeping Glutton: The Tearful Crocodile

Most of us by the time we have reached the age which can take *Alice in Wonderland* in its stride have probably learned to entertain some doubts about folk reports of the crocodile weeping heartily as it gnaws away at the flesh of its victim. In *Alice,* the Mock Turtle sobbed and wept a good deal, but there was nothing vicious or dangerous about him; and as for the crocodile, he "welcomes little fishes in, With gently smiling jaws," which is an easy concept to accept. In addition, by this time of life most of us have undoubtedly seen some sort of hypocrisy among our fellows and have been guilty of it ourselves—so we are able to understand the metaphor of the crocodile tears with no trouble. But tears in the crocodile's eyes—actual salt tears—surely do not occur, we tell ourselves with an uneasy laugh.

To ancient Greek and Roman storytellers, however, it was a matter of true fact, appearing in natural histories and proverbs which were beyond question. The crocodile "moans and sobs like a person in great distress in order to lure a man into its reach, and then, after devouring him sheds bitter tears over the dire fate of its victim."[37]

This belief had a life of hundreds of years. The famous travel tales of Sir John Mandeville, a contemporary of Chaucer, who supposedly had been just about everywhere—Palestine, Persia, Turkey, Egypt, India, Russia—referred to the "cokadrilles" which slew men and "eten hem wepynge." Bacon's essay *Of Wisdom for a Man's Self* informs us: "It is the wisdom of crocodiles, that shed tears when they would devour." Robert Burton's *Anatomy of Melancholy* substantiates the legend. It appears also in John Lyly's *Euphues:* "The crocodile shrowdeth greatest treason under most pitiful tears."

---

37. Charles Earle Funk, *A Hog on Ice and Other Curious Expressions* (New York: Harper & Brothers, 1948), p. 130.

Shakespeare in *Antony and Cleopatra, II Henry VI,* and *Othello* preserves the idea and Tennyson's "Dirge" has the line "Crocodiles wept tears for thee."[38]

Most Englishmen, of course, had never seen a crocodile, and were therefore ready to believe almost anything of a beast deemed so fearful. In fact, as any reader of early bestiaries knows, they were ready to believe almost anything of any strange beast. But so are we —and no wonder, since the scientific truth is often more amazing than anything the mind of man can invent: the jet propulsion and instantaneous camouflage of the squid, for instance. Unbelievable! While this book was being written, a newspaper published the following story, here given in its entirety: "OUT BY A NOSE. A newly-born crocodile cuts its way out of its egg shell with an 'egg tooth' which is on the end of its snout."[39] The statement was undocumented. Obviously the editor expected the assertion to be accepted without debate.

We may doubt the tears, in this enlightened age—if that's the word we are fumbling for—but there is no doubting the danger to man from this beast which has been known (in Madagascar) to reach a length of thirty feet (the largest American crocodile on record was twenty-three feet, in Latin America).[40] According to the Milnes, the Nile crocodile "is credited as the number-two killer of human beings, second only to poisonous snakes." Even Roger A. Caras, who is inclined to pooh-pooh most of the warnings about the malice of animals toward man, grants readily that "the ancient order of reptiles known as the crocodilia . . . are *by nature* man-eaters. With the possible exception of a few sharks, I know of no other animals that are normally so disposed."[41]

It is time now to reveal that the famous *crocodili lachrymae* (as

38. All of these entries are included in Burton Stevenson's *The Home Book of Quotations, Classical and Modern,* 6th ed. rev. (New York: Dodd, Mead, 1949), p. 1972. Stevenson also shows the British belief that crocodiles are traditionally associated chiefly with the Nile; he groups "Labour in Vain, or Coals to Newcastle" with "To bear pots to Samos isle, owls to Athens (Athenian coins were stamped with an owl in honor of Athena, goddess of wisdom), crocodiles to the Nile."

39. Boston *Traveler,* 11 April 1967.

40. Lorus J. and Margery Milne, *The Balance of Nature* (New York: Alfred A. Knopf, 1960), p. 57.

41. *Dangerous to Man* (Philadelphia: Chilton Books, 1964), pp. 202–3.

Erasmus called the crocodile tears) do appear very often as the beast gorges itself. There is no record of any sobbing, moaning, wailing, or human-type carryings-on of that sort—just the quiet tears. The crocodile is not a dainty eater: while it breaks up its larger victims into assorted pieces before attempting to swallow them, it will nevertheless gulp down, in its eagerness (perhaps after several days on an empty stomach), chunks of food larger than it can easily handle. When a big morsel goes down the red lane, "often the crocodile gasps for air . . . and at these times its tear glands discharge copiously. . . ."[42]

Hence it is fact, not myth, that crocodile tears appear as the victim is demolished; but, with all the respect due to the early observers, to attribute this to remorse is, of course, the sheerest anthropomorphism, the pathetic fallacy in full cry.

There is a charming postscript, which may not be new to readers who have followed the bestiaries: after gorging, the crocodile rests on the riverbank with his mouth wide open. In this engaging posture, he permits the spur-winged plovers to run all over the big tongue, pecking out bits of food stuck there as well as between the teeth—presumably with an up-and-down action rather than a back-and-forth one. Here, surely, we have dental hygiene at its most intimate. But there is a reason for this, like everything else: the birds are alert and very noisy if disturbed. Thus the croc can relax in the sun, certain that his postprandial nap will not offer a chance for an enemy to creep up on him unawares: if they try it, the birds will set up an alarm.

So Spartianus, Pliny, and Seneca were right after all: the croc has tear-filled eyes as he swallows his victim. Often he does. But he does not lure human victims by sobbing and all that. To balance his bad reputation as a man-eater, we must concede that under the pharaohs the Nile crocodile was sacred, an animal dedicated to Sebek; and up to the nineteenth century, the croc was a medical symbol for health because he supplied curatives for the relief of human ills. The dried blood was a sovereign remedy for snakebite and for the treatment of certain eye disorders. The gall bladder, desiccated and pul-

42. Milne, *Balance of Nature*, p. 65

verized, was worked into ointments which were said to improve the vision. For driving out fevers, there was nothing like a special lubricant made basically of crocodile fat. The dried and powdered skin was valued as an anesthetic in operations. And crocodile teeth hung around the neck in a bag warded off all kinds of bad luck—which is reminiscent of the contemporary "conjure bag" used by voodoo women in the American South, where alligator teeth are part of the charm.[43]

To add just one more curious association, the crocodile comes into the Bible just once—in Job (41: 1)—to illustrate as graphically as possible the might of deity as compared with the strength of man: "Canst thou draw leviathan with a hook? or his tongue with a cord which thou lettest down?" Even if, as suspected by some scholars, this is a later addition to the Book of Job, it is the only time "leviathan" definitely refers to the crocodile. Elsewhere in the Old Testament it refers "not to a crocodile but rather to a sea monster,"[44] as in the Jonah story.

Don't Swim After Eating

There were always two reasons why one should not go into the water "for at least an hour after luncheon," but behind them was a great, superior Cause tantamount to a decree from Sinai: "It's bad for you; you'll get cramps and drown." Not one child in ten million believed that and every single infant skeptic was ready, the instant attention wavered from himself, to test the theory with his life. And practically all of them could have done so safely and returned with empirical evidence to show that the myth is false. Among the parents it was an accepted fact, apparently an occupational hazard accompanying parenthood, that exercising after a meal slows down digestion, and therefore swimmers get cramps if they go in too soon after lunch; or that the chill of the water calls the blood to the skin, away from the digestive organs, and prevents digestion from

43. Ibid., p. 59.
44. Roy B. Chamberlin and Herman Feldman, *The Dartmouth Bible*, 2d ed., rev. and enl. (Boston: Houghton Mifflin Co., 1961), p. 463. This view is supported by the *Britannica*, 11th ed.

being accomplished. Both explanations have a reasonable sound and serve to continue the life of the myth.

There is a good deal of evidence, based on formal scientific research studies, indicating that a light repast (say, 500 calories) makes no measurable difference in the performance of an athlete in running or in swimming, and has no uncomfortable effects whatever. A glutton probably wouldn't *want* to swim or run after one of his huge meals; so the safety factor can be regarded as totally irrelevant. If you want the children to rest quietly on the beach for an hour after meals—light summer meals—then that's up to you. Chances are you'll weaken before the hour is up anyhow and encourage their working off energy at a distance from the spot where you'd like to get a little sunlit rest, and work up a tan to display to the neighbors when you get home again. The proposition that instant immersion or quick exercise will make any difference the evidence fails to prove.

One of the research teams consisted of Gene M. Asprey, Louis E. Alley, and W. W. Tuttle of the University of Iowa. At the end of the summer of 1966, they tested swimmers half an hour after eating, an hour after eating, and two hours after eating a meal consisting of 30 grams of cereal, two slices of toast (46 grams), 12 grams of sugar, 10 of butter, and 240 of whole milk—a total of 338 grams— and of 510 calories, with a balance of 16.2 grams of protein, 69.8 grams of carbohydrates, and 19.7 grams of fat. Twenty-four male undergraduates, eighteen to twenty-three years of age, swam eight trials each for the one-mile free-style swim; and as a control, the same men swam eight trials when they had taken no food for at least three hours. They swam, therefore, in all, thirty-two trials: eight after no food; eight within half an hour of the meal described; eight after one hour; and eight after two hours. Not every trial was exactly the same time; but there was no significant difference between what was established as a man's mean average and that after eating. The research team therefore boldly reported: "The eating of a small meal ½ hr., 1 hr., or 2 hr. before swimming has no adverse effect on swimming times for the 1-mile freestyle swim. . . . During the experiment the subjects were asked to report any adverse effects in the form of nausea or stomach cramps during or after the swims. None of the subjects reported that they had suffered any such effects."[45]

An equally detailed report in *Nutrition Reviews* (June 1968)[46] upset the idea, long held by the wait-an-hour authorities, that heavy exercise should be avoided immediately after eating. In fact, cross-country Olympic skiers are often given a glucose solution *during* the competition and appear to have benefited rather than been harmed by the feeding. "The effect of strenuous exercise on gastric emptying and intestinal absorption is essentially nil," this research shows.

Our children, on a summer's noon, taking their picnic on the beach or buying lunch at the local hot dog stand, are perhaps likely to absorb somewhat more than the spartan meal—500 calories—used to test the various swimmers. For instance, eight ounces of whole milk (320 calories), plus one hot dog (155 calories), plus one roll (115 calories), plus a slice of chocolate cake with thin icing for dessert (445 calories)—and we're twice as well fed as the athletes described.[47] Here, however, nature comes to help our cause: the stuffed child usually *wants* to rest a little before resuming battle. If he doesn't, the evidence indicates that no harm is likely to be done.

Yet there *is* truth in the myth that one should not swim right after eating *if psychic factors are involved*, because these do affect the digestive process. If your son is entered in a serious swimming competition that means a great deal to him, he should wait to eat until the event is over. Or if your child is afraid of the water, and is taking swimming lessons in order to conquer that fear and become master of the ocean waves—but has not yet gotten to the point where he is at ease in the water since he retains the fear still—then his swimming lesson should not closely follow his meal. Therefore, advises an editorial in *JAMA*, "since there will ordinarily be persons

45. Gene M. Asprey, Louis E. Alley, and W. W. Tuttle, "Effect of eating at various times on subsequent performances in the one-mile freestyle swim," *The Research Quarterly* 39, no. 2 (1966): 231.
46. "Exercise and Gastrointestinal Absorption in Human Beings," *Nutrition Reviews* 26, no. 6: 167 (unsigned).
47. Howe, *Nutrition for Practical Nurses*, pp. 219–48.

so affected in any group, prohibition of swimming immediately after meals is probably a wise rule *for schools and similar institutions*. [Italics added.] For the individual person it is a matter of personal reactions and practice."[48] Very likely the myth arose because it does apply in general. Now we know *why,* and are therefore more free: one of the lovelier effects of knowledge at all times.

In French circles, to judge from the old apothegm, there is less worry about these matters. They feel that anyone foolish enough to entrust himself to the waterways is going to end up dead, sooner or later; it's only logical. They say to each other, *"Bons nageurs sont à la fin noyés,"* just as the Englishman Thomas Fuller, a born pessimist, said, "Good swimmers are oftenest drowned."

Truth Is Safe in the Marketplace?

One of the most comforting of all proverbs is the widely believed aphorism that truth will prevail. Truth conquers all. We suffer under the tyrant's yoke, perhaps, but it cannot last, for "the first of all doctrines is this: that a lie cannot endure forever." Carlyle saw it that way. Galileo was condemned as a heretic in 1633 for teaching that the earth moves around the sun, when the Bible and other ecclesiastical authorities were teaching that it is the sun that moves, not the central and immovable earth. Copernicus had already been condemned by consulting theologians of the Holy See in 1616 for calling the sun the center. But in 1820 Pope Pius VII announced that the Copernican system might now be regarded as fully established. And in July, 1968, Franz Cardinal Konig of Vienna, at a meeting of Nobel Prize winners in Lindau on Lake Constance, announced that he had been authorized by Pope Paul VI personally to say that the Vatican has a plan to exonerate Galileo of the heresy charges. *Und sie bewegt sich doch,* to be sure. It does, nevertheless, move. But it takes a long time.

After we have examined a few dozen instances of this sort, we begin to give credence to the validity of the truth-conquers-all position. We have seen peoples who were exploited come to self-

48. *Journal of the American Medical Association,* 9 July 1960, p. 194.

government; we have seen tyrant bosses put down. But we are stung to attention by no less an authority than John Stuart Mill (in the famous essay *On Liberty,* which should be reread occasionally): "The dictum that truth always prevails over persecution is one of those pleasant falsehoods which men repeat after one another till they pass into commonplaces, but which all experience refutes. History teems with instances of truth put down by persecution. If not suppressed forever, it may be thrown back for centuries."

The idea behind the truth-conquers-all syndrome has roots at least as deep as the Elizabethan age, when the universe was thought of as a moral system initiated by God to work out purposes of his own. Since it was a unified system, moral in nature, it was automatically thrown out of kilter whenever an evil went unbalanced by punishment—and sooner or later the balance had to be adjusted. That explained why unnatural things happened in connection with the murder of a ruler. One recalls that in *Julius Caesar* (II. ii) strange celestial fireworks were seen; graves "yawned and yielded up their dead" and the clouds dripped blood while a lioness whelped in the streets, which, of course, no lioness in her right mind would ever do: she'd go into seclusion. And the night that Duncan was murdered, chimneys were blown down, "strange screams of death" were heard in the air, and there were earthquakes (*Macbeth,* II. iii). Things would not be normal again until the moral balance was set right through the punishment of the guilty ones. Thus truth *must* prevail in such a system, sooner or later.

It would not be difficult to document the case for John Stuart Mill, however. The injustice suffered by blacks in our own country for some centuries is as obvious an example as one could find of the failure of truth to overcome suppression; but there are plenty of others: the treatment of the American Indian; the innocent bystanders slain in Vietnam; the starved children in Biafra—to say nothing of Appalachia and Mississippi; victims of the McCarthy purges; the shameful violence at the 1968 Democratic convention in Chicago. . . .

Yet the belief in conquering truth runs through all the great prophets of our tradition and is deeply embedded in our literature.

Five hundred years before Christ, Aesop gave us the memorable story of the boy who cried "Wolf!"—the moral being that the joker lost all support from everybody as a result of becoming a known liar. This is supposedly the source of Aristotle's reply to the question "What is the reward of liars?" He answered, "When they speak the *truth* they are not believed." According to Scripture, at least one man died when he realized the enormity of his persistently perverting the truth. "Peter said, Ananias, . . . thou hast not lied unto men, but unto God. And Ananias hearing these words fell down, and gave up the ghost . . ." (Acts V: 3–5). Three hours later his wife, Sapphira, did the same thing in the same place, for the same reason.

Woodrow Wilson, in all earnestness, said, "The truth is the most robust, and indestructible and formidable thing in the world." There is something in us which cries for belief in these statements. Old John Gower (1390) held that "Trowthe mot stonde atte last." And who has not taken heart at the refrain of Chaucer's "Balade de Bon Conseyl," "Trouthe wil deliver, hit is no drede." We are still Elizabethans in our basic certainty that we live in an orderly and moral universe. Any experienced advertising man will tell you that unless a sales message carries conviction—unless people believe it's the truth, or enough of the truth to be worth an investment—the advertising is wasted. But in a case of desperation, once-disappointed customers will go back and invest again just on the basis of a *hope* that the medicine will help the cold, or the perfume will attract the suitor. When the drug Krebiozen was being pronounced worthless by the American Medical Association and other authorities, cancer patients (especially terminal cases) were loudly demanding it and claiming it had made them feel much better. In short, we like to believe that truth conquers all; but we are also guilty of that ancient and so human trait wishful thinking: we believe what we want to believe. Perhaps it was some such consideration that made the seventeenth-century divine Thomas Fuller assert: "I know how dangerous it is to follow truth too near the heels." The notion that to do so was to risk getting dust in one's eyes, or getting one's teeth kicked, and so forth, was also expressed by Raleigh, Robertson, Colton, Hare, and a good many others.

This can get very complicated, because one can raise the question that Pontius Pilate would not stay to hear answered, and then one has disturbed Cerberus for sure and hell begins to empty itself with the issues of Knowing and the Known, the various problems of human knowledge, and other deep-water monsters. Mark Caine has given a sophisticated answer that may serve for our day—possibly: "In a relative sense, everything is true; someone believes it. It is futile to deny anything. Merely invent something else. No one can ever prove that Jupiter or Thor or witches did not exist; people simply ceased to believe in them. Never deny anything, unless of course you want people to go on believing it." And then he delivers this classic: "The best way of defacing a poster is not to paste white paper over it but to draw mustaches on the participants."[49]

On Columbus Day in Nassau they celebrate the first sighting of the New World by the Admiral in the dark hours of October 12; but for many years the argument raged about which island was actually San Salvador. A Chicago *Herald* expedition in 1891 put up a memorial on Watling Island; but this did not convince the many people who thought it should have gone up on Cat Island. Finally, in 1926, the legislature of the Bahamas passed a law (this is always a handy way to establish truth) settling the first landfall at Watling Island. This was a step forward, but it did not help establish the spot on the island where Columbus landed, and there are three monuments on the small key today, one of which has the blessing of Samuel Eliot Morison, according to Jerome Beatty, Jr., who goes on to say: "Each one marks the spot where Columbus stepped ashore. If you ask the natives, they say that he landed everywhere at one time."[50] When shall we know the truth in such a case?

Yet we are of a mind to hold that the apothegm is true, in spite of everything: truth does conquer, but there is a danger in following it too near the heels. Every new research, every fresh investiga-

49. *The S-Man: A Grammar of Success* (Boston: Houghton Mifflin Co., 1960), p. 156.
50. *Saturday Review*, 1 December 1962.

tion turns up something which had been guesswork before. Who would have believed that three towering American leaders in 1777 were seriously considering pressing for an American attack on Liverpool and Glasgow, plundering and burning those cities? The author of the plan was Silas Deane; he proposed it in a letter to John Jay; and Jay shared the plan with Robert Morris, who helped finance the Revolution. The correspondence, hardly known of previously, was given to Columbia University in 1961 and some of it was reproduced in facsimile for the delectation of the judicious.[51] A little truth here, a little truth there—it all counts up.

51. *New York Times*, 2 July 1961.

IV

CHAPTER

Myths About People and the Facts They Rest On

Exposing the Voltaire Exposé: He Really Said It

The thundering, heroic phrase long attributed to Voltaire should have been suspect from the beginning, along with most of the postured statements one discovers chiseled on the bases of statues in the public parks. It is just too good. Too dramatic, too beautifully balanced, too eligible for a collection of epigrams. "I disapprove of what you say, but I will defend to the death your right to say it." As Bergen Evans points out in his monumental anthology, "The phrase has enough exaggeration to be striking and enough paradox to seem vaguely witty."[1] Also it fitted the facts, since Voltaire was a famous proponent of free speech. Whatever the reason, the sentence was accepted—and cited—as Voltaire's by more or less everybody. And why not? It makes a splendid quote, and one must attribute a quote *to* somebody, or it loses half its power.

But the day came when some skeptic tried to track it down in Voltaire's writings, and came back to the world with the triumphant information that it could not be found. Other literary detectives took up the trail, and ran the statement to earth in a book by S. G. Tallentyre (pen name of E. Beatrice Hall) called *The Friends of Voltaire,* published in 1907. She had used it as her own paraphrase, it seemed, of his attitude toward free speech. In his *Essay on Tolerance,* Voltaire had urged: "Think for yourselves and let others enjoy

1. *Dictionary of Quotations* (New York: Delacorte Press, 1968), p. 252.

96

the privilege to do so, too." Thus Tallentyre says, at the conclusion of her account, "I disapprove," and so on, "was his attitude now." Indeed, Paul Boller insists, "The Tallentyre piece never intended the famous quote to be taken literally, but only as a phrase interpreting Voltaire's attitude,"[2] much as one might report that Galileo said to himself, upon observing absolute proof of the earth's motion, "Aha! So you move, do you?" Yet the words are not to be found in the writings of Galileo.[3]

And that appeared to take care of *that*. Bartlett now gives this explanation, and acknowledges the help of a Harry Weinberger in establishing the point. It takes a well-armed challenger to dispute both Evans and Bartlett—and, incidentally, Will Durant.[4]

But now it turns out that a thoroughly established and accepted exposé of a folk "error" has done some toe-stubbing of its own. *Our* acknowledgment is gratefully given to Leo Rosten, brilliant creator of *H*Y*M*A*N*K*A*P*L*A*N* and other works, who drew our attention to the following words, written by Voltaire in a letter addressed on 6 February 1770, to M. le Riche: " *'M'sieur l'abbé, je déteste ce que vous écrivez, mais je donnerais ma vie pour que vous puissez continuer à écrire.'*[5] That's close enough to justify the Bartlett/Durant variation." It is, indeed. And it is a vivid reminder to beware of myths—they may be loaded.

Newton's Grade B Apple

One of the most famous anecdotes in the annals of science history is the story of Isaac Newton and the apple. The reader will recall

2. Paul F. Boller, Jr., *Quotemanship* (Dallas: Southern Methodist University Press, 1967), p. 324.

3. An almost perfect parallel is related in connection with Dr. Joseph Warren of Boston, who, after the Stamp Act of 1765, began to feel that it was going to be impossible to remain a loyal subject of the Crown. He wrote to his Harvard classmate Edmund Dana in England, complaining bitterly. The story continues: "He did not say, in so many words, 'We are different, we are Americans,' but it was the way he was beginning to feel, the way a great many of his fellow colonists were beginning to feel." Rhoda Truax, *The Doctors Warren of Boston: First Family of Surgery* (Boston: Houghton Mifflin Co., 1968), p. 39.

4. *The Story of Philosophy* (New York: Simon & Schuster, Inc., 1927), p. 271.

5. N. Guterman, *Book of French Quotations* (Garden City, N.Y.: Doubleday & Co., 1963), p. 188.

that according to the tale, Newton saw an apple fall from the tree—and that started the train of thought in his mind which ended up with the theory of gravitation. The story was given circulation by Voltaire, who admired Newton and Locke above all Englishmen, and who wrote a book called *Éléments de la philosophie de Newton*.

However, there is something so utterly pat about the narrative that the whole scene was believed to be contrived, and it has now become customary for the cognoscenti to smile indulgently at the mere mention of any association of Isaac Newton with the fruit of *Malus sylvestris* (or, if you prefer, *Pyrus malus*).

Wipe off that smile, men. Professor I. B. Cohen of Harvard, who has drawn attention to this matter,[6] will refer you to Jean Pelseneer's article "La pomme de Newton," appearing in *Ciel et Terre* I, no. 4 (1937), and in addition will assure you that full corroboration is supplied in a biography of Newton written "by his friend and admirer, the renowned antiquary, the Rev. William Stukeley (1687–1765)."[7]

Strangely enough, this biography, written in 1752, was not published for 184 years; there must be some sort of a story behind *that*. But the point for us is that Stukeley was an eyewitness and vouches for the Newton-apple story out of personal experience. He says that he was drinking tea under the apple trees with Isaac, and in the course of the conversation, Newton vouchsafed the information that it had been under precisely these conditions that the question of gravitation had entered his mind. "It was occasioned by the fall of an apple as he sat in a contemplative mood. . . . This was the birth of those amazing discoveries. . . ."

Even a skeptic has to admit this is believable: William Stukeley was a man of the cloth and a serious antiquarian; this is not the sort of thing his mind would invent, and if he says Newton reminisced, one sees no reason to doubt that this is what happened. Ever since the age of twenty-four, Newton had been trying to explain the motion of the moon by assuming the influence of gravitation; and

6. Bernard Cohen in *Nature* (16 February 1946), p. 197.
7. Hastings White, ed., *Memoirs of Sir Isaac Newton's Life by William Stukeley, M.D., F.R.S.,* 1752 (London: Taylor & Francis, 1936), p. 19.

the homely example of the apple—of small bulk and density—falling toward the earth—of vast bulk and matter—could develop into the idea that gravitation depends upon weight and that "this is the quality of all bodies whatsoever," including those in the heavens.[8] Newton and the apple is historic truth, not myth.

More than that: a descendant (scion) of the original apple tree in Newton's Woolsthorpe is now flourishing in Wellesley, Massachusetts, where it stands on the campus of Babson Institute, vigorously producing the very same mealy-textured fruit that the great man observed falling. This is because Roger K. Babson built up the best collection of Newtoniana in the western hemisphere, beginning in the early 1900s; and the curator at one time was the late Henry P. Macomber, who asked himself why, along with the Newton manuscripts, medals, maps, and portraits, there should not be a healthy descendant of the Apple Tree, whose authenticity the Babson people had recently established through the very same Stukeley reminiscences we have quoted. It was learned through the Royal Botanic Gardens at Kew that the tree was a "Flower of Kent," whose fruit is not crisp and juicy like the macintosh and therefore not particularly tempting to eat—which may be why Newton observed and did not devour. Macomber was told that the Woolsthorpe original had rotted and been cut down in 1820, but "that scions had been taken from the tree and propagated so as to establish a line of descent."[9] Sir Edward Salisbury, curator of the Kew Gardens, told Macomber he might be able to get a scion from Morrisville, Pennsylvania, because the Historical Commission in the 1940s had planted an English scion as part of the memorial to William Penn; and so it came that from Kew to Morrisville to Wellesley the line of the Flower of Kent found solid rooting in the good soil at Babson. Slips have since been sent from Wellesley to Hobart College in Geneva, New York, and to the Lamont Geological Observatory at Columbia.

8. Isaac Newton, *Philosophiae naturalis principia mathematica, Book III, Proposition VI, Theorem VI, Cor. 2,* quoted in William S. Knickerbocker, ed., *Classics of Modern Science* (Boston: Beacon Paperbacks, 1962), p. 70.
9. Paul J. Reale, "Sir Isaac's Mealy Apple Tree," *Yankee Magazine,* October 1967, pp. 96–97.

Thus the falling apple story is not only true, but we know what the brand is and could even eat one of the descending apples if we wanted to badly enough.

Cleopatra and the Wraparound Rug

Most of those who are familiar with the classic confrontation of Julius Caesar and the young Cleopatra at the first meeting of this immortal couple seem to discount, as sheer "Hollywood," the story that the queen had herself rolled up in an expensive Oriental rug which was then presented to the general as a gift. We are enchanted by the sheer drama of the strategy, and we exclaim, "What a marvelous entrance—what a gesture!" But then we think, "It's *too* good. It has to be contrived." Like Cyrano's nose, it must be an exaggeration.

For consider the total situation: The bald and aging Caesar was reaching the climax of his international fame as an apparently invincible military genius. Only four years previously he had ground the forces of Vercingetorix into bloody pulp (when the village of Uxellodonum surrendered, he fulfilled his threat to cut off the hands of every defender); and barely a year before his arrival at Alexandria he had crossed the Rubicon with the cry *"Alea jacta est,"* "The die is cast." Pompey had fled before him, but managed to get to sea at Brundisium. Before the summer was over, Caesar had defeated the legions of Pompey that were in Spain, and he had then pursued Pompey himself into the plain of Thessaly, where he thoroughly routed him at Pharsalus. Pompey fled again, seeking asylum in Egypt, and Caesar gave chase. Not until his arrival at Alexandria did he learn that Pompey had been murdered in Egypt. Clearly, at this juncture, Caesar was upon the point of becoming the top man. Cruel, calculating, ambitious, he was in his fifty-fourth year. Can such a man, with the cards all being dealt precisely to his order, be stopped in his tracks by some girlish whimsy, however delicious, contrived like an act in a masquerade ball by a child he'd never heard of?

Cleopatra, tall and slender in a family famous for plump women, was nothing but a slip of a girl—in her twenty-first year—inexperienced in intrigue and politics, the unknown queen of a beaten people, whose knowledge of men was rather confined to male slaves and her perhaps half-witted brother-husband. While we're at it, perhaps we should point to another popular fable: that Cleopatra was an Egyptian. She was not. "She was the daughter of Ptolemy XI, surnamed Auletes, who was the illegitimate son of Ptolemy VIII, son of Ptolemy VII. The Ptolemies formed the Greek dynasty in Egypt which ended with Cleopatra. Cleopatra was thus a Greek."[10] Not that being a Greek makes her exploit any less credible; even the good, gray eleventh edition of the *Britannica* tends to wax lyrical over this woman, saying, "In her the type of queen characteristic of the Macedonian dynasties stands in the most brilliant light. Imperious will, masculine boldness, relentless ambition like hers had been exhibited by queens of her race since the old Macedonian days before Philip and Alexander."

Young she was, especially in comparison with the world-conquering general; but nobody is calling her naïve. Her brother-husband was with Caesar in the city, no doubt being instructed in the general's plans for consolidating his empire and duly collecting various tributes and taxes. If there was a time to act—if she wished to make a bold play for her own rights in the kingdom—that time was now and the action had better be effective.

In a word, the legend appears to be true. It is told by one biographer in this manner:

Cleopatra was rowed to Alexandria in a small boat by a servant, Apollodorus, a giant of a man. At dusk the boat was tied to the quay just below the palace. Apollodorus rolled the slim girl into a rug, shouldered it, and carried it to the palace. The guards, who had already been bribed, conducted them to Caesar. Apollodorus unrolled the rug at Caesar's feet and Cleopatra sprang up before him.

She was young, vibrant, beautiful; her voice low and melodious. . . .

10. A. S. E. Ackermann, *Popular Fallacies Explained and Corrected* (Philadelphia: J. B. Lippincott Co., 1924), p. 474.

Some of her features were as violent as those of the Macedonian women; others might have come from the depths of gentle, brown Nubia. She had full, wanton lips under a thin curved nose. . . .[11]

This, assuredly, is one of the most interesting moments in history, and yet we find old Caesar writing sheaves of stuff about the butchery in Gaul and not a single word about the autumn evening in the palace at Alexandria, where, if one may say so, the waters of the magic Nile mingle caressingly with the sea. Heigh-ho. Anyhow, he stayed nine months, while mutinies began to threaten back in Italy and the sons of Pompey recruited more and more power in Spain.

Cleopatra did it, all right; and people have been talking about her ever since.

Baron Munchausen and the Working Press

Since it is palpable fabrication to tell of a horse cut cleanly in two at the middle and then sewn together again with "sprigs and young shoots of laurels" which afterward took root "in his body, grew up, and formed a bower over me" so that the rider went shaded and the animal unharmed; or to relate that a man climbed to the horns of the moon up a Turkish beanstalk; or that a hunter with an empty gun, attacked by a huge bear and having "nothing but two spare flints," threw the first into the animal's opened mouth, making him whirl in pain so that "I could level the second at his back-door," with the result that the two met in the middle, struck a spark, and "blew up the bear with a terrible explosion"—since these are obvious, self-evident tall tales, clearly intended by the author to be his entries in the Liars Club Contest, many people have assumed that the hero of these adventures is as mythical as his escapades. Surely there never really *was* a Baron Munchausen!

Almost as strange as the adventures of this famous traveler is the fact that no author has ever been made famous through the Baron— in fact, the chances are our reader does not know the name of the

11. Donald Day, *The Evolution of Love* (New York: Dial Press, 1954), pp. 115–16.

genius and social outcast who first wrote down the tales. Any volunteers?

The truth is that a younger son of the "Black Line" of the noble house of Rinteln-Bodenwerder in Brunswick, a chap by the name of Hieronymous Karl Friederich, Freiherr von Munchausen, was living in retirement at Bodenwerder, enjoying the life of a very hospitable country gentleman, setting a fine table, enjoying the excellent hunting along the meadows through which the Weser flows, and taking a certain impish pleasure in his reputation as a wit and raconteur—a sort of Buster Keaton style of narrating palpable nonsense—many years before the first Munchausen tale was quilled on paper. In his youth he had served as a cornet in the Brunswick Regiment supporting the Russians against the Turks—this would be in 1738 to 1740. Indeed, he was in the action when the Turks took Oczakov, turning the tides of war in their favor. He ended up a captain and retired to his estates when he was only forty, and for twenty-five years he lived in peace. Then, at age sixty-five, he suddenly found himself becoming a legend in his own time.

Some rascal in England had published a set of tales of the very kind with which the master of Bodenwerder "had once held his dinner-table in helpless laughter."[12] Worse, he had assigned them to Munchausen by name. German translations appeared. Sightseers began sneaking into the grounds to catch sight of the famous man. The fun went out of his tale-spinning. Seeking comfort, he married again at age seventy-four and died in 1797, sad and bitter.

It was a dirty trick, performed by one of the strangest writers since travelers' tales became popular, especially the genre which Carswell calls *Voyages Imaginaires,* which he traces back to the *Odyssey.*

Rudolf Erich Raspe was as German as Munchausen: he was seventeen years the Baron's junior and was born at Hanover and educated at the University of Göttingen. A redhead, he had enormous élan, unlimited ambition, and, apparently, no morals. Yet he was

12. John Carswell, "Introduction" to *Singular Travels, Campaigns and Adventures of Baron Munchausen,* by R. E. Raspe and Others (New York: Dover Publications, 1960), pp. xxvi–xxvii.

a fine scientist, an antiquarian, an æsthete, and a passionate devotee of Leibniz. He wrote his first book—it was an appreciation of Leibniz—when he was twenty-five; and the next year he published "an ambitious work on volcanic geology . . . which soon gained him international scientific fame."[13] His climb up the academic ladder was sciuroid—that is, squirrellike. At the university they admitted him to inner circles as *puer septem artium* because he could translate, interpret, write poetry as well as exposition, handle science with as masterful a hand as he did drama. He met Benjamin Franklin and devised improvements for the latter's glass harmonica. In 1769 he was elected a Fellow of the Royal Society of London. But all through this career, he was short of cash. He lived the sort of life that requires money, and money he never learned to handle. Since his academic honors did not bring wealth with them, he finally, in desperation, turned to the traditional solution, marriage. His eighteen-year-old bride made him richer by two thousand rix-dollars, which was a temporary relief, but not enough to hold off his creditors—largely professional moneylenders. So when he had spent all he had and borrowed all he could, he turned thief. As keeper of the famous collections of Frederick II, he had every opportunity to purloin choice pieces. This was discovered, and he fled to Holland and then to England; but from the moment of his flight in March 1775, he was a lost man. Expelled from the Royal Society, without a post, he earned what he could in any way he could—sometimes by working on translations, and once by selling certain fantastic stories to an Oxford printer named Smith. . . . He died in Donegal in 1794 of scarlet fever, poor man.

Perhaps the dirtiest trick of his whole life was his publication of *Baron Munchausen's Narrative of His Marvelous Travels and Campaigns in Russia.* There's no harm in composing impossible tall tales, especially when the obvious purpose is to amuse. Such collections have been popular in every culture with a literature, and in Germany there was the long tradition of the *Lugendichtungen,* and the *facetiae* or droll stories from the monasteries, in addition to a Munchausen-type hero in the Sixteenth century (Der Finkenritter)

13. Ibid., p. ix.

and another in the Seventeenth (Schelmuffsky). But to pin them deliberately on old Hieronymus, the retired cuirassier of Boden-werder, in mockery of the Baron's own "serious narration of palpable absurdities," and thus expose a harmless country gentleman and make him a public curiosity—especially when in all probability the author had been a guest at Bodenwerder years before—that is hard to forgive. And it was worse when Gottfried August Bürger translated the tales into German, where they won instant popularity, and increased the discomfort of the Baron.

No—Munchausen was no myth. And the clown with his name made him very miserable.

Back to Nature—with Brooks Atkinson

The myth is well established that naturalists, refugees from the skyscraper and the high-rise apartment, and others who have been lucky enough to get out of the city onto a few acres of their own in the country, become ecstatic about the bucolic life and worship every hour of it, every little jewel of an experience, such as looking a frog in the eye or counting the heartbeat of a chickadee. Writers such as Hal Borland, Loren Eiseley, Henry Beston, John Hay, and so on, like Thoreau before them, give added proof every time they put pen to paper. We read a four-inch essay in the editorial columns of the *Times* entitled "Hunter's Moon," and all the old magic swells around us like tones of a grand organ and we sigh enviously. How long is it since we have seen a sunrise, egad! We have given our hearts away, a sordid boon.

Yet there have been burlesques and parodies enough to indicate to us slaves of the encampment that all that glisters is not gold—stories of people who tried to build their dream houses; of tycoons who retired because of an age requirement and nearly went crazy trying to adjust to the quiet life on the sunny hillside; tales of men who tried to transplant themselves from Madison Avenue to West Tucket on the assumption that living yonder would be like one unending fishing trip with the peepers singing one to sleep each quiet night.

Now at last we have a nature writer (well, it is Brooks Atkinson *turned* nature writer) who sees through the trick. He is writing from Durham, New York, from his place on Prink Hill, and feeling pretty bitter about astronomers and the calendar makers who claim that autumn begins on 22 September and continues until 21 December.

"Don't they ever go outdoors?" he asks. "Autumn was concluded when ice formed on the bird bath and snow stayed on the mountain."

Instead of being ecstatic about autumn in early November, as tradition demands, Brooks Atkinson is depressed by it. Now everyone knows perfectly well that the nature lover at this season is supposed to be full of vim and delight. "There is something in the autumn that is native to my blood,/ Touch of manner, hint of mood,/ And my heart is like a rhyme. . . ." You don't say.

"The decline in the plenitude of nature from summer through autumn is always depressing," Atkinson wrote on 7 November.[14] "More than an hour of daylight has already dropped into limbo. Just about everything out of doors has been running down from delight and joy into melancholy." The bird migrations are over, the outdoors is without song. A month earlier there had been the blazing color of the fall leaves in the maples, birches and aspens, and the writer learned that the old notion of the first frost setting off a color explosion is a myth. "There had been no frost when the foliage was most ravishing in mid-October and none when the leaves fell in a downpour of color a week later." The land in November, however, is bare and dour. "The few compensations that autumn supplies for the decline of life outdoors are now over. We have nothing to take delight in." There are a few moody robins, he reports, but the deer who grazed nearby have disappeared, and soon the hunters will be at hand, manfully killing anything in the forest that moves. Regardless of what the calendar says, "Autumn is finished. It's winter and it's no good."

It is a good thing to have some sharp skeptic test the myth from

14. *New York Times,* 7 November 1968.

time to time—it is our protection against pure sentimentality, which can become infectious. There is another myth about the busy bee and one about "Go to the ant, thou sluggard; consider her ways and be wise." (Proverbs 6: 6) The idea behind both is industry, industry. It pays to be industrious. But a skeptic arrived at an anthill and challenged the theory. He claimed that the mindless, inchoate, random bumblings of a bunch of ants is more idiotically wasteful than any action he had observed in nature heretofore. He could find *nothing* here to make him wise except to go home and do exactly the opposite.

These testings are good, however, since in the end they show the truth of the myth. Ants may appear to be aimless—indeed, they do appear to be. But if you give them half an hour where they are building or manipulating or landscaping or whatever they call it, and watch closely, you will see the construction progressing with great precision, and with apparently exquisite planning.

So with the myth of the loveliness of nature. It is no use looking into an apple barrel for bananas—that is the wrong place to look. It depends what one is seeking. Atkinson, apparently, seeks the fullness of summer fruits and blossoms and the mad miracle of green. Take these away, and it's no good. Babette Deutsch ("The Hound") is shaken by the "blue and windy weather" more than by all the promises of spring; and Robert Frost ("My November Guest") gives us a lyric full of typical overtones expressing the beauty of lonely melancholy associated with autumn. The myth holds; beauty is of many kinds.

The Countess Godiva: What About That Ride?

When the Corporation of Coventry, particularly its Public Relations Department, was bestirring itself in 1967 to prepare a suitable celebration to commemorate the nine hundredth anniversary of Lady Godiva's death, a local historian by the name of Adrian Dobinson was quoted in a Reuters dispatch as saying that he had evidence to indicate that instead of being the heroine of the story, with her famous naked ride and all, Godiva herself *owned* Coventry and would have been the biggest tax collector to benefit from the hardship which tradition has her opposing.[15]

Now, a suggestion as dramatic as that is certainly indicative of the fact that the game's afoot and that the trail may lead straight to the mother lode in terms of myth and legend. We pursued it eagerly, only to have it disappear into the tall grass. Reuters, London, could tell no more than it had divulged; and we could not find the historian in question. But two months later a visitor to these shores, the Reverend Arthur Birtles of Birmingham, was sitting by good luck on the opposite side of our table, and we put the question to him. He went home and put the question to the writer of the "Mercian" column in the Birmingham *Post;* and *he* discovered at Coventry Council House that the Corporation was sponsoring an illustrated scholarly book to be written by Miss Joan Lancaster, city archivist at Coventry until 1948, and Dr. Hilda Davidson, "an expert in Anglo-Saxon and Scandinavian folklore."[16]

One begins to hazard a not uninformed guess as to why we could never reach Adrian Dobinson. When the reporter for Reuters got back to his typewriter, he couldn't read his own scrawl; where he had scratched "Hilda Davidson" he typed "Adrian Dobinson." All bets are being taken in the second room to the left.

To the American reader there is a real charm in returning to the England of A.D. 1050 and the days of Cnut and Edward the Confessor even if only to taste the names—place names and personal names. For instance, the Countess Godiva sometime before 1035 married the Earl Leofric of Mercia, and their son Aelfgar married Aelfgifu, and they had a son, Behrtric, who held lands in Baddesley Ensor, Compton Scorfen, and Stretton on the Fosse in Warwickshire as well as Coton-in-the-Elms in Derbyshire; and Leofric probably died at his manor of King's Bromley. It sounds more like a musical comedy burlesque than serious speech at first—until the richness of the nomenclature begins to be appreciated. One can find

15. *New York Times*, 12 March 1967.
16. Birmingham (England) *Post*, 26 May 1967.

samples at one's leisure now, however, since the special memorial book is in print.[17] And only 12s. 6d., too.

First of all, there is no doubt that both Leofric and Godiva were real people. He died in 1057, and she died ten years later, in 1067, the year after William the Conqueror arrived on the scene. All the abbeys kept chronicles of the times; and the various charters and records of deeds also bear testimony, as does the *Domesday Book* itself. She was christened with the Anglo-Saxon name Godgifu, but it has been Latinized to Godiva and nobody would know today whom you meant if the old name were used. "Leofric was one of the great magnates created by Cnut. . . . He was of his time, a politician, the harrier of Worcester, despoiler of the church's lands, and yet a devout man, who could see visions and miracles."[18] One had to be tough in those days in order to survive: one reads over and over again of persons being removed from high office by the simple process of assassination. There was no national police force; each noble had to depend upon himself and any allies he could muster for his protection. It was a rough-and-tumble world: when in 1041 Leofric learned that two of the king's housecarls, acting as tax collectors, had been murdered at Worcester, he saw to the punishment of the people of that town.

Thus the stories of Leofric's harshness toward the people of his own town of Coventry have some basis. This, we remember, was the basic motivation for Lady Godiva's intercession in the first place. King Edward the Confessor, about 1043, "issued a writ confirming to the Abbot of Coventry *sake* and *soke, toll* and *team* over his lands and men" in the same way that Leofric had these rights. The terms indicate the right to hold a court which tenants must attend and to exact taxes for every sale made in the territory. The taxes were sternly enforced—and they were not merely local taxes; otherwise Countess Godiva could have remitted them herself. They were national taxes, called the heregeld, levied to maintain the king's

17. Joan C. Lancaster, *Godiva of Coventry,* with a chapter on the folk tradition of the story by H. R. Ellis Davidson (Coventry, England: Coventry Corporation, 1967).

18. Ibid., p. v.

bodyguard, the housecarls. And they were of course very bitterly resented. However, it made the house of Leofric a great and powerful establishment. He himself was Earl of Mercia, and his son was Earl of East Anglia—so that between them they "controlled the great central area of England, from Worcestershire and Warwickshire in the south to Cheshire and Lincolnshire in the north, and from the Welsh Marches in the west right across to the East Anglian coast."[19]

Godiva was of different mettle. All the chroniclers agree that she was the possessor of all the highest virtues, was noble, religious, and obviously beloved of God. Apparently she did not wish to involve herself in politics, but she did try to influence her husband to make life a little easier for the citizenry. She was a great contributor to the church, in lands and income and in building chapels, endowing, restoring, and furnishing—including gold, silver, and gems as ornaments. She was a wealthy woman in her own right. Not only did she own Coventry, but she had vast land holdings in Warwickshire, Gloucestershire, and Nottinghamshire. They measured land by "hides." Coventry comprised five hides of land, that is, land producing value taxable at the rate of five hides yearly.

The situation makes sense—the gentle lady married to the tough administrator, and pleading for better treatment for her people in Coventry. But does the rest follow—the naked ride, Peeping Tom, and all?

None of the early chroniclers makes any reference to the ride. Miss Lancaster painstakingly lists the records and the writers, beginning with those who were making their testimony within the memory of men still living who remembered Godiva and Leofric, down to the *Anglo-Saxon Chronicle,* which also mentions no ride. But there is a manuscript at Corpus Christi College, Cambridge, of the *Flores Historiarum* of Matthew Paris, a monk of the Benedictine Abbey of Saint Albans. The writing dates to the early Thirteenth century—or about a hundred fifty years after the event, if there was an event. Here we read that the saintly Countess, *"villam Coventrensem a gravi servitute ac turpi liberare affectans,"* "wishing to free the town of Coventry from its burdensome and shameful

19. Ibid., p. 28.

servitude," pleaded with her husband. At first he refused to listen (probably telling her that business is business and she doesn't understand: one must run a profitable operation or give up). But she is persistent, and at last he says, in final exasperation, *"Ascende equum tuum nuda, et transi per mercatum villae ab initio usque ad finem, populo congregato . . ."* "Get on your horse unclothed, and ride through the market place from one end to the other when the crowd is there," and then ask me again. She did it, unseen by any soul, and Leofric relented and granted the town a charter.

As far as is known, there is no legend or folk story exactly parallel to this. Scholars have pointed out that it could be based on the memory of pagan rites in which nakedness played an essential part of a fertility magic. "The closest parallels found are examples of women stripping themselves naked to pull a plough, wade with a plough or harrow through water . . . in order to bring rain."[20]

Others have suggested as a source one of the Adam and Eve miracle plays in a series of biblical dramatizations that were popular favorites in the Middle Ages. Again it is put forward that the undressing merely symbolized the fact that Countess Godiva had been in the habit of selling her clothes for the benefit of the poor, or perhaps passing out clothes to the poor, and that this is a metaphor. To another commentator, it is the *horse* that was naked: that is, not adorned with the trappings that would ordinarily show his rider was a noble lady; and thus it could be seen as a penance.

The story had survival value, and other bits were added to it inevitably: at first the ride was to free the people from a painful servitude; then to free them from an abominable tax. The horse motif is said to symbolize that the one tax not remitted was the toll on horses in Coventry.

Then comes the Peeping Tom theme. In one version he is a tailor, and he looks out the window when Lady Godiva's horse whinnies —a natural enough, harmless enough reaction, one would say. But by this time there is also added the advance warning that the Countess has announced throughout the neighborhood: that she will take this ride at a specified time for the benefit of everybody, and no

20. Ibid., pp. 62–63.

fair peeking. Tom's act is thus punishable: it kills him. In another version, he is not a tailor at all, but a hostler familiar to this animal; and when the horse sees him he whinnies a greeting. In that case, the horse was guilty, not poor Tom. But we are reminded that in many a fairy story it is forbidden to mortals to see the fairies; and if one does, blindness or death follows. The classic version is the story of Actaeon and Diana, in which he sees the goddess in her ablutions, and she turns him into a stag, and his own hounds tear him to pieces. The oral tradition had Tom in the story by 1659, but nothing was in writing about him until the librarian of the Earl of Oxford set forth a little article in the City Annals sometime before 1670. There is a statue of Tom in the Leofric Hotel, Coventry, dated "c. 1600" and made out of one solid piece of oak; but again, there is some question whether this oaken personage, with his tight Elizabethan helmet, was actually *created* as Tom. He *looks* like some tough old footsoldier.

The first public procession honoring Lady Godiva was at the Corpus Christi Fair in 1678, a long time after the original ride. The mayor was there, and his armed guard, and workers from the various guilds with streamers and banners: the mercers, drapers, clothiers, blacksmiths, tailors, cappers, butchers, fellmongers, carpenters, cordwainers, bakers, weavers, woolcombers. . . . It was not an annual event, but was frequently put on as a trade fair attraction, the last time being 1951 and 1962, until the nine hundredth anniversary affair.

It is not unique to attach certain lasting virtues to historical personages, and if this happened to Godiva it also happened to George Washington, the forever truthful; to Abraham Lincoln, the forever honest; and, in certain circles, to Jean François Gravelet ("Blondin"), who walked a tightrope on stilts over Niagara Falls for the Prince of Wales, 8 September 1860.[21]

As for the Countess Godgifu of Coventry, it is not much of a risk to assert that no eyewitness is ever going to testify whether or not, arrayed solely in her lovely long hair, she rode the streets of the town

21. Jim Benagh, *Incredible Athletic Feats* (New York: Hart Publishing Co., 1969), p. 260.

on a whinnying horse. "An official" of Coventry told the Birmingham *Post:* "Modern critics generally repudiate the literal truth of the story, but on the other hand, the fundamentalists will always say she rode as she is supposed to have done—and will tell you the colour of the horse." In the same paper Miss Joan Lancaster, the archivist, is quoted: "I would say that the ride, as described in the story, almost certainly did not take place, but that there was probably some event in which Lady Godiva was concerned which gave rise to a grant of liberties of some kind to the inhabitants. . . ."[22]

There comes a time when a work of art becomes an objective bit of reality in its own right, and then one must deal with it as seriously as with any other real object. Miss Lancaster's book has seventeen plates at the end—pictures, paintings, statues, manuscripts, all interpreting the event and focusing chiefly on the naked horseback ride (the loveliest of which may be John Collier's painting of 1904). Paul Revere probably did not follow Longfellow's explicit instructions in his ride; but he rode. Lady Godiva may not have followed *her* script precisely; but she will never cease to ride. . . .

22. Birmingham *Post*, 26 May 1967.

V

Myths from History, Ancient and Current

Jolting the Cradle of Liberty

On Boston's Lafayette Mall, a forty-foot cement walk bordering the southern (Tremont Street) side of the Common, there is a bronze plate in a stone opposite the Cathedral Church of Saint Paul. It carries in bold relief a profile of Marie Joseph Paul Yves Roch Gilbert du Motier, marquis de Lafayette, gazing with imperious detachment over his patrician nose, westward toward Boylston Street. The metal is about thirty-four by forty-eight inches and reminds the visitor that Major General Lafayette, lately of the Army of the United States in the war for independence, "who nobly served the cause of liberty on two continents," had been "invited by Act of Congress to revisit the United States as a guest of the nation in 1824." On 17 June 1825 he laid the cornerstone of Bunker Hill Monument. The bronze relief was placed by the City of Boston with fitting ceremonies in 1924, and Lafayette was addressed with these words: "Heaven saw fit to ordain that the electric spark of liberty should be conducted through you from the New World to the Old."

Something about the handsome young French nobleman has always made him irresistibly romantic to the American imagination. Possibly he exemplified all the things we would like to be, despite our protestations of equality: he was top-echelon nobility; wealthy, courageous, idealistic, dashing in every way. Like Prince Hamlet, he was courtier, soldier, scholar—the "glass of fashion and the mould of form,/ The observed of all observers" . . . *Chevalier sans peur et sans reproche.*

Thus it was with a spirit of near idolatry that America opened her arms to Lafayette; and on 2 September 1824, the chevalier was in Concord and local hearts beat high as the Honorable Samuel Hoar introduced the Frenchman to the gathered multitudes, and in doing so inadvertently set off another revolution in one of those incredible accidents of history which can never be foreseen. The Senator reminded Lafayette that he was standing on the sacred ground where "the first forcible resistance" was made to British arms.[1]

One hopes that the noble Frenchman was not conscious of the family brawl that followed Hoar's assertion, in which clergy turned their backs on their reverend brothers and lifelong friends refused to speak to old comrades.

Fifty years earlier, on 19 April 1775, the people of Lexington had earned the right, they believed, to call *their* town the cradle of American liberty—for they had been taught that it was in Lexington that the first armed, organized resistance to British tyranny occurred. For Concord to rob them of these laurels was more than flesh could bear. The Concord upstarts must be put down with the full force of eyewitness evidence; and ten old-timers, who had been on the green at Lexington just before dawn on that faraway April morning, were called solemnly into court to give their depositions and settle this ridiculous matter once and for all.

Here we find a curious thing: depositions taken fifty years earlier and duly recorded had indicated that it was not the good citizens of Lexington who started the bloodshed and fired the first shot. It was the damned redcoats, that's who it was, murdering peaceful yeomen.

Paul Revere had heard Captain Parker of the Minutemen shout to his men, as they ran with their muskets to the green after the

---

1. Harold Murdock, *The Nineteenth of April, 1775* (Boston: Houghton Mifflin Co., 1925), p. 3.

alarm, "Let the troops pass by and don't molest them without they begin first."[2]

Parker, in his own deposition, 1775, said that he told his men not to "meddle or make with the said regular troops unless they should insult or molest us."[3] Such was the tenor of the depositions of eye-witnesses in 1775—and it is not hard to understand why their testimony should run to that sort of bias, especially when there was still hope in many American hearts that it would not come to a shooting war after all. Something could be worked out, eventually. But not, of course, if the colonists started firing on the regulars. Nobody wanted the blame for that first shooting. Not at the time. . . .

Later it was a matter of patriotism. We had won our freedom; two nations stood where only one nation had stood before. Somehow or other, we had convinced Britain that this fact had to be acknowledged. Now there was a certain glory in having been the first to fight. That Captain Parker, seeing the serried ranks of the British in an apparently endless column, "the six light companies out in front, with flankers off about a hundred yards to either side, and the grenadiers now only about a quarter mile behind,"[4] entertained any notion that his men could stop them is ridiculous. Seventy-six men had answered to the drummer's muster, and a nearby volunteer who heard the drum, a chap with the joyous name of Sylvanus Wood, came up shortly and joined them. Rapidly marching up the road, but hidden from the Minutemen by the meeting house, were seven hundred British regulars. Parker knew that Hancock and Adams had left town; and what else was there for the British to capture? Perhaps they would simply pass along up the Concord road, and not bother with the Minutemen at all. They had done this before in other marches out from Boston, without firing a shot—at Marblehead, Watertown, Cambridge. . . . The Minutemen were not blocking the road to Concord; the road curved left and the Americans were on the green, within musket shot, but

2. Frank Warren Coburn, *The Battle of April 19, 1775* (Lexington, Mass., Lexington Historical Society, 1922), p. 64.
3. Murdock, *Nineteenth of April*, p. 23.
4. John R. Galvin, *The Minute Men* (New York: Hawthorn Books, 1967), p. 134.

not in the path. But the redcoats were tense, and the leading company, marching fast, seemed to go out of control at the sight of Parker's men with guns in their hands. They left the road and tried to surround the farmers, and somebody fired a shot. Nobody knows who. Pitcairn was yelling at the Minutemen to lay down their arms and disperse. They had already begun to disperse, but took their muskets with them. In about ten minutes, eight Americans were dead and nine wounded and the British drummer was signaling "cease fire." One trooper was slightly wounded. Half an hour later the regulars had reformed their ranks and gone off toward Concord.

The scene was reenacted as a public spectacle in 1822. This time there was no hesitation among the Minutemen: they stood in bold defiance of the British. William Munroe, in the role of Captain Parker (he had been orderly sergeant under Parker in 1775), when he came to Parker's speech to his men, said firmly, "Stand your ground! Don't fire unless fired upon. But if they mean to have a war, let it begin here." Then, stepping out of character for a moment, Munroe told the audience, "Them are the very words that Captain Parker said."[5] Perhaps not exactly; but they are heroic words, memorably framed—and they are the words that appear today on a bronze plaque in a rock on Lexington Common.

Thus the available evidence in 1775 showed that the Minutemen had not been the first to shoot; and evidence from the same sources in 1824 indicated that they *had* been.

As for reenacting famous stories, Americans are no less fascinated by their history than other bipeds; we appear to have a profound delight in reconstructing famous events—as understood in later years by those to whom the torch has passed. During the Civil War centennial in the early 1960s, as many remember, no expense was spared to erect scenes and produce the action now regarded as immortal. Nor need the memorial drama or pageant wait a century —the reenactment at Lexington was staged forty-eight years after the event; and "The Return of MacArthur" was produced by Philippine troops in celebration of the twenty-fifth anniversary of the 1944 Allied landing on Leyte, a turning point in World War II

5. Coburn, *April 19, 1775*, p. 64.

—during ceremonies in which officials of the United States and the Philippines dedicated themselves to continuing the traditional friendship between the two peoples. (*New York Times,* 21 October 1969)

Today one hears no question of the reputation of Lexington as the cradle of American liberty. It is true that the first *bloodshed* of the Revolution occurred here on the Lexington green. But it is not true that the first armed, organized resistance to British tyranny took place here. There the myth goes astray.

The "first organized armed resistance of the Revolution," according to the Salem novelist and historian James Duncan Phillips, was at the bridge over the North River in Salem on 26 February, almost two months before Lexington.[6]

The story is told in detail in Major Galvin's recent book on the Minutemen. One of General Gage's spies told him that the rebels had collected a score of cannon at a forge in Salem. Gage sent for one of his officers, who knew Salem well, having guarded the general for a couple of years when he was living at nearby Danvers. This was Lieutenant Colonel Alexander Leslie, in command of the 64th Regiment. Gage ordered Leslie to sail by night to a point close to Salem and then march his men in to seize the cannon. Leslie embarked 240 men on Saturday night, 25 February. The transport arrived off Marblehead Neck at nine on Sunday morning, but waited to disembark until two in the afternoon, when it could be expected that almost everybody would be back in church for the rest of the day-long services. But there was no secret about his disembarking: he was seen by many people. No matter; he had his fifers playing "Yankee Doodle" in quickstep and the troops on the fast march before anyone could get away to warn the people at Salem.[7]

Leslie had only five miles to march. But somehow a courier got around the marching column and spread the alarm. There was no time to gather large numbers of defenders; but the Sunday services

6. *Pepper and Pirates: Adventures in the Sumatra Pepper Trade of Salem* (Boston: Houghton Mifflin Co., 1949), p. 103.

7. Galvin, *The Minute Men,* pp. 91–92.

were dramatically broken up and men went for horses to drag away the cannon, and for tools with which to pry off planks from the bridge. Colonel Timothy Pickering with a score of men ran for the North River bridge, which Leslie would have to pass over. They raised the drawbridge.

From this point on, there are two versions—the British report and the story which the provincials believed. The fact seems to be that Leslie at the drawbridge demanded passage for his troops; John Felt, a local shipowner, warned him against firing on the people, most of whom were not armed. He told Leslie that the alarm had gone out all over the countryside, and that pretty soon there would be hundreds of armed rebels on the scene. Leslie answered that he had orders to search for cannon. The guns which had not been hauled off had been covered with brush, so the local minister suggested a compromise: if the provincials let down the bridge, would Leslie simply march across, take a swift look, and march back to his ship? This saved face all around, and this was done. No guns were fired.

So the British report was that the spy's information had been incorrect: the brass cannon supposedly at Salem were only some old battered ship's guns not worth lugging away. The foray had been successfully carried out, and the provincials had not dared to offer resistance.

But the American report had a different tone. "The impact of the Salem affair on the minds of the provincials cannot be underestimated. To them, Leslie's march and his 'retreat' strengthened the conviction that the regulars could be faced down by determined action, and that the minute man system was the answer to British belligerence. On the following day the town of Beverly voted to raise two companies of minute men."[8]

We will probably never know what really happened at Salem. What we can be sure of is that Leslie sailed and marched with four companies of the 64th, and returned to his ship, and no shots were fired. He was confronted by organized armed resistance; and if

8. Ibid., p. 99.

there had been shooting, it is quite possible that Salem would be the cradle of American liberty.

Major General Thomas Gage faced an impossible job as governor of the province as long as the fatheaded peers in London insisted on treating the Americans like naughty children that needed spanking. They were too big to spank. Closing the port of Boston, trying to enforce the Intolerable Acts, and all the rest cured nothing. Gage arrived in 1774; he had seven regiments of regulars (2,500 troops) to pit against the unknown power of the Massachusetts countryside. His technique was to keep sending out the troops either for exercise or on legitimate forays, both in order to acquaint them with the area and to awe the natives. On 1 September 1774, he used the boat-transport technique to spirit away the government powder from Quarry Hill in Charlestown, starting at sunrise and being back in barracks before anyone knew what was going on. He was never successful again—provincial scouts and such riders as Paul Revere alerted the countryside before the redcoats could get there. So it was on 19 April . . . But before Lexington was Salem, and also forays into Brookline, Newton, Dedham, Milton. . . . The cradle of American liberty was big enough to hold them all.

How Black Was That Hole at Calcutta?

The Black Hole of Calcutta was a military prison at Fort William on the Hooghly River in Bengal. The fort and the troops were there for the protection of the East India Company, which was making money hand over fist for the benefit of British investors— the sole purpose behind the whole installation. Roger Drake, thirty-four-year-old senior Company official, was also the governor of Calcutta, and in the rigid hierarchy his power was absolute. He saw to it that the Moslem nabobs got their kickbacks from the trade with the British, and this kept them rich and contented. The area was a powder keg, however, because the Hindus were malevolently restless under Moslem rule, which had oppressed them for five centuries. In such a situation, a tight ship was called for: disciplined troops, strict policing, quick justice. But the commandant, George

Minchin, with a complacency which some have thought characteristic of the British (Braddock had it as he marched into the
American Indian ambush on the Monongahela almost exactly
thirteen months before the events of the Black Hole), was completely
careless about his defenses: there were shells that did not fit the
guns; fuses had not been prepared; the powder was damp; and
when the emergency came, nobody knew who was available to fight
and who was not.[9] Who cared? Everybody was getting paid off.
There was no danger. . . . Until suddenly the danger was viciously
upon them, like a leopard launching himself from the branch of
a tree.

But before we go into that, we must have a closeup of the Black
Hole—a nickname the military prison had earned long before the
crisis which brought it infamy. "One room with two small barred
air-holes and a door. This was the prison: a room about eighteen
feet by fourteen feet, intended to house at the most three or four
drunken soldiers for a night. Its dim interior was as hot as an oven,
only pencils of light coming through the windows. . . . The room
was filled with the stench of sweat, foul air, urine, excrement and
rats. Along the wall at the rear ran a platform on which soldiers
could sleep. It was the only furniture except for a pot."[10]

Most of us have heard, at least in a general way, of the four-day
battle which was launched against the British by the new young
nabob, Siraj Uddaula, who, at twenty-seven, hated the British and
the East India Company and, after due warning, marched against
the 515 Europeans with fifty thousand troops, including four
hundred elephants, two thousand camels, and a large detachment
of artillery with thirty yoke of oxen to each gun. . . .

Of course we have forgotten the details; but we know that at
the end there were 146 prisoners who had "honorably surrendered"
to the nabob under his promise to treat them as prisoners of war
—that is, not to take vengeance on the defeated men. The story we
have heard relates that on the night of 20 June 1756—in the middle

9. Noel Barber, *The Black Hole of Calcutta* (Boston: Houghton Mifflin Co., 1966),
p. 51.
10. Ibid., p. 36.

of the hottest Indian weather—the 146 prisoners were jammed into the Black Hole at 8 P.M., and that twenty-three were technically alive at six the next morning when the prison door was opened. The imagination falters in the face of that terrible night during which death came most horribly to 123 men. Incidentally, there was one woman among the prisoners, a Mrs. Carey; her husband died but she survived.

When we have wanted to refer to the uttermost horror, the blackest abysm, the quintessential evil of man's treatment of man at its complete worst, we have often used the Black Hole of Calcutta as a symbol. How can there be a brutality beyond that of the Black Hole? Novelists and poets, preachers and dramatists have made the Black Hole idiomatic for an ultimate blackness. In fact, the *Britannica* asserts: "The chief event in the history of Calcutta is the sack of the town and the capture of Fort William in 1756 by Suraj-ud-Dowlah, the nawab of Bengal. . . ."

Yet there have been careful students and famous people who have held that the story is a hoax, deliberately fostered by the British to justify England's iron grip on the territory. George W. Hartmann has written: "Sir Rabindranath Tagore and other distinguished Bengalis have publicly voiced their skepticism. . . . There is certainly grave doubt whether this alleged event ever actually occurred, at least in the manner in which it is usually transmitted and understood," he concludes, while conceding that much evidence is simply lacking and presuming that positive proof will probably never be forthcoming.[11] J. H. Little, writing in the official journal of the Calcutta Historical Society, was entirely convinced that "the whole thing is a gigantic hoax."[12] One has to admit that Little is quite correct in pointing out that the "massacre"—if that's the word—is attested to by one chief eyewitness, John Zephaniah Holwell, and that his testimony is the only written evidence to go into any detail. (Little is mistaken in saying Holwell is the *only* witness who survived the experience to testify; there were two others,

11. "The 'Black Hole' of Calcutta: Fact or Fiction?" *The Journal of Social Psychology* 27, (1948): 17–35.

12. "The Black Hole—the Question of Holwell's Veracity," *Bengal, Past and Present*, no. 21 (1915), pp. 75–104.

as Noel Barber shows in his more recent study.[13] But only Holwell wrote at length or in detail; and his word is certainly the most important. If his fifty-page pamphlet is a hoax, serious doubt falls on the whole account.)

Another recent work that questions the story is Harvey Einbinder's fascinating, if somewhat wildly swinging, *The Myth of the Britannica,* in which the author discusses over six hundred articles still being printed in 1958 which need revision in the light of newer knowledge—and one of them is the article on India in which the story of the Black Hole is narrated. Einbinder says that Little "demonstrated that Holwell was a liar and a grasping mercenary." He tells us that the Black Hole incident "is not mentioned in the chief Indian historical work of the period, the *Seir Mutaquherin,* which records other atrocities inflicted on the English. . . . No official report on the Black Hole was ever forwarded to the directors of the company, and Holwell's personal narrative contained many inconsistencies."[14] Similar doubts have been raised by both American and English authors, and very likely will continue to be unless on some great day of illumination a definite proof is exhumed from someplace. The learned Bergen Evans has questioned the story in *The Spoor of Spooks and Other Nonsense* (1954), and so has MacDonald Critchley, in *The Black Hole and Other Essays* (1964), not to mention various magazine articles from time to time.

It is true that John Zephaniah Holwell had something to gain by narrating a heroic story. He had come out to Calcutta as a surgeon's mate in 1732 and by the time of the siege had advanced to the position of zamindar or chief magistrate, "by far the shrewdest man in Calcutta."[15] There is no doubt that he was among the captured prisoners at the time of the storming of Fort William— although he had a chance to sneak away privately and escape by way of the river. However, the prisoners had no reason to believe that they were going to be tortured—the nabob had promised them

13. *Black Hole of Calcutta,* p. 20. Captain Mills of the garrison wrote a brief entry in his diary confirming Holwell; and John Cooke, the governor's secretary, gave verbal testimony at the official inquiry, also supporting Holwell.

14. *The Myth of the Britannica* (New York: Grove Press, 1964), pp. 184–85.

15. Barber, *Black Hole of Calcutta,* p. 34.

the traditional honorable treatment of prisoners of war, and there is no evidence to indicate that Holwell understood they were receiving anything else. The weather was viciously hot; it was black night; the battle had raged all day; parts of the fort were in flames; riot, pillage, and drunkenness howled through the compound; and a drunk Dutch soldier happened to shoot and kill an Indian. The authorities decided it was time to clamp down. The nabob ordered the erstwhile defenders of the fort clapped into prison until morning—possibly as much for their own safety in the half-lit chaos as for the general peace. He had never seen the Black Hole. He merely sent the captured fighters to prison. The rest we are familiar with.

Holwell wrote his eyewitness account six months later; and partly as the result of his narrative, he became the all-powerful governor of Bengal, supported by the armed might of Her Majesty's forces in India. Granting all this, however, would it be reasonable to expect a man who had lived through that black, superheated hell, in which men half out of their minds tried to drink sweat and urine in their desperation, to tell a calm, wholly objective story about the experience? With no inconsistencies or contradictions?

The foregoing is admittedly slanted and colored by Noel Barber's reply to the doubting Thomases. Barber is a trained investigator and reporter: as foreign correspondent for the London *Daily Mail,* he spent two years checking original documents, official correspondence, minutes of proceedings, reports, court records. And he concludes: "It is a true story; its characters live and die as they lived and died two hundred years ago."[16]

Barber seems to be familiar with the various critics who have written to question the historical fact. Of them all he says, "Invariably, one curious omission marks the arguments of those who claim the night of the Black Hole never occurred: if the one hundred and twenty-three British prisoners did not die in the Black Hole, where did they die? It is inconceivable that the standard three-volume reference work on this period of British history (*Bengal in 1756–57* by C. R. Hill), which contains over a thousand

16. *Black Hole of Calcutta,* p. 19.

pages of documentary evidence and verbatim testimony by sur-
vivors of the Black Hole, should ignore the fate of these men when
the fates of all the others are carefully recorded. . . . If Holwell
invented the story, how was it that not one of the twenty-three
persons he names denied the story when evidence of the fall of
Calcutta was being taken? This, then, is the story as I know
it. . . ."[17]

We conclude that if the story of the Black Hole is a myth, it
is a myth containing a great deal of truth. For us, the most incredible part of the story is the extreme pinnacle of inefficiency
attained by the commandant, George Minchin. It was known that
the nabob had sworn to throw the British out and that he was
on the march with a huge array. Yet in Calcutta there was no
requisition of food; trenches were not dug; no hospital wards were
set up; no plan of defense was drawn up; no evacuation of women
and children was undertaken; some of the walls were so rotten
from neglect that they would not support the weight of cannon;
fifty guns which had been unloaded three years previously lay on
the docks still, rusted and useless. The report on reserves of powder
showed that there was plenty—but failed to state that most of it
was damp. "No shells fitted the guns. No fuses had been prepared."
The governor asked Minchin for a full report on the strength of
the garrison. "Incredibly, Captain Minchin did not know."

One would be glad to believe that *this* part of the story was a
myth; sadly, it seems to have been all too true.

America Is Getting to Be One Big City

Ever since the Housing Act of 1949, and perhaps before that, the
idea has been more and more widely accepted that the United
States is an urban civilization. Probably today it would be hard
to find many persons of average literacy who would be willing
to deny that. It seems to be an accepted truism of sociology. "Everybody says so," said Grandfather Frog (we *think* it was Grandfather
Frog), "and what everybody says must be true."

17. *Ibid.*, pp. 19, 20, 21.

The *Reader's Digest Almanac* for 1967 was a little more cautious: "The United States is fast becoming an urban nation," it said, "with nearly 70 percent of the population now living in urban areas" (page 381).

That 70 percent figure came from the 1960 census; and the Census Bureau defines as urban any incorporated community of more than 2,500 inhabitants. And there's the rub. That definition belongs to the early nineteenth century. It would have been just dandy for 1828, for instance, when Mrs. Trollope was braving the rigors of travel in America, trying to dodge the pigs in the streets of Cincinnati (after all, people threw the garbage into the streets, and why should the pigs miss a good thing?) and trying to get her shopping done without having tobacco juice sprayed on her gown by one citizen or another (they all chewed).[18] The Cumberland Road was then the only paved highway in the country; there was no hard-surface turnpike in the continuous highway system between Boston and Savannah; coach travel from Philadelphia to New York required three days, with the coach moving eighteen hours per day.[19] And 2,500 people constituted an urban situation.

It is true that John L. McAdam, the English contractor, about 1815, made "the first substantial improvement in roadbuilding since Roman times," with his solid base of crushed stone topped by an inch of finely crushed stone and stone dust (this is the macadam road)[20] but it was not until the 1870s that asphalt began to be used as a binder in this country (the dust on an original macadam road in the dry season would choke a hippo) and road building was not undertaken seriously until after 1900. Why should they bother, after all, when nobody was taking the automobile seriously either? (There were eight thousand passenger cars in the United States in 1900).[21] It is difficult to imagine an urban society in the absence

18. Mrs. Frances Trollope, *Domestic Manners of the Americans* (New York: Vintage Books, 1960), pp. 16, 88, and passim.

19. Richard B. Morris, ed., *Encyclopedia of American History* (New York: Harper & Brothers, 1953), pp. 411, 420.

20. James R. Newman, ed., *The Harper Encyclopedia of Science*, rev. ed. (New York: Harper & Row, 1967), p. 689.

21. Morris, *Encyclopedia of American History*, p. 434.

of the motorcar and good roads. At least, it would have to be a different *kind* of urban living from ours. However, the prophets who said that the automobile would never replace the bicycle (the *Literary Digest* quoted such a spokesman in its issue of 14 October 1899) turned out to be wrong, and by midcentury there were nearly two million miles of surfaced roads and forty-two million registered passenger cars (excluding trucks).[22] By that time a population of 2,500 indicated a country village. But a country village in 1950 was an urban settlement by comparison with a country village fifty years before: radio and television had opened up the ways, the gadgets, and the conformities of city style.

A new way of thinking about America was introduced when the U.S. Bureau of the Budget defined Standard Metropolitan Statistical Areas (SMSAs), of which 231 were examined in detail for the first time in *Statistical Abstract of the United States* for 1967. "The general concept of a metropolitan area is one of an integrated economical and social unit with a recognized large population nucleus. Each SMSA contains at least one central city with at least 50,000 inhabitants. . . ."[23]

Tables were prepared which anaylzed these SMSAs in terms of 144 items of information: population totals, rank in population, nonwhite population, area size, estimated population 1965 (showing five years' growth or loss), births, deaths, marriages, votes for President, Social Security employment figures, taxable payrolls, construction, manufacturing, transportation, trade, finance, public services, government, unemployment, housing, etcetera.

Using the definition of the Budget Bureau—50,000 inhabitants—instead of that of the Census Bureau—2,500 population—changes that overwhelming "70 percent urban" figure to one which shows that as of 1960, "only 32.3 percent of the American population lived in cities of 50,000 or more; another 21.2 percent lived in the suburbs of these cities (the urban fringe). Nearly half of the American

22. Ibid. The figure for 1966 was 71,152,000 (*Statistical Abstract of the United States, 1967*). In May 1969 the Review and Reference Edition of *Automotive News* stated that there are 200 million registered motor vehicles in the world.

23. *Statistical Abstract of the United States,* 1969, p. 897.

population (46.5 percent) resided in areas the Census Bureau classified as small town or rural!"[24]

Thus the statement that we are today a predominantly urban civilization is a myth. Between the passage of the Housing Act of 1949 and autumn 1966 the U.S. Government had spent five billion dollars as the 90 percent federal share for 1,700 urban renewal projects in 800 cities, as the *Reader's Digest Almanac* for 1967 points out in a summary article. By this time we were facing problems of overcrowding, air and water pollution, traffic jams, education and welfare, race and crime problems, issues involving health, drugs, poverty, decayed areas, and so forth, and we were really getting urbanized just fine.

As we become more and more urbanized, it is interesting to cast a backward glance at the American record and the difference in our way of thinking. The big job for this country after the Treaty of Paris in 1783 was, of course, the development of this practically untouched continent: improving harbors and riverways, establishing lively new industries and trade relationships, and enjoying the fruits of independence. Travel by road was so bad that in many places four-wheeled vehicles were out of the question and in fact one went afoot or horseback, or one stayed home—unless one went by boat. That's why inauguration of the President took place in March—to give him time to get from wherever he was to Washington. Naturally those eyeing the new western lands wanted roads to open them up. The first real start was in 1811, the Cumberland Road, which was stopped in its tracks by the Panic of 1819. To get federal money for roads in those days was impossible. As his last official act, President Madison vetoed the road bill to maintain the Cumberland turnpike. Said it was unconstitutional. In 1822, President Monroe vetoed another road bill for the same reason. Areas like New England and the South, in particular, could see no dad-gummed reason why *they* should help pay for roads in *Ohio*. Let individual states pay for their own roads. It wasn't until 31 May 1830 that a president (Jackson) felt

24. Harold Wolman, University of Pennsylvania, in *Commonweal*, 25 October 1968, p. 103.

he could support such projects as the Cumberland Road. . . . But in our own day we have seen a plan launched for an interstate highway system projected to reach 41,000 miles by 1972 (and already totaling about 22,000 in 1966), with the federal government paying ninety cents out of every dollar spent.

Changes are coming rapidly; but it will not do to jump the gun. Possibly by the time this manuscript is translated by some half-understood magic into printed pages, we will have placed an airport on the moon. But as this is written, we have not done so, and we mustn't say we have if we want to keep our thinking straight. And the fact is that at the present moment, a clear majority of the congressional districts (actually 51.3 percent of them) "are primarily small town or rural in which television provides most of the experience so far as inner-city problems and disorders are concerned."[25] That is 223 out of 435 congressional districts. And it may explain why congressmen have not been speedier to take action on poverty programs, ghetto and race disorders of the metropolitan centers, and so on: they are somebody's else's problems—because we are not yet primarily an urban nation.

Yet the myth is coming to be true. We *will* be an urban nation. A recent Gallup poll showed that we reject the idea of a guaranteed income (58 to 36 percent) but we accept the idea of a guarantee of enough work to supply at least a low-level income to every family with an employable wage earner (78 to 18 percent). It is a sign, surely.

Down with London Bridge

"London Bridge," the excited and shrill chorus assures us, "is falling down, falling down, falling down!" But as the game increases in dramatic tension up to the sudden physical capture of "my fair lady," with its accompanying screams and laughter, we see that any reference to the possibility of real demolition or delapidation of any actual London Bridge is the last thing in the

25. Ibid., p. 105.

minds of the players. It's just a figure of speech they are using in the imagery of their game.

Even so, why London Bridge? Where did the idea come from? Are we to believe that some child plucked it out of the air to use in his singsong doggerel for the purpose of timing the action of the game?

Or do we have here another one of those folk words which the child picked up because it was in the texture of the culture? A folk word with factual experience behind it, perhaps. . . .

The engineering problem involved in throwing a bridge across the Thames as near the mouth of the river as London was probably too complicated for simple tribesmen or even for such sturdy invincibles as Hengist's Saxons, great warriors though they undoubtedly were. According to Dio Cassius, the Roman engineers succeeded in placing a more or less permanent bridge there in A.D. 43, however, because "as long as there was no bridge to join the north and south banks of the Thames the great object of Roman rule remained unfulfilled. This object was the completion of a system of roads connecting all parts of the Empire with Rome. . . ."[26]

Here was a river three hundred yards wide at this point, with a swift tide which raised the water level twenty feet in full flood. Anyone familiar with the carrying power of flowing water can understand the almost insuperable difficulties of setting up a permanent bridge in such a place. Finally in 1176 the foundations were set on artificial islands, called starlings; but these "so constricted the channel as to make the rush of water dangerous to boats."[27] In fact, the water was so swift under London Bridge that in the eighteenth century waterwheels were used at the bridge to develop power in order to raise water for the city's use. Old London Bridge had four arches of stone and a drawbridge; there was a gatehouse at each end and a chapel or crypt in the middle dedicated to Saint Thomas of Canterbury. This edifice stood for

26. *Encyclopaedia Britannica*, 11th ed.
27. T. K. Derry and Trevor L. Williams, *Short History of Technology* (London: Oxford University Press, 1961), p. 184.

centuries until a new one was started in 1824, designed by John Rennie and completed by his sons in 1831—one of three famous masonry bridges planned by the great engineer. (His first Waterloo Bridge introduced granite for bridge building to London and made such a beautiful structure that the sculptor Canova said it was worth traveling from Rome to see it.)

Sophisticated engineers, in short, were able to build a nearly permanent bridge at the mouth of the Thames; but it was well known that old bridges often collapsed because of insecure foundations, ice and spring floods, and the first attempts at constructing London Bridge met the same fate in the primitive days. An early form of the rhyme begins to give us a clue to the darker, myth-clouded meaning of the rubric. It runs: "London bridge is broken down," thus establishing the nature of the problem; then the advice is given: "Build it up with wood and clay, wood and clay, wood and clay," to which the response comes: "Wood and clay will wash away." Then: "Build it up with bricks and mortar . . . Bricks and mortar will not stay," and so on to iron and steel, silver and gold, and finally to the establishment in the bridge of a sleepless watchman, a guardian spirit—and of course this is the crux of the matter.[28]

It is at this point that we establish contact with a well-nigh universal myth, with our rhyme of "a mysterious bridge which must ceaselessly be rebuilt," and of "children singing lightheartedly as they play a game upon which there still rests an element of fear. . . . It is one of the few, perhaps the only one, in which there is justification for suggesting that it preserves the memory of a dark and terrible rite of past times."[29]

The dark and terrible rite is of course a human sacrifice, usually of a child. Living people were indeed built into the foundations, walls, and gates of bridges to act as guardian spirits; and until this was done, the structure would not stand, according to the legend. "All over the world," the Opies report, "stories of human sac-

28. Iona and Peter Opie, *The Oxford Dictionary of Nursery Rhymes* (London: Oxford University Press, The Clarendon Press, 1952) p. 270.
29. Ibid., p. 272.

rifice are associated with bridges, to the erection of which the rivers are supposed to have an especial antipathy. . . . When the Bridge Gate at Bremen was demolished in the last century the skeleton of a child was found embedded in the foundations. The bridge of Aryte in Greece is said to have kept falling down until they walled in the wife of the master mason." In Brittany, the building of a bridge at Rosporden was unsuccessful until a four-year-old boy was buried in the foot of it. With him were immured symbols of food and light—a piece of bread and a candle—so that the guardian would remain watchful.[30]

This game of capturing a victim as the players file through the narrow passage is found all over Europe, as the Opies point out. In France, the game is played to the following quatrain:

> *Trois fois passera,*
> *La dernière, la dernière;*
> *Trois fois passera,*
> *La dernière y restera.*

The Opies provide evidence of such practices from Denmark, Italy, Spain, and Germany; and they hold that in London itself, "there is a tradition that the stones of this great bridge, too, were once bespattered with the blood of little children."

Now as for London Bridge falling down in our own day, we can cite the royal assent of Queen Elizabeth to a bill in 1967 "empowering London to tear down the old bridge and build a new one at a cost of £2.4 million ($6.7-million),"[31] because it had been discovered that London Bridge was settling into the muddy bed of the Thames at a rate of an eighth of an inch yearly. Engineers were confident, it was reported, that the bridge could last another three or four decades, but eventually it had to come down. This is the Rennie-designed bridge finished in 1831; therefore, at least *sub specie aeternitatis,* a permanent bridge at this spot has been impossible to date, guardian spirit or no guardian spirit.

So the myth is true: London Bridge has always been falling

30. Ibid., p. 275.
31. *New York Times,* 5 March 1967.

down, in a manner of speaking. But the origin of the rhyme is not the fact that in the thirteenth century "great ice blocks crushed five of the bridge's arches," as a Reuters dispatch writer believed, but arises from a much darker source.

The memory of it is recalled when in the construction of any building a coin is laid beneath the foundation stone: the coin is a modern substitute for an animal or human sacrifice.[32]

It is seldom possible to trace the origin of a custom, but in the case of these "foundation sacrifices" or charms, as they are sometimes called, there is good reason to believe that they originated in the idea that those who are thus sacrificed turn into spirits who haunt the place where they were killed, doing mischief to those who attempt to harm the place. As Sir James Frazer remarked, "This theory would explain why such sacrifices appear to be offered most commonly at thoroughfares, such as gates and bridges, where ghostly warders may be deemed especially serviceable in keeping watch on the multitudes that go to and fro."[33]

As a final note, the ten thousand tons of granite blocks composing London Bridge have all become the property of Robert P. McCulloch, Jr., and the McCulloch Oil Corporation of Los Angeles, as Mr. McCulloch announced in mid-April 1968 in the Lord Mayor's Mansion of London. Many of the Cornish slabs were already stacked and numbered. They would be trucked to the Surrey commercial docks and thence shipped overseas to Long Beach, California, where trucks would pick them up again to transport them to Lake Havasu City, Arizona, one of America's newest resort cities, 232 air miles east of Los Angeles. Havasu is a forty-five-square-mile artificial lake; and there will be an artificial island across from an artificial river to be called the "Little Thames." The McCulloch Corporation paid $2.4 million for the bridge, which it is hoped will attract tourists. In this way, wrote

32. S. Baring-Gould, *Curious Survivals* (London: Methuen, 1905), p. 2; idem, *A Book of Folk-Lore* (London: W. Collins Sons, n.d.), p. 117.

33. Sir James Frazer, *The Golden Bough,* vol. 3, *Taboo and the Perils of the Soul* (London and New York: Macmillan, 1935), pp. 90–92. On foundation sacrifice see also Edward B. Tylor, *Primitive Culture,* 2d ed., vol. 2 (New York: Henry Holt, 1889), pp. 104 ff; also Edward Westermarck, *The Origin and Development of the Moral Ideas,* vol. 1 (London: Macmillan, 1912), pp. 461 ff.

George H. Favre in the *Christian Science Monitor,* "London Bridge thus will probably become the world's largest and most expensive effort to connect a city with a nonisland in a nonlake over a nonriver."[34] Here in this desert country (the center of a triangle formed by Las Vegas, Nevada, Palm Springs, California, and Phoenix, Arizona), surrounded by mountains which shoulder the sky, perhaps London Bridge will stop falling down at long last.[35] But what would Shakespeare and Dickens say?

National Birthday, July 4?

No doubt we will have to answer to the House Un-American Activities Committee for this, but it is nevertheless a fact that the members of the Second Continental Congress did *not* sign the document known to fame as the Declaration of Independence on 4 July 1776. American independence was *not* proclaimed to the world—as so often asserted—on that date. The official name of the document was *not* "the Declaration of Independence." Famous historians, in repeating the error, do not establish it as fact. Samuel Flagg Bemis, for instance, is correct in stating that "Total independence was resolved on July 2," but wrong in continuing with the statement, "and the famous Declaration proclaimed to the world July 4, 1776."[36] While Edmund S. Morgan does not go quite that far, he permits the reader to unpack his firecrackers for the Fourth: "On July 2 this resolution was adopted and two days later [was adopted] the famous declaration to the world, drafted by Thomas Jefferson."[37] With backing of this caliber, it is surely no wonder that the myth persists and that millions of Americans believe that the Fourth of July is the national birthday.

34. 20 April 1968.
35. "Sir Gilbert Inglefield, Lord Mayor of London, arrayed in his medieval robes of office, has laid the cornerstone of his city's historical old bridge. The bridge will span the Colorado River here." *New York Times,* 10 October 1968 (story datelined "Lake Havasu City, Ariz.").
36. *The Diplomacy of the American Revolution* (Bloomington, Ind.: Indiana University Press, 1957), p. 31.
37. *The Birth of the Republic 1763–1789* (Chicago: University of Chicago Press, 1956), p. 76.

In fact, one feels faintly subversive merely to mention that technically the tradition is in error. However, the risk is worth it if one can at the same time issue a caveat, an effective and memorable warning, against all oversimplified absolutes in the reconstruction of history—for no event leaps fully grown in complete armor into the arena of human affairs after the example of Pallas Athene from the head of Zeus. The demand of public opinion for independence did not find a voice suddenly, although it did grow fast once born. Ten years previously it would have been difficult to find any sizable group in the Colonies which would even consider a separation: the colonists were Englishmen—largely—and proud of the fact that, standing shoulder to shoulder with British troops, they had fought the French successfully so that from 1763 on, they could farm without a musket in the bushes and get on with the exciting business of peaceful development and growth. Englishmen with the rights and privileges of Englishmen. They asked no more.

But no war is cheap; and now the British national debt was huge—in addition to which Britain had new territorial responsibilities in two hemispheres. The ministry's attitude of "salutary neglect" changed quickly to a demand that the colonies share in the cost of defense. So there followed the Sugar Act (1764), the Stamp Act (1765), the tax on tea—and the growing resistance in the Colonies, answered by sterner measures by the ministry in the form of the punitive Coercive Acts, in turn igniting open rebellion in the Colonies. Good men died on 19 April 1775—both among the farmers and in the soldier ranks. The siege of Boston, which followed immediately after the British retreat from Concord, lasted nearly a year. May '75 saw Ethan Allen at Ticonderoga; 17 June saw Bunker Hill. In the fall, Arnold marched to Quebec. . . . Thus one event was piled on top of another until public opinion in America became quite the reverse of what it had been a decade earlier, and John Adams, looking back, reflected that the real American revolution "was in the hearts and minds of the people," and the trial by arms simply measured the depth of conviction. It must be said that a snotty ministry helped the colonists make up their minds: in the summer of 1775, three months *after* Lexington, the Continental Congress made the gesture of the so-called Olive Branch Petition to the king, begging him even at this late stage to intervene and help restore "the former harmony." The answer came a month later when George III proclaimed that a general rebellion existed which must be suppressed by whatever means necessary. The king did not receive petitions from rebels. This was followed by a prohibition against all trade with America; American ships were declared lawful prizes if they could be taken; and American sailors were subject to impressment.

It was against this background that Richard Henry Lee of Virginia, on instruction from the House of Burgesses, rose in Congress on 7 June 1776 to offer three resolutions: the first declared that "these United Colonies are, and of right ought to be, free and independent states, that they are absolved from all allegiance to the British Crown, and that all political connection between them and the State of Great Britain is, and ought to be, totally dissolved." (His second and third resolutions urged making favorable foreign alliances and offered a plan of American confederation.)

Five delegations were prepared to vote for the Lee resolutions immediately, but consideration was postponed by a 7–5 vote to give the delegations from New York, Pennsylvania, Delaware, and South Carolina more time to get specific instructions.[38] Thus it was 2 July before Congress actually adopted the Lee resolutions. Meanwhile, however, a Committee of Five had been appointed to prepare a statement in formal language which would explain to the family of nations the reasons for the American action, and to show why it was necessary and unavoidable. The new nation was going to need friends and allies; and it was important to show that its actions were responsible and that the new government was going to prove stable and trustworthy. This Committee consisted of Thomas Jefferson, John Adams, Benjamin Franklin, Roger Sherman, and Robert R. Livingston; and they asked Jefferson to prepare a first draft, which he did.[39] With some minor corrections

38. Samuel Eliot Morison, *The Oxford History of the American People* (New York: Oxford University Press, 1965), p. 221.

39. Merrill D. Peterson, *The Jefferson Image in the American Mind* (New York: Oxford University Press, 1960), p. 306.

from the Committee, the Jefferson draft (formally the Report of the Committee of Five) was presented to Congress on 28 June, "taken up four days later, debated on three successive days, and finally adopted with a number of amendments on the fourth of July."[40]

It would be fascinating to have the detailed discussion for those three days of debate. Anyone who has ever sat on a committee whose duty it was to make a statement which might satisfy all representative opinions can understand where the time went. But the Congress was sitting as a Committee of the Whole Congress, and the discussions were not recorded. We know what some of the changes were from Jefferson's notes; for example, the Report had severely censured the people of England, and there were those who felt we ought to keep any friends we could in Britain. Jefferson commented: "The pusillanimous idea that we had friends in England worth keeping terms with, still haunted the minds of many." If anybody is curious to see precisely what was done, Becker prints the entire Declaration, running a line through material deleted by Congress and adding in italics everything that Congress added.[41]

So we have Lee's resolution on independence voted by Congress on 2 July; and we have the Committee Report, "with the title and stile of 'The Unanimous Declaration of the Thirteen United States of America,'" agreed to on the evening of 4 July and "signed by order and in behalf of the Congress" by one person—John Hancock, president. "Contrary to a tradition early established and long held, the Declaration was not signed by the members on July 4."[42]

As for proclaiming the matter to the world, two Pennsylvania papers (the *Journal* and the *Gazette*) printed the news on 3 July: "Yesterday the Continental Congress declared the United Colonies free and independent states. . . ."[43]

40. Carl L. Becker, *The Declaration of Independence: A Study in the History of Political Ideas* (New York: Vintage Books, 1958), p. 3.

41. Ibid., pp. 174–75.

42. Ibid., p. 184.

43. Arthur M. Schlesinger, *Prelude to Independence: The Newspaper War on Britain 1764–1776* (New York: Vintage, 1965), p. 281.

In short, the *principle* of independence was voted on Tuesday, 2 July; the newspapers carried it on Wednesday, 3 July; Congress voted the Declaration itself on Thursday, 4 July; printed copies were sent to the various colonies and to the Army on Friday and Saturday; and on Monday, 8 July, the document was read publicly from the balcony of Independence Hall. The actual signing by the members took place on 2 August, after the copy which had been engrossed on parchment was returned and diligently compared with the original. There were fifty-six signers, eighteen of non-English origin, "nearly half of them immigrants," as Schlesinger points out.

Sam Adams said the people looked upon this Declaration as if it were a decree straight from heaven; and John Adams said 2 July would ring down through the corridors of time as the most memorable event in the history of the country. As sacred writ, it was inevitable that mythology should create a certain amount of statuary for the public parks around this theme; and it is of record that a Thomas C. Donaldson, having located the site of the house where Jefferson wrote that first draft (the corner of Seventh and Market Streets), went to the spot after the building had been demolished to make room for a bank, and "fondly gathered up its remains."[44]

Myth likes its subjects simple, bold, specific, and colorful. Here the myth is that on a day in Philadelphia early in July 1776—simply and specifically 4 July—the Continental Congress rose as one man, togas firmly wrapped and eyes stern, and, at the frayed end of its patience, informed George III of England where he and his ministry could go.

It is a good myth and has in it the basic truth underlying all such stories, whether the precise dates are as scheduled or not. No less an authority than Samuel Eliot Morison gives the opinion that the words now to be quoted are "more revolutionary" than anything from Robespierre, Marx, or Lenin:

We hold these truths to be self-evident, that all men are created equal, that they are endowed by their Creator with certain unalienable Rights, that among these are Life, Liberty, and the pursuit of Happiness. . . .

44. Peterson, *Jefferson Image*, p. 304.

So once again, despite the annual discovery by newspaper feature writers of the postponed signing, we have a myth which is true the moment it is correctly interpreted: a man has the right to freedom if he can defend it, and he will be applauded on all sides if he succeeds. At one time the United Colonies were British; and on the other side of that time the United States were independent. Whether one selects the day the peace treaty was signed in Paris, 1783, or the Fourth of July, 1776, is a detail.

Since the foregoing was written, we have seen additional evidence that the original broadside printed for distribution and repeating the edited words of the Committee of Five still has more than passing interest in the national scene. One of the sixteen extant known copies of the first printing was discovered in a scrapbook and was auctioned off at the Samuel T. Freeman & Co. rooms in Philadelphia on 7 May 1969. It brought the "highest price ever paid at auction for a printed or manuscript book or document," to wit, $404,000. The previous record price for such a piece had been $155,000 for a copy of the first printing of the Constitution, in April 1969. The *Declaration* was, of course, purchased by a Texan, Ira G. Corn, Jr., of Dallas.[45]

The United States Is a Christian Nation?

The statement that "America is a Christian nation" is considerably more than an expression of popular opinion. Somehow or other the idea seems to be so thoroughly rooted in our society—despite the obvious pluralism of our national makeup—that it is not to be doubted and has even been asserted in court decisions as an assumption beyond any reasonable questioning. As early as 1811 the high court of New York State in *The People* v. *Ruggles*—a blasphemy trial—held that "a reviling is still an offense, because it tends to corrupt the morals of the people, and to destroy good order," and therefore blasphemy is a civil crime as well as a religious evil, "and for this plain reason, that the case assumes that we are a Christian

45. *New York Times,* 8 May 1969.

people, and the morality of the country is deeply ingrafted upon Christianity. . . ."[46]

The United States Supreme Court said practically the same thing thirty years later: "It is unnecessary for us, however, to consider what would be the legal effect of a devise [gift of real estate by will] in Pennsylvania from the establishment of a school or college, for the propagation of Judaism, or Deism or any other form of infidelity. Such a case is not to be presumed to exist in a Christian country; and therefore it must be made out by clear and indisputable proof. . . ."[47]

"We are a Christian nation." The phrase slips easily off the tongue, and it is not difficult to understand why the country should accept it—indeed, welcome it as a characterization devoutly to be wished. "Whatever makes men good Christians," said stern old Dan'l Webster, "makes them good citizens." And Samuel Johnson, the all-time great egghead, averred, "Christianity is the highest perfection of humanity." The assurance that we are not aliens in a world we never made, but instead that we are at home and cared for and secure in our future and that love is the law of our being—this is a doctrine of comfort, a haven from fear. Who *wants* to question it?

It must be true. Henry Ward Beecher, the "most influential minister in America" in the 1870s, assured his wealthy merchant parishioners in Brooklyn that "God has need of rich Christians . . . and He assigns particular duties to them . . . in this Christian Republic where all men are declared to be free and equal."[48] Yes, it makes sense: for the first couple of hundred years, the New World was peopled from the Christian nations of Spain, France, and, particularly, England. Even after that, from 1820 to 1967, the largest portion of immigration was from Great Britain and Ireland

46. Joel Prentiss Bishop, *New Commentaries on the Criminal Law,* vol. 1 (Chicago: T. H. Flood & Co., 1892), pp. 294-95. Cited, with interpretative comment by Associate Judge Edward O. Weant, Jr., Fifth Judicial Circuit of Maryland, in a Memorandum Order filed 1 May 1969 declaring Maryland's 246-year-old blasphemy law unconstitutional. Personal correspondence.

47. Vidal, et al. v. Girard's Executors, 43 U.S. 126 (1844), p. 198.

48. Digby Baltzell, *The Protestant Establishment: Aristocracy and Caste in America* (New York: Random House, 1964), pp. 101, 119.

—about 9.5 million of the total immigration of 44 million, 1820–1967, or 9.4 percent, came from the British Isles; the closest second is Germany, with 6.9 percent—that is, over the whole eighty-seven-year period—and Italy supplied 5.1 percent. All the immigrants were from Christian countries, or at least from countries of which the rulers professed some brand of Christianity—with the exception of Asia and Africa, which together contributed only 1.4 percent over the whole period.[49] Irish immigration reached its high point after the famine of 1846, and the Germans came in greatest numbers after the revolutions of 1830 and 1848, both nations giving stout peasant stock mostly, strong to build railroads and canals in a country racing westward.[50]

The evidence we have seen points to the probability that people using the phrase "Christian nation" for America have been largely churchmen, opinion leaders, politicians, and the bosses; and what they have meant is "Protestant." For the truth is that until the middle of the twentieth century, "at the top of the pyramid of wealth and social prestige . . . there is a White-Anglo-Saxon-Protestant establishment" which only very recently has been losing its power and authority.[51] The roots of this power structure are found in the era between Francis Drake and Benjamin Disraeli, during which the authority of the white man was built up largely by the gentlemen of England; it received a tremendous fillip after 1859 when Darwin's *Origin of Species* appeared and social Darwinism as a philosophy developed as an analogue, with Herbert Spencer as its standard-bearer. Now all of a sudden we are assured that it is inevitable that the strong should survive and the weak become extinct; and thus, clearly, the American Anglo-Saxon millionaire is the fittest to rule and to command—his very possession of the wealth is the proof of this—and he should be left alone (laissez-faire) by the government to pursue his path, ordained as it was by the will of God, no less, as Henry Ward Beecher continually assured the public. Socialism, in consequence, was a

49. U.S. Bureau of the Census, *Pocket Data Book*, 1969, pp. 70–71.
50. Morison, *Oxford History*, pp. 479–80.
51. Baltzell, *Protestant Establishment*, p. ix.

thwarting of God's will. He had established that the fittest should survive and the weak perish. Better not interfere with *that!* Especially in a Christian nation . . .

The foregoing are some of the ideas clustered around the term "Christian nation." Our money says "In God We Trust." A chaplain addresses prayers to the God of Our Fathers as the legislature opens each session. Our pledge to the flag has the words "under God." We attend churches—at least at Christmas and Easter. We contribute billions to the ecclesiastical establishment. We send missionaries to the heathen. And we acknowledge the primacy of the ethics of Jesus as an ideal system: love, mercy, justice, charity, forgiveness, humility.

Do these things, in fact, make America a Christian nation? In the last third of the twentieth century, are we a Christian nation? Were we a Christian nation to start with? According to some scholars, the answer is a resounding and impatient No. The "Christian nation" notion is one of the stickiest myths ever to attach itself to this country, with the collaboration and support of the dominant white Anglo-Saxon Protestant leadership. Franklin Hamlin Littell is emphatic. He is professor of church history at Perkins School of Theology, Southern Methodist University, an international scholar who has published extensively in both English and German. He asserts:

The whole image of early America as a "Christian nation" (i.e., Protestant-controlled) is a lie which must be struck down: America was, in her colonial period—like continental Europe—officially religious and in fact characterized by "baptized heathenism"; in her early years as a nation she was overwhelmingly unchurched and heathen, regardless of pretensions and public claims. . . .

The idea that the American people were once Christian and have subsequently declined is false, and the historical perspective involved is unsound. America has never been a Christian nation except in the nominal sense. In the colonial period, state churches were maintained at public expense, as was the case in the home countries of Europe. . . . The course of American church history has been marked, by and large, by the effort to win a people back to the churches they had frankly abandoned when support ceased to be compulsory. . . .[52]

As the colonial state churches collapsed, according to Littell, the revivalists held aloft the memory of the Pilgrim fathers, "creating thereby the most persistent myth of American history: that the 'Founding Fathers' of the colonies came to found religious liberty and that the 'Founding Fathers' of the Republic were above all dedicated to the cause of liberty. . . ."[53] The colonists won their independence with a population of about three and a half million, Littell asserts; among them were about twenty thousand Roman Catholics and six thousand Jews. Hence it was largely a Protestant nation that faced the world with the Treaty of Paris in 1783—but there is "ample statistical evidence that the established Protestant churches by no means commanded the loyalty or willing support of the vast majority of the population." We were actually heathen, and the Protestant and Catholic missionary societies of Europe sent missionaries, tracts, and money in an unremitting attempt to save the new world from irreligion. The figures Littell gives are as follows:

1776	5% of the population held church membership
1800	6.9% of the population held church membership
1850	15.5% of the population held church membership
1900	35.7% of the population held church membership
1926	50% plus of the population held church membership

He adds, "With the census of 1960 we stand at a high tide of successful mass evangelism, with voluntary church membership at nearly 70 percent and popular identification with the churches even higher."[54]

One of the reasons politicians, and other people who want to keep the conversation peaceful and safe, stay away from religious controversy as far as they possibly can is that when one deals with re-

52. *From State Church to Pluralism: A Protestant Interpretation of Religion in American History* (Garden City, N.Y.: Doubleday Anchor Books, 1962), pp. xx, x.
53. Ibid., p. 48.
54. Ibid., p. 32.

ligion, one is playing Pandora with the very most profound, most important, ultimately most threatening center of human passion. For if the term "religion" has any meaning, it relates man to the Unknown; it answers the most persistent question: Why am I here? What is the meaning of life? And if we have embraced a religion which we believe answers this sort of thing and in addition gives us a clue to what's going to happen when we pass over Jordan, then we're *not* going to sit by and see that holy faith disturbed. We have our answers; and we are poised to fly at any intruder who tells us we're wrong. We've got too much invested in our religious system; it is the one thing that ties together all the loose pieces of life and forces them to make sense, thus maintaining our very sanity. Destroy this, and we are lost indeed. Which explains the unleashed ferocity of our attacks on heretics of all kinds, whatever we say on Sunday about the brotherhood of man and the fatherhood of God. Death by torture is, we feel, the only reasonable reply to those minions of the Devil who would tempt our very souls from everlasting paradise—and their punishment should be adapted to the enormity of their crime. In addition to which, of course, they are mistaken; their truths are falsehoods. We have had our revelation and *in hoc signo vincamus.*

In discussing the proposition that America is a Christian nation, it is therefore extremely important that both writer and reader should agree to hold any strong personal prejudices within control, to make the attempt to keep the chariot on the narrow road with the full use of reason—in the faith, held so firmly by John Milton, the scholarly Channing, and a hundred other free minds—that reason is safe in the marketplace and that a truth does not suffer by being questioned by the keenest interrogators. Because if the writer starts using loaded language or the reader adopts an attitude of defense, our whole purpose is defeated and we end where we started.

"Our ability to reason," says Kathleen Nott in her brilliant essay *The Emperor's Clothes,* "is based on inference, on our attachment to human experience, and this can never give us more than a high approximation to certainty. Our world is probability . . . [But there are] those whose emotional hunger for certainty is so great that they choose intellectual starvation if they cannot have their preferred diet. . . ."[55]

That the United States of America is a Christian nation is stated as fact by persons who consider themselves Christian. They use the statement in support of some moral or ethical point of view, usually with political intentions. The famous radio priest, Monsignor Fulton J. Sheen, used to equate Christianity with Americanism indeed, as did the widely popular opinion leader Norman Vincent Peale ("Let the churches stand up for capitalism").[56]

All of the wars in which America has engaged have been *defensive* from this point of view, because America is a Christian country and would never force a smaller nation to do its bidding under threat of physical power, except for its own good. We would never pick a fight, we always say.

Before we try to decide whether such a characterization is a reflection of external truth or merely one of internal wishful thinking, we have to agree on what we mean by "Christian," much to the disgust, no doubt, of those who are saying to themselves, "*Everybody* knows what one means by 'Christian.'" But that is not true. The meaning could be: "A person who consciously and habitually tries to follow the ethics of Jesus." Or it could mean: "An adherent of an organized religious group which looks upon Jesus Christ as Lord and Savior, the only begotten son of God, a member of the Trinity . . ." and so forth, until the whole creed is stated. Besides which there would be groupings of all descriptions: "I was born a Methodist, so I'm a Christian," or "I was baptized in the Congregational Church, which makes me a Christian." Even "I was never baptized anywhere, so I'm an atheist," as we heard this question answered lately. People seem to know about as much on the subject of religion as they do in the field of biology. The most important mechanism we can ever have anything to do with is the

55. *The Emperor's Clothes* (Bloomington: Indiana University Press, 1958), p. 3.
56. William G. McLoughlin and Robert N. Bellah, eds., *Religion in America*, from *Daedalus* (Boston: Beacon Press, 1968), p. ix.

organism which bears our name and pays taxes in our name; and we know almost nothing about how it works or what's healthy for it. Too busy. And the most important spiritual, ethical, moral, inspired fruit of human intelligence is expressed in terms of religion —where meaning and interpretation and values can alone find expression; and we take it from where the preachers leave it on Sunday (if, indeed, we study so deeply!). Too busy.

Let the reader ask himself—whatever his views on the subject of Vietnam (and we have no intention of preaching on this subject)— whether he believes that American forces would *ever* withdraw if it was believed that *the cost of remaining was nominal* and that *victory was possible,* regardless of the morality of American troops using napalm (by comparison with which burning at the stake was almost merciful) and defoliation gases and other tools of a Christian and gentleman foe? The nonsense is in the question: the only reason so many voices were demanding an end to Vietnam is that it was becoming unbearably *expensive* and there was *no* promise of victory. Christian ethics were out of it.

Therefore it was no idle question to insist on a definition of the word "Christian." The supreme authority in America on the American language is *Webster's Third New International Dictionary.* The first definition of "Christian" is: "One who believes or professes or is assumed to believe"—those are important modifiers!—"in Jesus Christ and the truth as taught by him: an adherent of Christianity: one who has accepted the Christian religious and moral principles of life: one who has faith in and has pledged allegiance to God thought of as revealed in Christ. . . ."

Here the emphasis is on the ethics of Jesus. Of course, it was Paul and not Jesus who adapted the message for the non-Jewish world and had to meet the competition of the many Greek and Persian savior-sects and, in doing so, adopted so many of their rituals and salvation mysticisms into what became, with the years, accepted orthodox doctrine. One could ask, "Is America 'Christian' in the light of the Council of Nicaea?" But that was A.D. 325! We would not argue—and shed blood—today over the "iota contro-

versy" revolving around the question of whether Christ was of
"identical" or "similar" substance with God. . . .

Our own national history can be illuminating on the "Christian
nation" controversy. Many religious groups came to these shores not
to establish freedom of religion, but to set up an oligarchy where
their particular form of religion would be free. Roger Williams
and men like him became famous in the American archives because they refused to play that game, and demanded freedom for
everybody. The subject was of local importance until American independence had been won—and then suddenly the thirteen sisters
beside the sea, who often trusted each other less than they trusted
Britain—had to learn to live together. Fearful of any single religious dominance (like the Church of England, with its customary
bloodshed and repressions) they wrote into their Constitution and
into each state constitution that this society would never support
any specific religion. It was open to all churches; but they had to
find their own support.

Thus, when the Barbary pirates (1812–15) attacked American
merchantmen in the Mediterranean and sold American sailors into
slavery (obviously on the theory that there was no "United States of
America" except on paper, and that sleepy watchdogs make for easy
theft), it took a Stephen Decatur, acting on behalf of all, sailing
with ten vessels from New York (10 May 1815), to move against
these rascals with disciplined might and crumple the entire naval
strength of the Dey of Algiers and the governments of Tunis and
Tripoli as well. In the treaty with Tripoli we find John Adams
saying: "As the government of the United States of America is not
in any sense founded on the Christian Religion—as it has itself no
character or enmity against the law, religion or tranquility of Mus-
selmen . . ."[57]

Actually the history of the word "Christian" is itself full of interest. The word appears only three times in the New Testament
(Acts 11 : 26; Acts 26 : 28; and I Peter 4 : 16). It was first used at Anti-
och and according to Tacitus it was used by the populace to indi-

57. George Seldes, *The Great Quotations* (New York: Lyle Stuart, 1960), p. 45.

cate followers of someone whose proper name was thought to be Christ; there was no reference at all to the notion of "Messiah."[58] Followers of Jesus themselves avoided the term, which was considered a pejorative. They called themselves "the brethren," or "the disciples," "the saints," "the faithful," "the elect"—but *never* "Christians."[59] Historians like Tacitus and Suetonius used it freely, however, apparently feeling that the termination *-ianus* meant "follower of" as in *Caesariani, Pompeiani,* and so on. ". . . *quos vulgus Christianos appellabat*" ("whom the ordinary person called Christians"), says Tacitus. Hastings says, "If it did not originate as a sarcastic *jeu d'esprit,* it very soon came to be used with a contemptuous signification. It occurs with an implication of scorn in the mouth of Agrippa."

The contempt was because the Christians worshiped a crucified man; that they were mostly slaves themselves; because they seemed to be "morose and unsociable Puritans," and because they were believed to be part of a worldwide subversive organization: which is a thought for the next John Bircher who shows up—although, unfortunately, he would not be able to enjoy the parallel. Christians had a mysterious worship ritual; they met secretly; they opposed theater and conscription . . . a pretty suspicious lot indeed.

Then there was the pagan confusion between *Christus* and *chrestus,* the first referring to Christ and the second to any good or generous thing, so that "Christian" gradually attracted to itself, as a term, the idea of brotherly love, quite by accident.

Finally, in the consideration of our character as a Christian nation, we have to look at a few tables from the Bureau of the Census (ecclesiastical statistics, doubtful as they are, have to be used here) and we find that totals which come close to half the population of the United States are claimed by organized religion. Of church groups with fewer than 500,000 members there are 78,000; and with the huge Baptist totals (2 million plus), along with Lutheran, Methodist (combined total, 15 million), and many smaller groups

58. F. L. Cross, ed., *The Oxford Dictionary of the Christian Church* (New York: Oxford University Press, 1957), p. 275.

59. James Hastings, *A Dictionary of the Bible* (New York: Charles Scribner's Sons, 1902), 1: 384–85.

with 2 and 2½ million each, it is possible to say that America seems to be somewhat more than half Christian, in terms of church membership. Certainly there is no doubt at all that, as Gaustad says, "In the heritage of America, religion's role has always been significant and has often been crucial."[60]

So be it. But the cultural attitude toward Christianity—toward the whole field of religion—has undergone such a revolutionary change in the last few decades that it has exactly reversed itself; and in no place more clearly than in statements by the United States Supreme Court. As Paul Blanshard, pioneer Protestant scholar and critic of Roman Catholicism, put it in his definitive *Religion and the Schools:* "It is quite startling to go back a hundred years or more and see how American judicial opinion ignored religious rights before the United States Supreme Court had adopted modern attitudes." He then summarizes the case of *Permoli* v. *Municipality* (1845), in which the court ruled that the City of New Orleans could constitutionally prevent a Roman Catholic priest from conducting a funeral in any Catholic church in the city, saying, " 'The Constitution makes no provisions for protecting the citizens of the respective states in their religious liberties; this is left to the state constitution and laws' (44 U.S. at 589)." The Supreme Court in the sixties, using the Fourteenth Amendment as a bridge, "takes precisely the opposite view. . . ."[61]

That new view was expressed by Justice Black in the classic and oft-quoted words of the Everson decision (1947): "The 'Establishment of Religion' clause of the First Amendment means at least this: Neither a state nor the Federal Government can set up a church. Neither can pass laws which aid one religion, aid all religions, or prefer one religion over another. . . ."[62]

So there we have two completely antipodal statements by the Supreme Court: in the New Orleans case, the national court is not interested and it's up to the state; in the Everson case—103 years later—the national court is very much interested and no state may

60. Edwin Scott Gaustad, *A Religious History of America* (New York: Harper & Row, 1966), Preface.
61. *Religion and the Schools* (Boston: Beacon Press, 1963), p. 78.
62. Ibid., p. 79.

give preference to one religion over another—not even to Christianity. The court went further in 1961 and guaranteed the right of a man to occupy public office even if he was an atheist (*Torcasso* v. *Watkins,* 367 U.S. at 495). Here Justice Black added a sentence to his Everson statement, asserting that neither a state nor the federal government "can constitutionally pass laws nor impose requirements which aid all religions as against non-believers, and neither can aid those religions based on a belief in the existence of God as against those religions founded on different beliefs." He added in a footnote: "Among religions in this country which do not teach what would generally be considered a belief in the existence of God are Buddhism, Taoism, Ethical Culture, Secular Humanism and others."[63]

Says Blanshard in summary: "It has taken the public a long time to recognize the fact that, in strictly legal terms, the United States is not a Christian country. It is a pluralistic nation guaranteeing all believers and unbelievers equal rights. In the nineteenth century the United States moved from being a Protestant country to being a Protestant and Catholic country; then it moved to the status of being a tri-partite Protestant-Catholic-Jewish country. Finally in the inaugural ceremonies for Presidents Eisenhower and Kennedy, the United States became a quadruplicate religious society, granting ceremonial recognition to Protestant, Catholic, Jewish and Greek Orthodox faiths" (January 1961).[64]

If one says, then, that "America is a Christian nation," one means "exclusively" Christian or at least so predominantly Christian that one could assume his neighbor on the subway to be a Christian. We believe we have shown that attitude to mirror a myth. Yet if one grants that the ideal of men living together in peace is a Christian ideal, then there is this much truth in that myth: that out of the melting pot has come a democratic ideal which gives legal and iron-bound protection to every citizen—to believe or not to believe, and to be held harmless therefor. This in contrast with the terrible and hideous religious wars conducted in other parts of the world in the

63. Ibid., p. 83.
64. Ibid., p. 82.

name of Christ, and the dungeons and torture and slow death inflicted on those who differ. We have our own follies, to be sure; but
that particular insanity we do not have and we are the first nation
to have won to this freedom.

The Gettysburg Address—an Instant Classic?

It seems to be rather widely believed that when Abraham Lincoln
finished his assignment at Gettysburg (19 November 1863), to "formally set apart these grounds to their sacred use by a few appro-
priate remarks,"[65] a solemn and awe-filled hush fell over the vast
assembly on Cemetery Hill (the crowd was variously estimated at
fifteen thousand, thirty thousand, and fifty thousand, according to
Sandburg). The story goes that everybody was struck mute by the
President's eloquence—too stunned to applaud, thus giving Lincoln
the notion that he had been a miserable failure.

The last part is easily documented: Lincoln told Colonel Ward
Hill Lamon, according to the latter's written word, that he re-
gretted not having prepared the speech with more care. He told
him, "Lamon, that speech won't *scour*. It is a flat failure and the
people are disappointed." (In Lincoln farm country, when wet soil
stuck to the mold board of the plow, they said it didn't scour.) Like
every public speaker, Lincoln had a dream of the impact he wanted
his speech to have; but he had been harried mercilessly in the
period preceding it, and never did have an hour to himself to prepare and polish it.

But the first part of the legend is myth. There was no general
or universal acceptance of it as a grand speech. In fact, a good
many people were hardly aware that it had been given. For the
preceding two hours they had listened, with various degrees of interest, to the last of the great orators. ("Webster, Clay, Calhoun
gone, he was the last of the orators. No more great men left to us,
only Everett," said John Russell Young, who covered the event for

---

65. Carl Sandburg, *Abraham Lincoln: The War Years* (New York: Dell Publishing Co., 1960), 2:401. This was the wording of David Wills, acting for the governors
of the states involved in the dedication.

the Philadelphia *Press* and the New York *Herald,* as well as the New York *Tribune.*)[66] Edward Everett's address was already in type, and Lincoln had seen a copy, so he knew just when his turn came. But after Everett finished and he and the audience were regaining their breath, the Baltimore Glee Club sang an ode written especially for the occasion—things were accomplished more leisurely in those days—and after *that* Colonel Lamon stood up and said, simply, "The President of the United States"—not a word more.

The reader will find, if he cares to test the theory, that reading the Gettysburg Address word by word—even *con espressione* and with gestures, which Lincoln did not ("He spoke slowly, with deliberation, reading straight on," Young reports)—it is hard to expand the elapsed time much beyond two minutes and a half. Stretching it to three minutes appears to be exaggeration to the point of artificiality.

"The President of the United States," says Lamon. Flutter of applause. Lincoln speaks in a nervous, high voice for less than three minutes, and sits down—he sits down so quickly that the poor news photographer, who with the help of some members of the audience has managed to set up his tripod and has been trying to focus on the speaker from an angle that will permit the face to be shown attractively (Lincoln keeps holding his notes in front of him), in desperation uncovers the lens and pulls the trigger that sparks his magnesium—to light an empty sky, while the puff of smoke floats off and those around him laugh in commiseration.

Many newspaper accounts indicated applause at various parts of the speech, and some recorded "Long continued applause" at the end; but John Russell Young, who took the whole thing down in shorthand directly from Lincoln's mouth, says he didn't notice any applause. Lincoln had given the Associated Press his speech beforehand, of course, so that Young's papers didn't use the shorthand notes. He believed the applauses were inserted either out of respect for the President or because they would be expected to occur and were therefore inserted.

66. John Russell Young, *Men and Memories: Personal Reminiscences* (New York: F. T. Nealy, 1901), 1: 59 ff.

Anyhow, it was over almost before one could settle oneself to listen; and the audience thereafter began to wander around to see the various battle scenes which had been set up in the fields to dramatize the events of four months before. Young, well-trained as a reporter, leaned over and asked the President if that was all he was going to say. "Yes, for the present," Lincoln answered.

After all, Lincoln had not been asked to give the official address at the dedication. In terms of today's usage, indeed, the manner in which he was invited to attend would be considered downright insulting. He got a printed notice that the exercises would be held and that Edward Everett would be making the address. His notice was not sent to him until 2 November, more than six weeks after Everett had been invited to speak. In fact, asking Lincoln to be present was, according to the Illinois representative of the Board of Commissioners, "an afterthought."[67] But it occurred to somebody that the nation's chief executive ought to say a word on such an occasion, perhaps.

Lincoln agreed to appear, but he had little enthusiasm for it. He had a few things to do in Washington. . . . Meade and Grant were in trouble; the wedding of Kate Chase (daughter of the Secretary of the Treasury) involved top national society and millions in wealth—and there was no escaping it. There were enormous pressures on him. Important men wanted him to proclaim to the nation that the war was not between North and South, but between the people and the aristocrats; some newspapers openly predicted that he would go to Gettysburg merely to strengthen his political fences and take advantage of the helpless dead to play the demagogue. Thaddeus Stevens, the Pennsylvania congressman who wanted to arm the slaves and liquidate the plantation owners, said that Lincoln was a dead card politically, and remarked in anticipation of Gettysburg, "The dead going to eulogize the dead."[68] Besides, his son Tad was sick in bed and the doctors had not been able to diagnose the trouble; the boy's mother was almost hysterical—she

67. Sandburg, *Abraham Lincoln,* p. 401, quoting Clark E. Carr of Galesburg.
68. Ibid., p. 404; Morison, *Oxford History,* pp. 636, 714.

was still in mourning for Willie. No, Lincoln was not *eager* to go to Gettysburg. . . .

Nor was the address universally applauded. "We pass over the silly remarks of the President; for the credit of the nation we are willing that the veil of oblivion shall be dropped over them and that they shall no more be repeated or thought of," said the Harrisburg *Patriot and Union,* with that generous sweetness of spirit which our newspapers reserve especially for those they oppose politically. The *Times* of Chicago went further: "Mr. Lincoln did most foully traduce the motives of the men who were slain at Gettysburg. . . . The cheek of every American must tingle with shame," and so forth. It is incredible. The Providence *Journal* and the Springfield (Mass.) *Republican,* as well as *Harper's Weekly,* thought it was great, however, and so did other people, including Everett himself, who wrote to Lincoln wishing that he had been able to reach the heart of the matter in his two hours as well as Lincoln had in two minutes. Sandburg gives a good summary of the reactions of the press and of leading personalities.

The Gettysburg Address *became* a classic as people read and reread it—there cannot be any debate about that. But as John Russell Young recalled, "I have read many narratives of the scene, of the emotions produced by the President's address, the transcendent awe that fell upon everyone. . . . There was nothing of this, to the writer, at least."[69]

In short, it was better than an instant classic, because it had a quality that caused it to grow upon people as they examined it thoughtfully in the quiet of their libraries, apart from the heady emotions of the occasion. In its symbolism, the myth is true.

America Is a Nation of Readers?

Of the many myths associated with books and literature, one of the most widely believed in this country is that practically everybody reads a good deal. On the subway trains, on the streetcars, on the

69. *Men and Memories,* vol. I, pp. 59–72, and quoted in Bulkley S. Griffin's symposium, *Offbeat History* (Cleveland: World Publishing Co., 1967), p. 25.

buses, in the waiting rooms, and on the jets—everywhere, apparently, except on the tramp steamers—paperbacks are being devoured, newspapers and magazines are open: surely we are a nation of avid readers. Also we talk a lot about what we read. The standard cliché in vaudeville, second only to "Who was that lady I seen you with last night?" used to be "Have you read any good books lately?" True, both remarks were considered inordinately funny and aroused cheerful merriment from audiences to whom the remarks seemed always fresh and new; but the book question, if it satirizes the uneasy situation when two strangers are trying to get a conversation going at a cocktail party, nevertheless illustrates the fact that a discussion of books is a standard opener. News of books is suitable material for headlines, particularly when combined with that favorite American dream of rags to riches—for example, the experience in the early sixties of Harold Robbins, whose flamboyant sex reveries helped sell *The Carpetbaggers* to the movies and won him an advance payment of one million dollars for his next book, whatever it might be—and at the time it was not even a title. Obviously, then, we are readers all, interested in what is being published. We *care*. That is the myth which we are about to dissect.

For the fact is most people *don't* care.

The ones who *do* care appear to care a great deal, some to the point of fanaticism—they hardly dare to enter a bookstore because they know that they will come away penniless. But not most people.

In the census of 1960 there were about 128 million Americans of fourteen years or more. If we add the 17 million children who were ten to fourteen, we have a total of 145 million potential readers (the estimate for 1970 was 183,540,000).[70] A quick calculation in simple arithmetic informs us that if most of the potential readers in the 1960 census had been devotees, as the myth holds, then the market for books, magazines, and newspapers would have to consist of 72,-500,001 persons. The American people spent $3,497,000,000 in 1960 for books, maps, magazines, newspapers, and sheet music.[71] Which

70. *The U.S. Book of Facts, Statistics & Information* (New York: Essandess Special Edition, 1967), p. 8.

71. U.S. Bureau of the Census, *Pocket Data Book*, 1969, p. 212.

means that in 1960 those 72½ million fans of literature spent about
$48.23 each in a whole year. But of course not all the money spent
for books and magazines was handed out by the fanatics, and some
went for sheet music, so perhaps that $48.23 should be cut consider-
ably: how about $35, arbitrarily? In any case, it amounts to less
than a dollar per week per fanatic—which does not mirror a particularly frenetic enthusiasm. A 10-cent newspaper per day, with
forty cents for Sunday—that uses up the dollar.

So it's no wonder that publishers of trade books refuse to endorse
any such figure as 72 million book fans. They estimate usually
something more like 18 million enthusiasts. In a nation of over 200
million! Undoubtedly the truth is, as Omar said, neither here nor
there; but it at least indicates that the number of Americans who
are bookstore customers, members of book clubs, or regular visitors
to the library does not make up a majority of our citizens.

How does such a myth become established? For one thing, it is
a flattering myth. The reading of books is associated with culture
and wisdom, and we like to think of ourselves as a literate nation
rich in culture and wisdom. Also, in our school days, there was a
great emphasis on books, which were our learning tools and which
probably always will be, despite the new projectors and visual aids
and push-button educational techniques of various kinds. Our teachers, who were so influential in forming our opinions, were usually
book enthusiasts. . . . And then we read about runaway best sellers
occasionally—Erskine Caldwell was reported in 1964 to have 43 million of his books in paperback editions;[72] and fairly astronomical
figures were attached to Dr. Spock's famous guidebook and William Hillcourt's *Handbook* for Boy Scouts (both in the neighborhood of 20-odd million copies, according to *Publishers' Weekly,*
17 August 1964). It was no secret that Senator Robert Kennedy's
short (25,000 words) book on the Cuban missile crisis was purchased by the McCall Corporation for an advance of one million
dollars, or that President Johnson had several similar offers for his

72. *New York Times Book Review,* 5 January 1964.

Memoirs.[73] Hence, in terms of our most familiar criterion, money, books have times of being very important and commanding high public interest, opening up many a cocktail conversation and many a lecture at the women's club.

More than that, certain books have admittedly changed the world almost by magic. It doesn't matter whether we have read them or not: their status is secure. Passing by the curious paradox that the most influential book in western civilization is the least understood —the Bible—we cannot help baring our heads at the mention of Nicolaus Copernicus and his *De revolutionibus orbium coelestium* (1543); Andreas Vesalius' *De humani corporis fabrica* (1543); Galileo Galilei's *Dialogo sopra i due massimi sistemi del mondo* (1632); Sir Isaac Newton's *Philosophiae naturalis principia mathematica* (1687)—and so on down to Charles Darwin's *The Origin of Species* (1859) and Albert Einstein's papers on the special theory of relativity in the *Annalen der Physik* (1905), resumed in his book *The Meaning of Relativity* (1922), and even to Ralph Nader's *Unsafe at Any Speed* (Grossman, 1965), which touched off the whole program of recalling defective cars and requiring certain safety standards from manufacturers; or Rachel Carson's *Silent Spring* (Houghton Mifflin, 1962), which first revealed to the masses the dangers of insecticides as agents of bird slaughter. One could spend a rich day listing books which have changed our lives. It is not hard to see why books themselves have retained a position of high status; nor can one deny that at times they have commanded high money values also. (Incidentally, the fourteenth-century classic *Piers Plowman* (c. 1362–98), known to practically nobody but scholars, turned up in manuscript at Sotheby's in London a few years ago and brought the nice round figure of $78,400.)

Books seem mighty important to Washington visitors who want to see the world's largest library—the Congressional Library, covering six acres of land and containing 279 miles of bookshelves for 14 million books and pamphlets.[74] (The famous New York Public

73. *Publishers' Weekly,* 30 September 1968; and *New York Times,* 1 November 1968.

74. *Guinness Book of World Records* (New York: Sterling Publishing Co., 1966), p. 167.

Library at Fifth Avenue and Forty-second Street has something like 4,750,000 books and 80 miles of shelves.)[75] But talk of this nature is not concerned primarily with books and reading, but about books and money, or books and monuments: not about ideas, characters, narrative style, excellence in exposition, language usage, characters, plots, interpretation of life—things which are the true intestines of books, and in which, contrary to the beloved myth, most people are not interested very deeply—at least, not in *reading* about them.

American publishers produce, in the course of a year, something over twenty thousand new "trade" titles, as they are called—meaning books as merchandise, volumes for bookstore customers or book club buyers. This does not include the technical books on law, medicine, and electronics, and various textbooks used in universities and schools. (And this is where the real money is in the book industry, despite the occasional flamboyant runaway best seller.) Of the twenty-odd thousand new trade titles—an average of perhaps 450 books per week—most of them strut and fret their hour upon the stage and then are heard no more, like that poor player, that walking shadow that Macbeth compared human life to. Perhaps thirty titles per week are reviewed here and there, and the rest sell a thousand copies—or perhaps even six thousand—and are then remaindered, for six cents up to possibly sixty cents, to a big wholesaler, who dribbles them out for the Big Sale Value specials in bookstores that feature bargain books, from three for a dollar to half the list price.

We know this sounds terribly sad. It *is* terribly sad. It means that some wonderful manuscripts never get published at all because no commercial publisher is willing to risk the investment—he's afraid that there is not a large enough market to consume, let's say, eight thousand copies (at which point he would have almost certainly recovered his raw cost and overhead, if the book were realistically priced). If we were really a nation of readers, we could have some certainty that almost any *important* book would have a chance: all we have to find, in this hypothetical case, is eight thousand buy-

75. *New York Times,* 27 May 1969.

ers in a population of nearly 200 million readers—which is one out of every twenty-five thousand. Sometimes they're there; but more often, alas, not.

Seen from another angle, the weekly magazine that gives more information about books than any other—so much so that it is considered the bible of the book trade—is *Publishers' Weekly*. *Reader's Digest* sells something like 13 million copies in America. *Publishers' Weekly* has a circulation of about twenty-five thousand. The *Digest* is bought by 520 times as many people.

Here, then, even in the hallowed groves of book publishing, the shadow of the dollar casts its chill. But cheer up: it may not be as bad as it sounds. We are adding new readers every year. And when you see a warning in your favorite paper or magazine that the time is coming when audiovisual aids, teaching machines, and computers of various kinds will shortly be replacing the book as a learning tool, remember the words of Mr. Daniel Melcher, former chairman of the R. R. Bowker Company, and a man who knows as much about book publishing perhaps as anyone in this country. He told the National Association of College Stores convention: "Books have been and books remain the number one mainstay of the learning process. Education without machines and teachers is possible, but education without books is unthinkable. . . . There is mounting evidence that the innate adaptability of the book to the reader's needs, in terms of letting him start anywhere, race ahead, refer back, skip, etc., is definitely more in tune with the way the brain actually works than any externally programmed learning or lecturing. It is beginning to appear that all of us know more about how to instruct ourselves than about how to instruct others."[76]

As book lovers, we hope Mr. Melcher is right; but as students of human nature, we are sharply aware that people believe what they *want* to believe; and as observers of science, we realize that it is only under circumstances of total control that one can read the future—and these restrictions apply equally to Mr. Melcher. Publishing, especially the fiscal aspects of the work, is in his blood and was equally in the veins of his revered father. Of course he wants

76. *Publishers' Weekly*, 19 May 1969, p. 34.

to see the book triumphant. But he cannot arrest the progress of
technology at, say, M.I.T., where they are already producing robots
more "intelligent than any single man could ever be," to quote
a recent letter from the banks of the Charles. And Mr. Melcher's
view of the future is contradicted by that of an intelligent and experienced college bookstore manager. Ray W. Vanderhoef, of the
Iowa Book and Supply Company, states:

I believe that in the not too distant future [the textbook will decline as
a teaching tool]. This will be a rapidly accelerating trend in all major
four-year colleges and universities. The only possible area where the
textbook may hold its former position is in the junior, two-year college
and the vocational-technical schools, provided publishers are willing to
meet their requirements. . . . The textbook is not necessarily a dying
product, but only if publishers are willing to become truly selective [pro-
ducing material specifically useful to the student and not to build academic reputations].

Today's student is no longer a passive individual. It used to be that
the student accepted the system as it was. . . .[77]

77. "This Textbook Thing," Publishers' Weekly, 5 January 1970, pp. 47–48.

VI

CHAPTER

Myths from the Cliché, the Ipse Dixit, the Proverb

The Rock-steady Permanence of the Law

In our whirligig world where new knowledge is developing so fast that we seem to wake up every morning in a strange country, it is comforting to have the assurance that at least there is one arena of human endeavor which is permanent, solid, dependable, firm, and steady: the Law. We see the great courthouses sitting in our city squares in granite or marble, unfaltering and indomitable. We know that they shelter the great twenty-pound volumes full of discussion of precedents, torts, libels, contracts, felonies, misdemeanors, misprisions, and remises. Perhaps we visit a courtroom in session and see some great black-robed figure presiding over the ants below, and we are filled with abiding awe as this judge listens, sifting the true from the false and directing and ordering the lives of men as if he were Odin the all-wise. What a relief!

We hate to spoil the reader's day, but the unchanging, rockbound law is a myth. This was proverbial knowledge to Aeschylus 2,500 years ago; he wrote in *Seven Against Thebes:* "The laws of a state change with the changing times." Sydney Smith was sharper. "Whenever I hear any man talk of an unalterable law," he wrote in the *Plymley Letters* (1807), "the only effect it produces upon me is to convince me that he is an unalterable fool."

It is not hard to understand that a law which seems ridiculous to many people and which runs counter to public opinion will not be respected or enforced except by a dictator or a police state; and for that reason, Aeschylus was right. Our own Great Experiment with the Eighteenth Amendment in this country is the all-time exemplar. But we can at least say that the law does not change whimsically, overnight, irresponsibly. When Solon was compiling his Laws (about 600 B.C.), Anacharsis gave him a certain amount of good-natured kidding, asking him if he really thought that greed, injustice, theft, and so forth could be removed from human affairs by writing laws against them. No, Solon said. He didn't think it would work just that way. "Men keep their agreements," he said, "when it is to the profit of both parties to do so, and they will observe the law when they realize that the practice of justice is advantageous to them." Which is earthy realism of the same kind employed by Cicero when he said that we are servants of the law "to the end that it may be possible for us to be free."

But since the law must attempt to cover every type of activity and speak in terms which allow the fewest loopholes or exceptions, it is obviously never going to be a perfect instrument, being man-made. For example, Justice Thurgood Marshall, speaking for the majority in a Supreme Court decision in an obscenity opinion (*Stanley* v. *Georgia,* 7 April 1969), reversed the Georgia statute which made mere possession of obscene materials a crime. "Fundamental is the right," he said, "to be free from unwanted governmental intrusions into one's privacy." But that decision immediately brought up the dilemma whether it is really possible to protect the right to possess obscene materials if it is still unlawful to sell or distribute them. That question will have to be handled sometime. . . .

This subject of the evolution and growth of the law to the point where one can demonstrate that a contemporary decision of the United States Supreme Court completely reverses an earlier decision of the United States Supreme Court (composed of different men, of course, and living in different times) was brought up lately by two news reports dealing with blasphemy charges. We had somehow not heard much about heretics and blasphemers in recent years—except for the abortive attempts to try Bishop Pike for heresy in 1966–67—and now all of a sudden we find two blasphemy trials making news: one in Maryland and one in Delaware. In Delaware, William F. Bertolette had been arrested along with Matthew Allen Bennett—both young men were seventeen—on the charge that in an underground newspaper which they published an article referred to Jesus as a bastard. This violated Delaware's 143-year-old statute, still on the books. A judge of the court of common pleas had retired the charge, but the state Department of Justice pursued it and a grand jury indicted young Bertolette. Now the state superior court must decide whether the old statute is constitutional.[1] We should point out that the young man must be convicted of a *civil* crime: he cannot be judged on the basis of having committed an ecclesiastical or religious evil; our courts today cannot handle that class of trial, since we have no established church as part of our government—in which we differ from Britain. It was otherwise before the Constitution. "The Massachusetts Bay Colony," for example, "in its Body of Liberties of 1641, made blaspheming of 'god, the father, Sonne or Holie Ghost, with direct expresse, presumptuous or high-handed blasphemie' or the cursing of God 'in like manner' a crime punishable by death."[2] So did the Act of Toleration of Maryland in 1649. The only "tolerant" part of this famous document (often called "the first decree granting complete religious liberty to emanate from an assembly") is in the fourth of its four sections, where it is made law that "no person or persons within this province . . . professing to believe in Jesus Christ, shall henceforth be in any ways troubled . . . in respect of his or her religion. . . ."[3]

Pfeffer adds: "The courts that have sustained blasphemy statutes have done so on the ground that blasphemy was a civil offense at English common law, and therefore could properly be made a civil offense under American state statutes. But, like Sunday laws . . . blasphemy laws were religious and ecclesiastical in origin; and the sole reason for intervention by the English secular courts was the

---

1. *New York Times*, 13 July 1969.
2. Edwin Powers, *Crime and Punishment in Early Massachusetts, 1620–1692* (Boston: Beacon Press, 1966), pp. 158–59.
3. Leo Pfeffer, *Church, State and Freedom*, rev. ed. (Boston: Beacon Press, 1967), p. 83.

desire to protect and sustain an established church as a part of the apparatus of government."[4]

Even after the adoption of the American Constitution there were instances in which our courts maintained that blasphemy is a civil crime—but for another reason. This fact was dug out by Carroll County Circuit Judge Edward O. Weant, Jr., who judged the 246-year-old Maryland blasphemy law to be unconstitutional, in the other trial referred to above. Judge Weant's ruling in this case overturned the conviction of Irving K. West by trial magistrate Charles J. Simpson of Westminster, who found West guilty and sentenced him to pay twenty-five dollars and serve thirty days. "Judge Weant's 16-page opinion traced the history of the blasphemy laws back to 1656 in England when the penalty for a first offense was that 'a hole be bored in the tongue.' "[5] Judge Weant discovered in the case of *The People* v. *Ruggles* (8 Johns. Rep. 290) that the high court of New York State found blasphemy more dangerous as a disturber of the peace than as a danger to Christianity. Said the court: "The consequences may be less extensively pernicious in the one case than in the other, but in both instances a reviling is still an offense, because it tends to corrupt the morals of the people, and to destroy good order." The people of New York State, it said, are Christians; and any mockery of that faith "is a gross violation of decency and good order" and must be considered unlawful in civil law.[6] This was in 1811. What Ruggles had, in fact, said was that "Jesus Christ was a bastard and his mother was a whore." Chancellor Kent held, then, that Christianity being "the religion professed by almost the whole community," this blasphemy must be punished as a civil crime.

That ruling was overturned in 1895 when Judge Parker overruled the grand jury of Lexington, Kentucky, in a similar decision. He said, "In the code of laws of a country enjoying absolute religious

4. Ibid., pp. 663–64.
5. *New York Times,* 17 June 1969.
6. Edward O. Weant, Jr., Memorandum Order filed 1 May 1969 (No. 2814 Criminals in the Circuit Court of Carroll County), p. 10, and citing Joel Prentiss Bishop, *New Commentaries on the Criminal Law,* vol. 1 (Chicago: T. H. Flood & Co., 1892), p. 303.

freedom, there is no place for the common law crime of blasphemy."[7] Actually, "the last recorded criminal trial where a conviction of blasphemy was appealed to the Supreme Judicial Court of the Commonwealth (Massachusetts) and upheld . . . was the famous case of Abner Kneeland in 1838 that stirred the city of Boston and brought many liberals to his defense." Kneeland had been a Universalist minister; but later he became editor of the Boston *Investigator,* in which he published an article that caused his prosecution; he held that the Universalists' God was "a mere chimera of their imagination" and that their story of Christ was as much fable as the Prometheus legend.[8]

Although we seldom hear of a blasphemy trial any more, Judge Weant says that "approximately half of the states of the Union have blasphemy statutes while the balance have recourse in the common law," to this day.[9] One might be surprised to learn what large numbers of our citizens are profoundly in favor of punishing blasphemy. We see so much "free" expression in even such formerly conventionally good gray magazines as the *Atlantic Monthly* and *Harper's*—even to the use in our day of that classic of four-letter words of which all three editions of Webster have denied the existence—and we hear such unbuckled speech on stage and screen, that it is easy to get the impression that conventions of speech have passed all considerations of propriety in our society as a whole. A case could be made to the contrary. For example, *The Interpreter's Bible,* an enormous work in twelve volumes published by the official Methodist publishing house, in the volume covering Leviticus (where death by stoning, in which "all the congregation" must participate, is the required penalty for blasphemy), carries this editorial comment:

"Generally the state is not expected to tolerate the expression of seditious opinions; yet revolution does not necessarily spell disaster for a people, whereas a loss of reverence for the name of God can only lead to the dissolution of society and in the end to death."[10]

7. Pfeffer, *Church, State and Freedom,* p. 666.
8. Powers, *Crime and Punishment,* p. 159.
9. Memorandum order, p. 9.
10. *The Interpreter's Bible* (Nashville, Tenn.: Abingdon-Cokesbury, 1951), 2: 119.

This point of view is found among strongly orthodox Christians everywhere, particularly the fundamentalist, Bible-belt millions and earnest followers of Billy Graham's type of evangelism in all corners. The fact that "the law against blasphemy has practically ceased to be put into active operation," as the *Britannica* points out (11th ed., 1910), does not mean that blasphemy is not regarded in hundreds of thousands of households as a very black religious crime. Perhaps not all of the more than ten million Methodists in America would agree with the opinion about the loss of reverence for the name of God, but even so, people who have been closely associated with the story of Jesus and whose emotions are stirred by the drama surrounding him are not likely to forget that it was blasphemy for which Caiaphas the High Priest condemned Jesus in Marks' account. "Art thou the Christ?" "I am." And then Caiaphas, as a man must who has heard blasphemy, ripped his robe across the breast— not as a mere histrionic gesture, according to Craveri, but as part of a strict ritual "prescribed for anyone who heard a blasphemy uttered. The garment must be torn not along the seam, but in the middle of the fabric so that the damage was irreparable."[11]

There appear to be various definitions of blasphemy; but at bottom it means "evil-speaking" (Gr. *blas,* "evil" or "profane," *phemos,* "speaking") and sends off a branch which gives us the English "blame."[12] In the Old Testament, the word is "almost universally confined to language or deeds derogating from the honor of God and his claims to overlordship of men." In the New Testament it is more commonly "railing or slanderous talk"; but in either case, the punishment is death.[13]

The roots are deep, and it is no wonder that the blood chills a little, even in a relatively sophisticated culture, at the word "blasphemy." For the day was when a word was more than a symbol; it was a thing in its own right; it was magic. How widespread this

11. Marcello Craveri, *The Life of Jesus,* trans. from the Italian by Charles Lam Markmann (New York: Grove Press, 1967), p. 397.

12. *The Oxford English Dictionary;* supported by Eric Partridge, *Origins* (London: Routledge & Kegan Paul, 1959).

13. James Hastings, *A Dictionary of the Bible,* 1-vol. ed. (New York: Charles Scribner's Sons, 1921), p. 101.

"word equals thing" syndrome is, as the decade of the 1970s gets under way, might well make a book-length study. In the age of exploration and colonization it was certainly basic. "The King's lawyers who wrote these commissions [for such navigators as Ponce de Leon] believed that naming was part of holding empire, that no one could well lay claim to a nameless city, and that a province without a name was hardly a province at all."[14]

But deeper than that is the personal magic. "The person who knows the name of a god can invoke and obtain help from him by calling upon him by his name. . . . The knowledge of the names of demons constituted the chief power of the magicians of olden times."[15] Even in some American Indian tribes, a person had a public name and a secret, private name. Pocahontas, for example, had the secret name of Matokes; and the name taboo—the prohibition against saying the name out loud—is well documented in Indian legends. Uttering the name aloud commands the presence of fiend, devil, or god in many cultures. Thus the Jews, anxious to hide the name of Jehovah from the pagans, "pronounced the Name only once a year. This was by the High Priest in the Temple on Yom Kippur . . . and then in an indistinct manner while invoking the blessing (Numbers: vi: 24-26) during the chant of the priests, so that the people listening could not hear it."[16] This taboo became so strong that the ancient Jews avoided even the suggestion of writing the Most Holy Name "when some other word is intended. The Jews have a special way of writing the number fifteen. It would naturally be *Yod-He* (ten and five); but *Yod-He* spells *Yah,* a short form of the Ineffable Name. So for fifteen the Jews write, in Hebrew, *Teth-Wau* (nine and six).[17] The enunciation of YHVH, *Yod-He-Vav-He,* the tetragrammaton, is simply not worth the risk.

This basic fear of control through the name is, of course, the basis for such stories as the tale of Rumpelstiltskin and others like it—

14. George R. Stewart, *Names on the Land* (New York: Random House, 1945), p. 12.

15. Elsdon C. Smith, *The Story of Our Names* (New York: Harper & Brothers, 1950), p. 187.

16. Ibid., p. 169.

17. Ibid.

and the myth bites deep. We can never forget it. We speak of identity, of alienation, and of blasphemy, and we try to smile—but our *name* is the way to reach us, and this we all know, and this we fear. . . .

The Average Man and the Man in the Street

With the advent of the contraceptive pill and various other convenient and inexpensive—and surprisingly reliable—methods of preventing conception, one of the chief fears blocking premarital sexual intercourse was removed. Thereafter, as various surveys indicated, there was a significant statistical change upward in the number of college women who admitted to having engaged in intercourse before marriage. The figures for men, while slightly increased, were not so dramatic.[18] Thus our society is unquestionably faced with the fact of a new morality totally at variance, for example, with the Victorian. To some observers, the new situation is more honest, healthier, and less destructive of personality. Many conservatives, however, are outraged. Hence there is a debate. How does "the country" feel about it? What says the "Man in the Street"? What does the "average citizen" think?

To get answers to such questions, several television programs are accustomed to sending out a team with microphones and mobile equipment, and obtaining statements of opinion from people who *are* in the street. If they could include all the civilian resident population of voting age (that is, 118,465,000 in 1968),[19] then they would be in a position to give some average figures that would be a fairly accurate reflection of the true situation. However, interviewing close to 120 million people is out of the question. Even if each interview were to be restricted to two minutes, it would require 4 million hours to record just the time spent in talking to that number of people; that is, 500,000 eight-hour working days, or 1,370 years. By

---

18. "Sex in Academe," by the Editors of *Playboy,* September 1969, p. 193, is a typical study. Five colleges are surveyed in depth (San Francisco State, Brown/Pembroke, Bryn Mawr, University of Illinois, and University of Alabama) and there is a chart covering attitudes and usages at twenty-five American colleges and universities.

19. *Statistical Abstract of the United States,* 1969, p. 369.

the time the answers were available, they would be so profoundly out of date that nobody would be interested: it would be as if we finally had the results of a survey undertaken in the year 600 A.D.

But of course opinion polls are not taken in that manner. The poll queries a cross section of the real population—a selection which is so truly representative that the answers from a few hundred will be indicative of the whole population—and with computers at work, the whole thing can be projected very rapidly, as those who saw the predictions of the results of the last presidential election will remember.

Even so, it is rather widely believed that the "average man" is nonexistent: a myth. "There is no such creature as the average man," a recent study asserts with finality. "The phrase is meaningless. It is as empty as 'the typical American.' It is a lazy man's cliché by which the speaker makes a weak attempt—not a thoughtful attempt, but a feeble one—to refer to a basic type that does not in fact exist."[20]

If we say, "The average literate reader," do we mean someone very like the speaker, only not quite as intelligent? "The average businessman is a crook." Does this mean that we think most manufacturers, buyers, and sellers are thieves, or do we mean to give the uncomplicated ancient warning *caveat emptor,* "let the buyer use caution"? It is most important that we avoid easy generalizations in the attempt to cite some opinion and give it the force of a mathematical certainty. Let's say your car is all paid for. Yet it could be maintained that you owe about $168 on it. That is because so many automobiles in America are not all paid for: in fact, the unpaid part amounts to nearly $34 billion, according to the Federal Reserve Board; and "divided equally among the population, this represents about $168 owed by every man, woman, and child."[21] This supports the view that the average citizen is a mythological character: and nobody is going to collect that $168 from us who have a paid-in-full receipt.

20. Ashley Montagu and Edward Darling, *The Prevalence of Nonsense* (New York: Harper & Row, 1967), p. xi.
21. *Christian Science Monitor,* 7 November 1968.

But we are a nation of statistic lovers. Statistics give one the feeling of being authoritatively informed on one's subject. Those in the computer field warn us, however, that if we feed "garbage" into the computer, we cannot avoid obtaining the same sort of material in output, although it may have a very serious aspect as the machine feeds it back to us. For example, there was the famous survey that solemnly reported that at Johns Hopkins $33\frac{1}{3}$ percent of all the coeds had married faculty men. It was absolutely true: at the time of the survey, the university had precisely three women students, one of whom had married a professor.[22] The same technique is used, of course, by advertising agencies in order to be able to state, with documented certainty, that eight out of ten doctors find Woodman's Pine Dust the best coagulant obtainable: the agency spends time and money assembling panel after panel until the desired result has been obtained; and then it can be quoted. The "average reader," seeing the statement in print, tends to believe it. Only there *is* no average reader.

The attempt to find a median, an average, a typical person or figure in order to make the statistics more real, can lead to some delightful considerations, however, such as the statistical assertion that the driver who has the best chance of escaping accidents is a seventy-five-year-old woman riding a motorcycle at fifty-one miles per hour on a Thursday between two and three in the morning. Or Irving Chernev's calculation that "if everyone in the world were to spend every waking hour playing chess, at the unlikely rate of a game a minute, it would take 217 billion years to use all the possible variations on the first ten moves of Black and White."[23] We simply won't be here to see it done.

Darrell Huff showed us long ago that one can say that the average income of families in a certain suburban neighborhood is $15,000 per year, when one is trying to persuade a buyer that it's a nice neighborhood; or one can say the average income is $3,500—and both would be right, because the first is an arithmetic average: add them up and divide by the number of participants; and the second is a

22. *Time*, 8 September 1967.
23. *New York Times Book Review*, 7 September 1969.

median: half the families have more than $3,500 and half have less. Or one could say the average is $5,000 annual salary if the neighborhood has more families earning that figure than there are earning any other figure—and here $5,000 is called the modal income. Huff's conclusion is that when one is dealing with data having to do with many human characteristics, such as "average height of the male," you get a normal bell-shaped curve and the mean, the medium, the mode are all at about the same point—the average. But not when you deal with *incomes,* which range from very high to very low, as in a large city where salaries may range from $50,000 to below $10,000—with 95 percent of the incomes under $10,000.[24] (In passing, we should remember that Huff was writing in 1953–54, when a salary of $15,000 was high and $3,500 enough so that one could buy one's own home. The figures sound a little fantastic in our own time. Between 1953 and 1968, private nonfarm industry increased salaries from $3.50 per employee man-hour with a purchasing power of $3.10 to a figure of $7.30 per employee man-hour with a purchasing power of $2.90. In the sixties alone, "average weekly earnings" for the nation jumped from $89.72 in 1960 to $122.51 in 1968.)[25]

It seems to be the case that whether the idea of "average" is realistic or not, we do keep turning to it as a tool for thought. Sometimes it is misleading, but often it is very useful. One must remember that "average," like most English words, has more meanings than one black-and-white denotation; it is more like a halftone or a coarse-screen etching that shades off here and again there into related but not identical configurations and connotations. The Arabic *'awar* meant "fault," and eventually we have the French *avarie,* meaning damage to goods from being shipped—damage at sea— and the equitable sharing of such loss among the partners concerned (the basic idea behind insurance); and thus we slip easily into the notion of a relative proportion, the arithmetic mean, and a representative type.

24. Darrell Huff, *How to Lie with Statistics* (New York: W. W. Norton, 1954), pp. 28–29.
25. *Statistical Abstract of the United States,* 1969, pp. 228, 229.

To the student of anatomy, the average is a reality: most human bodies are like the descriptions in the anatomy texts. There will be some variations, but the medical student following the manual of dissection and Gray's immortal *Anatomy* will discover that the cadaver under his scalpel is *almost* precisely as described—so substantially the same that for all practical purposes the description of the average is correct and stands for the reality on the table.

The word "average" is perfectly valid in comparing the typical Englishman with the typical American, for instance. They do differ —in general, in speech, in dress—and yet some Americans are very like some Englishmen, and the word must not be used to indicate total behavior. It is in the latter usage that the myth is true: the average man is nonexistent. But the average height of the Hottentots can be determined.

It's a Free Country: You Can Say What You Like

"This is a free country, and I'll say what I please!" So do the truculently naïve expose their slavery to a widely held myth. It is true that we have heard in thousands of classrooms and repeated to each other in scores of bars that freedom of speech is guaranteed to Americans in the most basic law of the land, the Constitution. But what the First Amendment says is that "Congress shall make no law . . . abridging the freedom of speech, or of the press." That, of course, means also that the individual states are likewise forbidden to make laws of that kind. But to equate that basic law with the statement that an American is free to say what he wants to say, wherever he wants to say it, and whenever the mood strikes him, is, as we have said, naïve.

"The most stringent protection of free speech would not protect a man in falsely shouting fire in a theater and causing a panic," said Mr. Justice Oliver Wendell Holmes. "It does not even protect a man from an injunction against uttering words that may have all the effect of force."[26] He then shows how freedom of speech is a relative freedom: "The question in every case is whether the

26. Opinion in *Schwenck* v. *U.S.*, 249 *U.S.* 47 (1918).

words used are used in such circumstances and are of such a nature as to create a clear and present danger that they will bring about the substantive evils that Congress has a right to prevent. It is a question of proximity and degree."[27]

Two extraordinary cases were reported as the 1960s came to a close, both dramatically illustrating the idiocy of taking freedom of speech as an absolute. In the first story, two business executives were returning to Boston from a three-day convention and display of new products in Chicago. Something was wrong at O'Hare Airport that day, and the call for passengers was delayed almost two hours—which time our two conventioners devoted to consuming martinis. They constructed an atmosphere of such hilarious bonhomie at their table that other waiting travelers were attracted and joined the little group, so that by the time the Boston plane was called there were ten people gathered around the two Bostonians; one forgot his hat and another his briefcase as they all hurried out to the plane, laughing and jesting merrily. No one was actually stoned, of course. But none was in great pain, either. The last to enter the plane was one of the men from Boston. Adopting an extremely sober face, he whispered to a stewardess that the other Bostonian, the one with the pink shirt, was carrying a bomb in his attaché case. She seemed to understand, and everyone was duly seated. Then came one of those periods when nobody did anything. Just sat. No explanations of any kind. No motors warming up. No air blowing through the vents. Nobody serving comforting libations. The laughter died down and gave way to grumbles.

After about twenty minutes, the stewardess who had been told about the bomb returned with several policemen. They went to the Bostonian with the pink shirt and demanded to see inside his attaché case. He made things worse by falling into a fierce rage; but in the end he handed the case over. Inside, among some shirts and socks and papers, was a shaving bomb. The Bostonian instantly proved this to everyone's satisfaction. The law then turned to the informer Bostonian. He must return to the main building with the police, while the much-delayed flight took off. Nothing is

27. Ibid.

harder to take than a great practical joke that miscarries. Suddenly the whole thing was no fun. But he could see that argument, bribery, tantrums, demands to see his lawyer—nothing would change the fact that he must leave the plane with the police now.

He explained that it was all a joke. They'd had a drink, waiting two hours for the plane. He had told the stewardess there was a bomb in his friend's bag. There was: it contained shaving foam. His friend would be embarrassed, but everybody would end up laughing. What's the harm in that? Isn't this a free country?

Yes, it's a free country. But a bomb threat in a crowded airliner is no joke, and according to U.S. Code, Title 18, Section 35 (as amended 7 July 1965 by Public Laws 89-64, 79 Stat. 210), "Whoever . . . conveys . . . false information . . . concerning an attempt . . . to do any act which would be a crime prohibited by this chapter . . . shall be fined not more than $5,000, or imprisoned not more than five years, or both. . . ."

The story is a true one, but the names must be withheld. In the second story, the names were widely published. Tilford E. Dudley, director of national affairs for the United Church of Christ, an able and law-trained executive of sixty-two, had been seated on American Airlines flight 511 from Boston to Washington on Thursday, 3 July 1969. The Church had just finished a convention in Boston. A stewardess paused beside his seat and asked the routine question about his destination. Dudley, who admitted that he likes to tease pretty girls, replied, "How long does it take to Cuba?" The stewardess, Miss Janice Nika, 21, testified later that she said, "Please be quiet; don't say any more!" But he said he had been wondering about this with some of his friends. She said, "Please shut up! Don't say any more!" She left him laughing and went to the cockpit to tell Captain Eisemann about Dudley; and Eisemann instructed the tower that he was returning to the loading area with a passenger who was talking about making Havana.[28]

In any event, Dudley was handcuffed, taken to a police station,

28. Boston *Globe,* 10 July 1969; Boston *Herald,* 5 July 1969; *Time,* 18 July 1969. (*Time* magazine reminded its readers that "a number of people have been escorted off airplanes in recent months for asking similar questions—Marlon Brando, for one.")

and booked for disturbing the peace. For a descendant of the founder of Cambridge and a Harvard Law School graduate—to say nothing of his position in the contemporary church—this was something less than a joke by this time. All the more so when District Court Judge Guy J. Rizzoto, in East Boston District Court, fined him two hundred dollars, which he said would be instantly appealed. Judge Rizzoto, brushing off the testimony of eleven witnesses who said no one had been disturbed on the plane by Dudley's talk, used Mr. Justice Holmes's famous theater example to emphasize his decision.

Freedom of speech, of course, remains. One may jest with comely lasses—within reasonable limits—to one's heart's content; but where the public safety can be involved, and especially where the public is profoundly aware of bombs and hijackings that were *not* in jest, the tradition of verbal freedom may run through pretty narrow channels. One would suppose that the judicious would be aware of this; but we ourselves are a living testimony to the further truth that no master of the jocose can win them all.

Mad as a "What"?

Seeking colorful rhetorical expression of madness at its apogee, many authors have found reasonable satisfaction in simple similes: "mad as a buck," "as a hatter," "as a March hare," "as a weaver." Dryden perhaps carried the idea a little further:

> Free from all meaning, whether good or bad,
> And in one word, heroically mad.
> —*Absalom*

Polonius thought he could do better, one recalls, but found himself on very thin ice, wishing he'd stayed on the dock. "For, to define true madness/ What is't but to be nothing else but mad?"

In the meaning of "mentally disordered," "mad" is thought to derive in oblique ways from the Latin *mutare,* "to change," which finds its way into Gothic as *maidjan,* "to change or corrupt"; and into Anglo-Saxon as *gemaedd,* "foolish." Thus a mind which is

erratic, illogical, totally inconsistent—in a word, moonstruck, lunatic, and disassembled—is mad. It was Thackeray who wrote "mad
as a hatter" (*Pendennis,* Chapter 10). That does not necessarily
mean that Thackeray *invented* the phrase—it was a folk saying long
before. In fact, when John Tenniel adopted Lewis Carroll's suggestion that the Hatter (Chapter VII, *Alice in Wonderland,* "A Mad
Tea Party") should be a caricature of a chap named Theophilus
Carter, a furniture dealer near Oxford, the artist was quite aware
of the fact that Carter was known in the neighborhood as the Mad
Hatter because he always wore a top hat and had crazy ideas. Good
casting at Paramount in 1933 had Edward Everett Horton as the
Hatter and Charles Ruggles as the March Hare, incidentally; and
Norbert Wiener, in *Ex-Prodigy,* gave his opinion that Bertrand Rus-
sell looks almost exactly like the Tenniel drawing.[29]

In short, "mad hatter" or "mad as a hatter" has long been accepted in the vernacular. But until the latter part of the nineteenth
century, no one had any scientific reason for it—merely the observed
phenomenon that there appeared to be an occupational hazard
which afflicted some professional hatters with mental looseness.

However, the popular belief can be once again justified: Dr. Alice
Hamilton, the first woman to teach at the Harvard Medical School,
"was one of the first doctors to investigate occupational diseases,
discovering, for example, that 'mad hatters' were poisoned into that
condition by the mercury they inhaled while working."[30]

The fact is that mercury poisoning is one of the oldest occupational diseases known to man. Both mercury and its many com-
pounds are sources of poisoning and can cause gastrointestinal
inflammation, urinary disorders, ulceration of the skin, neuromuscu-
lar lesions—and mental deterioration. In the art of felting—which is
said to be older than that of weaving—furs are treated with a solution of nitrate of mercury. This is called "carroting" or "secretage,"
and vastly improves the felting properties of the furs.[31]

29. Norbert Wiener, *Ex-Prodigy: My Childhood and Youth* (New York: Simon &
Schuster, 1953), pp. 194–95.
30. Deane Lord, "The Arthur and Elizabeth Schlesinger Library on the History of
Women in America," *Harvard Today,* Autumn 1968, p. 19.
31. *Encyclopaedia Britannica,* 11th ed.

Hence workers in hat factories using felt were subjected to the risks of mercury poisoning and sometimes the toxins affected the brain. So there was some reason to characterize hatters as mad— even heroically mad.

The Comics Have No Cultural Influence?

Most thoughtful people would agree, perhaps, that the comics, the funny papers, are for children and do not have any significant cultural influence one way or the other. We catch old Dad reading *Terry* when he doesn't think anybody is watching him, possibly; and he may grin sheepishly when we accuse him of reading escape literature. But he is just a boy caught in the apple tree. He is not *affected* by the funnies, and neither are the children. Right? It's hardly worth a serious question.

At this point we advise the passengers in the open compartments to hold onto their hats, because measured by audience response the comics are more influential than Longfellow, Emerson, Thoreau, and Walt Whitman put together. And one could add Whittier, Emily Dickinson, Edna St. Vincent Millay, and William Carlos Williams. In fact, a case could be made for the proposition that the comics get more response from the public to which they address themselves than all the authors writing in this country since George Washington fought it out with the icecakes on the Delaware.

"A single strip, such as *Blondie* which appears in some 1,200 papers throughout the world, may be read seventeen billion times in a single year," according to one eminent authority, who notes in another place that this strip attracts 600 to 700 million readers a week.[32] Longfellow had a best seller in 1839 (*Hyperion*); William Cullen Bryant's anthology *Library of Poetry and Song* rated very high in 1871; Mark Twain's *Connecticut Yankee* was at or near the top in 1889; Edna Ferber was a best seller in 1924 with *So Big* and again in 1930 with *Cimarron*—but these books merely reached their

32. David Manning White and Robert H. Abel, *The Funnies, An American Idiom* (Glencoe, Ill., The Free Press, 1963), pp. viii and 3.

thousands of admirers, and practically the only public response was buying (or borrowing) the book or perhaps seeing the movie.[33] Even taking into account some of the seemingly astronomical figures that have come in with new printing processes, new paperback markets, and fabulous new distribution systems, book sales of *any* title or *any* author appear unable to compete with the extraordinary popular acceptance which has been accorded to the cartoonists of comic strips. In a way, the comparison is not fair: it takes only a moment daily to keep abreast of Orphan Annie—if one is inclined to do that—but reading a book calls for considerably more investment in time. Besides, there's a compulsion to read *some* sort of newspaper, and the comics are right in there, handy to the news— except for the dignified *New York Times,* which even *Time* magazine credits with being "the world's greatest newspaper" and to which it assigns a circulation of one million daily.[34]

We were speaking of reader response, however—not just the gigantic audience. What we had in mind was action on the part of the readers: as when Al Capp offered a prize for the "most gruesome" face for Lena the Hyena and received one million answers. And when Dagwood and Blondie were debating what to call their second child, they got more than 400,000 letters from readers offering to solve the problem for them.[35]

Readers project a strange identity with some of the comic characters—to the point where they cannot permit disaster to overtake the cartoon personality. Our own favorite here is the experience of cartoonist Raeburn Van Buren, creator of *Abbie and Slats.* When a beloved character in the strip died, there were so many letters of protest that the artist had to write an open letter promising to restore the character to life and urging readers to try to forget the whole sorry episode.

Some readers will remember that Skeezix was in the service in the war against Japan. One of the know-it-all columnists happened

33. Frank Luther Mott, *Golden Multitudes: The Story of Best Sellers in the United States* (New York: Macmillan Co., 1947), pp. 318–19.
34. *Time,* 4 July 1969, in a review of *The Kingdom and the Power,* by Gay Talese.
35. White and Abel, *The Funnies,* p. 6.

to reveal in his syndicated space that the cartoonist, King, planned to have Skeezix wounded by a Jap bullet in the future. This evoked a response so violent that the newspapers had to take serious space in the news columns to reassure people that Skeezix would be safe: the Pittsburgh *Post-Gazette* did this in a page-one headlined announcement. When Milton Caniff permitted the death of Raven Sherman, he got 1,400 letters of sympathy and a host of angry objections to the murderous deed.[36] Actual gifts as well as thousands of congratulations came in when Chester Gould recorded the marriage of B. O. Plenty and Gravel Gertie.

The huge audience and the incredible response this readership is known to give spell out an influence which many commercial interests would like to engage, and more than one advertiser has attempted to create his own comic strip for sales purposes; but there is no confusing the impostor with the genuine prince, and the public has not been confused. However, governments were very happy to have the cartoonists helping out with the problem of public morale during World War II: the British Ministry of Information kept Ham Fisher apprised of General Montgomery's progress at Tunisia so that the *Joe Palooka* strip could be planned in consonance with current maneuvers; and FDR paid Fisher a personal compliment for helping to make the draft acceptable to the public.

In order to command their enormous readership, the comics stay close to the basic beliefs of their readers and show the prevailing taste and customs of their times. Thus they reflect the culture and indeed reinforce it. To do this, they change as the customs change. Mutt began as a hustler and sportsman, but now is a suburban husband facing all the customary frustrations and harassments.

Originally the comics were used merely to gain circulation. In the 1890s the feud between Pulitzer and Hearst gave them their serious start; and their entry into the mass market came with syndication by Moses Koenigsberg in 1913. They have developed from unenlightened crudeness in both drawing and script to the realism of Caniff and the gentle satire of *Pogo*—not *always* so gentle; Walt

36. Ibid., pp. 6–7.

Kelly pulled no punches in his caricaturing of Senator Joe McCarthy—and the sophistication of Charles M. Schulz's *Peanuts*. Along the way the comics have created folk heroes and supported such institutions as the family; provided soap opera (*Prince Valiant, Mary Worth*); and offered social criticism (*Li'l Abner*). It's a far cry from Richard Outcault's *The Yellow Kid* (1895) and the first complete section of color comics—which appeared in the New York *Journal* the next year (including *The Katzenjammer Kids, Happy Hooligan,* and *Alphonse and Gaston*)—to Charlie Brown; from the convention that each separate strip should develop a single wisecrack or contretemps or pratfall with no continuity between today's event and the following strip, up to the skilled draftsmanship and the continued story, the use of material from current history and medicine and psychiatry along with the rising status of women (Maggie used to go through Jiggs's pockets for cash; Mary Worth wouldn't think of such an approach). This has been the evolution of the comics over the last half century. The dramatic contrast between *The Captain and the Kids* and *Dennis the Menace* exemplifies most clearly what has happened. Comics reflect the culture and have helped to form the culture.

So while we began with the myth that the comics are mere toys for child minds and are insignificant in their impact—and while that myth was true in the first decade of this century—we have to say today that the comics *become* important as they more and more fulfill human needs and provide the folk heroes we require. Li'l Abner remains forever the hillbilly simpleton of giant strength; but he is always ready to oppose the strong-and-evil: and he always does. Illiterate, yes—and deliberately so. When the Pittsburgh *Press* censored him for some local political reason, Al Capp said, "'. . . they got fourteen thousand letters of protest. Who would ever have thought that so many people who like my strip are actually able to write?'"[37]

If the comics of the early period had continued as they were and if new comics had not been added as the culture advanced, the myth of childish insignificance would doubtless be true still (for

37. Ibid., p. 41.

instance, in the order of their appearance, *The Katzenjammer Kids, Mutt and Jeff,* and *Bringing Up Father*). But Maggie, the social climber, is replaced by Blondie, the emancipated woman; the merely mischievous Hans and Fritz have become Dennis and Charlie Brown; and Mutt, as we have said, has become the harassed suburbanite. In the course of their evolution, the comics achieved their incomparable, incredible popularity: and in reaching their huge audience, they can no longer be regarded as mere bagatelle.

The funnies have demonstrated their power to get reader response. Crystal City, Texas, put up a statue in honor of Popeye because he made spinach acceptable to the young—as acceptable as it could be made to them. Ham Fisher was crowned the Cheese King of 1937 by the National Cheese Institute because Joe Palooka trained on cheese and sales consequently zoomed. Flash Gordon started the craze for wedgies. Sparkle Plenty dolls earned three million dollars in sales in their first year. The Shmoos of Al Capp helped build the sales of no fewer than sixty-five various products "such as glassware, underwear, soap, fishhooks, egg cups, banks, birthday cards . . . household deodorizers. . . ."[38] Some scholars have gone so far as to claim that the comics have unified American culture in reaching more people than the public schools could. In our own day, such strips as *Rex Morgan, M.D.* and *Judge Parker* —both of which probably would have been incomprehensible to comic readers of the time of World War I—were planned on the basis of scientific public opinion surveys. They are masterminded by Dr. Nicholas Dallis of Toledo, an M.D. who came to the city to head up the Mental Hygiene Center; the characters are drawn by Marvin Bradley, and backgrounds by Frank Edgington. "Not like the old days, when one man transferred his own genius to paper. But the purpose of *Rex Morgan* and of its companion strip, *Judge Parker,* is different: it is to reflect life much as it is lived, adding dramatic emphasis and a dash of romance."[39]

That this technique gains wide readership; that the comics are

38. Ibid., pp. 21–22.
39. Stephen Becker, *Comic Art in America* (New York: Simon & Schuster, 1959), p. 275.

no longer simple blackouts trying to get one laugh; that the strips reflect and help form our culture—these are the reasons why the myth of their jocular insignificance is becoming less true all the time.

First Taste Is Best?

Some famous English master of taste was quoted in the press recently as being envious of those who had not yet read *War and Peace,* which, in the accepted mode of the best-thought-of people, he characterized as "the greatest novel in any language," and it may be, for all we know: any book that requires charts and guidelines to help the reader must be up there near the top. This *arbiter elegantiarum* was sorry that he could never again read the book for the first time, and thus he envied those who were about to undertake the journey. That first primal delight, as of the First Garden in the first dew-wet sunrise, as of the first discovery of love—all innocence and trust, untouched as yet with a single hint of the commonplace—this is what he envied. This is what we see in the eyes of children. Until they get educated.

Apparently some such experience overtook John Keats when he began reading the translation of Homer by George Chapman, the Elizabethan: he compared himself to an astronomer gazing through his telescope at the very moment that "a new planet swims into his ken," or to the little band of conquistadors on the mountain peak at Darien seeing the Pacific Ocean for the first time through European eyes (although, of course, it was not "stout Cortez" at all, but the ill-starred Vasco Nuñez de Balboa who led the Spaniards).

This is the belief, widespread in our literature, that one's first contact with a masterpiece is somehow the best or most pleasurable. Which is palpable nonsense. One's first contact with *anything* is necessarily tentative. That new tennis racket may seem to have perfect balance, and one's initial pleasure may be titillating indeed; but the performance in emergencies, the stroke-after-stroke excellence, the way the instrument adapts to one's needs until it seems to be an extension of oneself—these are the things which grow on the user and create an appreciation which could only be guessed at, that day in the sporting goods store.

In the same way, the perfection of George Chapman's art as a poet and translator grew upon John Keats as he experienced different facets of Chapman's skill, as he perceived nuances not noted at first, as he felt with the absolute assurance of intuitive knowledge that Chapman's redaction had conveyed Homer's spirit as well as his meaning in ways never previously accomplished by anyone—these are the things that must have grown upon Keats as he continued his exploration.

One may be struck dumb with the beauty of some painting, sculpture, ballet, concerto, or even scent, and sense the shock of recognizing excellence; but it has to hold up. And if it holds up, it has to increase. The moment it begins to stand still, it has started to regress and one has reached the point where the charm fades. "Give me excess of it, that, surfeiting, / The appetite may sicken, and so die," says the Duke of Illyria in the opening lines of *Twelfth Night*.

Psychologically the reason for the surfeit is lack of contrast, lack of variety. Gertrude Stein showed us that a word repeated endlessly becomes nonsense; and we know, for example, that an attempt to repeat such syllables as "coat, boy," five or six times rapidly finds the tongue disobeying orders and saying such lunatic things as "coyt, bo," almost at once. A synapse most recently employed tends to be used again; but after a while weariness sets in and fatigue mixes up the procession. We need the contrasts, the changes. There is no sweet if there is no sour. Not everyone is enough of an artist to use the available varieties when they are called for, of course. Saki tells us, in "The Stalled Ox," of a painter whose *Noontide Peace* was a "study of two dun cows under a walnut tree." His next painting, by contrast (Saki does not say "by contrast," being too subtle for that) was entitled *A Midday Sanctuary*, and was "a study of a walnut tree with two dun cows under it."

But *up to that standstill point*—which would be necessarily different for varying works of art and for different viewers—it is a matter of progression from first impression to greater appreciation as richer elements are recognized; and then, as Enobarbus (who was loyally biased, we grant) said of Cleopatra to Maecenas in one of the most impressive tributes ever paid to a woman: "Age cannot wither her, nor custom stale / Her infinite variety; other women cloy / The appetites they feed, but she makes hungry / Where most she satisfies."

The myth of the first being the best is involved in some of mankind's most curious customs—for example, the *jus primae noctis* in feudal days, where the lord of the area was entitled to the first night with any girl just married. It really must have gotten awfully tiresome.

Furthermore, to do justice to the myth, one must bear in mind the number of experiences which were not seen as pleasurable at all the first time but later grew to be more and more appreciated —like the taste for ale. Bitter stuff! Quite. But what about that slow-creeping warmth along the veins? And the first thing one knows one is holding hands with that old Latin teacher, Alfred Edward Housman, and clinking mugs as the recitative intones "Ale, man, ale's the stuff to drink / For fellows whom it hurts to think. . . ." Our first exacerbating experience with Shakespeare probably occurred in sophomore year in high school. One need not ask the reader to join in the almost unanimous vote that this was not love at first sight. . . .

Nevertheless, the ancient and widespread belief that the first is the best has this much truth in it: that the wild surmise never appears again in just the way it did that first time—and therefore we treasure that first. But it might be best not to work it out in a needlework sampler.

The Poor Little Rich Girl

The idea—should one say the hope?—that the enormously wealthy are enormously unhappy is to be found in the writings of mankind all over the globe from tribal and bucolic cultures to the great sophisticated systems of the educated and literate world. Said old

Periander (about 600 B.C.): *"Plus est sollicitas magis beatus"*—"the greater your fortune, the greater your care." Croesus of Lydia, the archetype of unlimited wealth, was warned by Solon about the divine wrath which haunts the rich—and Cyrus, it will be remembered, took Croesus finally in a manner similar to that employed by Grant in taking Richmond in the famous American adage. And one of the favorite Grecian fables relates the gift of the touch of gold to Midas, the Phrygian king, from the god Dionysus, who happened to be pleased with the king at the time. We all know the raspers *that* led to.

"The rich knows not who is his friend," said George Herbert; and the writer John Clarke remarked, "A rich man's money hangs him often." (One is tempted to suggest that once would be almost enough; but apparently not.) S. G. Champion held that "Riches take away more pleasure than they give," and Jesus himself is on record that it is easier for a camel to work its way through the eye of a needle than for a rich man to enter the Kingdom of Heaven. (There have been many attempted changes in this camel translation, trying to make it "more reasonable," such as pointing out the *kamelos,* Greek "camel," is easily confused with *kamilos,* "rope," and suggesting that it makes more sense to see a person trying to thread a needle with a rope—although he is obviously doomed to failure in this case also—than to find a camel trying to shoulder its way through. In fact, these translators hold, the figure is ridiculous. Chances are a camel couldn't even *see* a needle, to say nothing of the eye. Hence the original must have been "rope" and not "camel." Others have said that "the needle's eye" is the name of a gate in Jerusalem, a tight squeeze for a thin man and an impossibility for a camel—and *that's* what Jesus meant. But George Arthur Buttrick, writing the Exposition for Matthew in *The Interpreter's Bible,* holds that the accepted translation is correct and that Jesus was deliberately making a ridiculous—and rather colorful—parallel for a completely and unthinkably impossible act. "The eye of a needle does not mean the wicket gate in a large door, and camel is not a miswriting of the Greek word for rope.

The Babylonian Talmud twice speaks of an elephant passing through a needle's eye."[40] In fact, Elton Trueblood has traced in the saying of Jesus irony and other forms of humorous discourse, and ends up with thirty outstanding examples, including the camel-needle figure.)[41]

However, if the proposition that the very rich are unhappy people is to make any sense, it has to be a relative statement: are the rich any more unhappy than the other 202,252,000 Americans who saw the dawn of the year 1969? ("A total of 202,254,000 Americans are on hand to welcome in the New Year, the United States Census Bureau estimated Tuesday.")[42] George G. Kirstein makes the statement that "one out of every two thousand Americans is a millionaire," and he throws down the following gauntlet: "I challenge you to pick him out on your subway train, on your walk down the street, or in the theatre audience." By contrast, he says, one could have picked out the millionaires easily in 1900; but today they are, as a class, unobtrusive—possibly for purposes of safety.[43]

Kirstein quickly concedes that "anyone familiar with the potentially corrosive qualities of vast wealth can cite examples of miserable, lonely people, so separated from the environment in which they live that life offers little enjoyment," and he also quotes Dr. Philip K. McAllister, the doctor who attended Golden Girl Doris Duke when she was broken up because of having run down a friend with a car: "Wealth does not bring happiness," the doctor soberly told the New York *Daily News* (10 October 1966). "I am convinced that enormous wealth brings great handicaps."

This attitude is fed heaping portions of evidence by the newspaper feature writers whenever an opportunity occurs. For example —and for contrast—United Press International sent a story out to subscribers for use with the good-cheer conventional stuff for Christmas, 1969, which the Boston *Globe* adorned with a six-column headline: "$2500-A-DAY PRISON FOR BARBARA HUTTON." In the text we learn that the fifty-seven-year-old Woolworth heiress is sick,

40. *The Interpreter's Bible*, 7: 485.
41. *The Humor of Christ* (New York: Harper & Row, 1964), p. 127.
42. *New York Times*, 2 January 1969.
43. *The Rich—Are They Different?* (Boston: Houghton Mifflin Co., 1968), p. 206.

alone, spending Christmas day in the Mark Hopkins (the entire sixteenth floor), none of her seven husbands being present, no member of the family at hand, and requiring waiting upon, hand and foot: they have to carry her to the table. She weighs only ninety pounds. Has cataracts on her eyes. Other "unexplained ailments." She says, "I am lonely here. I have no home and no anchor." And the assumption seems to be that the disaster that put her in this sorry condition was the $50 million from the dime store fortune plus other millions from various husbands.[44]

Surely the moral is plain—and salutary: we must be happy with what we have. Riches do not bring happiness!

It would be pleasant for some of us to think so, perhaps, but how often do you find the extremely wealthy—and thus presumably the most afflicted with the sorrows of affluence—divesting themselves of the incumbrance so as to live happier lives? If some well-meaning friend should lay a hot coal upon the palm of my hand, and I found it unpleasantly hot, would I not drop it rather than encourage it by blowing additional oxygen upon it? Isn't it possible that the very rich have changed from being flamboyant, as at the turn of the century, to being as inconspicuous as possible (with some exceptions) so that the public will think they live simply and that one cannot buy happiness? Today's Morgan yacht is a 62-foot motor sailer instead of the massive 350-foot *Corsair* of three decades back.[45]

Some students of the subject have pointed to suicides as indicators of the truth of the theory that being rich is an unhappy state and that losing one's wealth in the crash of a bad market sends the tycoons down from the forty-seventh floor in a sky-darkening flock of death seekers. The classic work *Suicide* by Emile Durkheim, with which his editor, George Simpson, agrees, would indicate that suicides are high among the privileged. But Gregory Zilboorg says the statistics "as compiled today" deserve little credence. Too many suicides are reported as being something else; attempted suicides that result in death later on are never included in vital statistics;

---

44. Richard M. Harnett, UPI, Boston *Globe*, 25 December 1969.
45. Kirstein, *The Rich*, p. 206.

who can tell whether a suicide by automobile is really that or an accident?

The unhappy rich . . . It's a very old legend. Ptah-Hotep, 3550 B.C., commiserated with the wealthy, saying, "Riches are of no avail if one be weary." And also there is the sly pejorative, suspicious of wealth, and saying, with Solomon, of all people, "No one gets rich quickly if he is honest," or, with Plato, "A rich man can't be good." The poet Lucretius stated that "A contented mind and a frugal existence are riches enough for any man." But Ben Franklin turned the whole cart on its side. "Who is rich?" he said. "He that is content. Who is that? Nobody."

The old legend is, of course, partly true—like most generalizations. If one happens to be a person with a built-in fear of being robbed, then one is probably unhappier with fifty dollars in one's pocket than with ten cents.

Franklin P. Adams once did a lovely verse called "The Rich Man," showing the tycoon at his country estate, his town estate, smoking his fifty-cent cigars and jeering at fate. "He frivols through the livelong day," sang FPA. But does anybody think for one moment that the poet, committed to his muse, would change places with the playboy? And the poem ends, like the old vaudeville blackout, its contemporary, "You bet I would!"

Old Shoes Are Good Luck?

Seeing how important it is to be able to walk in comfort, it is no wonder that the homely subject of shoes has been one of the most familiar to have been made the center of fable and folklore. Whether the footwear was in the form of moccasins of one kind or another, or regulation soles-and-uppers, it was essential that they should be suited to the wearer. No matter how handsome, one shoe fits not all feet—as people have been saying ever since they stopped going barefoot—and the one absolute requirement is a good fit. This characteristic has even been used as a test of identity in discovering the owner, as we know from the story of Cinderella (whose slippers, incidentally, were not *verre*, "glass," but *vair*, "ermine")[46] and from various magic tales. A generation before Christ, Horace was writing in his *Epistles: "Metiri se quemque suo modulo ac pede verum est"*—"For still when all is said the rule stands fast / That each man's shoe be made on his own last." Montaigne agreed: *"A chaque pied son soulier."* (*Essays*, III. 13; 1595) So we say, "If the shoe fits, put it on," and having put it on, if it's comfortable then one is a lucky person. It seems like a simple truism, but the idea is so natural and earthy that the depth of its integrity is not seen and the notion is merely taken for granted. He who tries fifty feet of travel in shoes that have a stone in them knows how essential the comfort is—if anything is going to get done that day.

The Scottish proverb runs: "Rice for gude luck and bauchles for bonnie bairns," "bauchles" meaning old shoes. Rice is a fertility symbol; but we want our children healthy and normal and well formed, not giving the appearance of the unlicked bear whelp that carries no impression like the dam. Old shoes, then, for good luck.

Thus when the bride leaves the house of her parents, slippers and shoes are thrown at her—not only for good luck but also to indicate the hope of a lasting marriage: she is leaving this home for good, and the footwear should go, too.

Another symbolism reflects the supposed mastery of the husband over the wife. When Luther was attending a wedding on one occasion, he whispered to the groom that he had placed a pair of the groom's shoes on the head of the bed, *"afin qu'il prit ainsi la domination et le gouvernement"*—so that the groom should thus assume control and direction of the household.[47] It's a pleasant dream, and according to the European view of matrimony, a lucky situation to achieve.

Old shoes stood for good luck; new shoes, then, by corollary, indicated taking a chance. *"Mutavit calceos"*—"he has changed his shoes"—they said when a Roman became a senator. Roman senators wore black buskins reaching to the middle of the calf, with a

---

46. See Montagu and Darling, *Prevalence of Nonsense*, pp. 234–35.
47. E. Cobham Brewer, *The Reader's Handbook* (Philadelphia: J. B. Lippincott Co., 1902), p. 1000.

silver letter C on the instep.[48] (R. D. Jameson says senators and magistrates wore red shoes before Marcus Aurelius changed the rules; he also finds a charming illustration showing why old shoes are preferable. This is from the Omaha Indians: the mother cut a hole in the sole of the young child's moccasin "so that the child can refuse to accompany an other-world messenger because his moccasins are worn out.")[49]

No doubt we would be held accountable by today's readers if we omitted the widely held hypothesis that shoes, old or new, are symbolic of the female genitals. Indeed there are writers who insist that everywhere, in all cultures, this is recognized. Which explains the act of the Manchu bride in giving shoes to her new husband; and of the Arab divorcing his wife, who says she is his slipper and he is putting her off. Very likely, as Jameson suggests, the old woman who lived in a shoe and had so many children was a nymphomaniac.[50] In this connection, the curious might ask why it is necessary, in so many cultures, to remove the shoes in the presence of the deity? Moses and Joshua were told to go barefoot on holy ground; the Rhodians were forbidden to carry shoes into the temple of the Tegean Mother; it was required to enter temples barefoot in Crete; nobody wearing shoes could enter the temples of Cybele and Isis; the Moslems take off their footwear at the door of the mosque. . . . Or why is it good luck to place a shoe on the housetop, heel up?

But we were discussing the legend that old shoes stand for good fortune; and unhappily we must report that there are holes in the theory, especially if one refers to the product of the modern shoe-maker, who is so likely to employ the allergen mercaptobenzothi-azole.

Prior to 1940 the news that a person could be allergic to his own shoes was regarded as what we can only call a dermatological curiosity, and in doing so we are appropriating a phrase originated

48. Ibid., p. 1001.
49. Maria Leach and Jerome Fried, eds., *Funk & Wagnalls Standard Dictionary of Folklore, Mythology and Legend*, 2 vols. (New York: Funk & Wagnalls, 1949–50), 2:1008.
50. Ibid., p. 1008.

by Dr. Ernst Epstein of the San Mateo Medical Clinic and the Division of Dermatology, University of California San Francisco Medical Center. His interesting article "Shoe Contact Dermatitis," demonstrated that today shoe allergy is recognized as a fairly common problem, but that it does not appear often enough for its presence to be the first suspect: the diagnosis is more likely to be fungus infection, atopic eczema, or psoriasis.[51]

"Rubber-based adhesives or lining materials are the most commonly encountered offenders," Epstein says; and the first observers to point this out were P. Bonnevie and P. V. Marcussen in a report published in 1944. Therefore the fact of allergies based on rubber is of fairly recent knowledge. Patients having the same symptoms were customarily treated as having dermatophytosis, a skin disease originating with a fungus.

If one is allergic to something—pollen, vegetable oils, bacteria, certain proteins, or even light, heat, and cold in some cases—it does not require a large quantity of the allergen to produce the symptoms. Fishbein says "a millionth of a milligram" will do it.[52] The allergy can be caused by something one is closely associated with, or it can be something one dislikes—or it can be something one craves and needs. There is no curing it, to date. The treatment is to remove the allergen, if one can discover what it is. The mercaptobenzothiazole to which we referred a moment ago, which is an accelerator used in the vulcanization of rubber, proved to be an allergen for most of the patients of Drs. Bonnevie and Marcussen, for instance.

Dr. Epstein points out that routine clinical examination of inflammation of the foot does not reveal the fact that an allergy is at work; in the old days (before 1940) it probably would not have even been suspected. And today it is not the first answer to suggest itself, as we have pointed out. But there is sufficient documentation now to demonstrate that some people are, indeed, allergic to their own shoes, and since "rubber-based adhesives are universally used

51. *Journal of the American Medical Association*, 209, no. 10 (8 September 1969): 1487–88.
52. Morris Fishbein, *Modern Home Medical Adviser* (Garden City, N.Y.: Doubleday & Co., 1949), p. 192.

in the shoe industry, they are apparently the cause of much shoe dermatitis."[53]

Admittedly, coping with shoe allergy is a complicated and tiresome process, and we have no intention of attempting to summarize the procedure here. Patch-testing is the diagnostic method; but avoidance of contact with the allergen is not a simple matter, "Since the precise allergen as well as the exact composition of the shoes is rarely known." Dr. Epstein names one company which "manufactures a shoe made of vegetable-tanned leather and nonrubber adhesives, a most helpful product (Brockton Shoe Co., Derma Pedic shoe)," which indicates that industry is alert to the new problem.

On the whole, however, we believe we have strengthened rather than weakened the grand old apothegm that old shoes are good luck: because if you've worn them this long without dermatitis, you're home safe. And even if you're not home safe, you are more fortunate than those patients who are allergic to *themselves.* One can go barefoot if necessary; but fancy running about without oneself. . . . This is no joke: Dr. Lamar S. Osment, associate professor at the Medical College of Alabama, reported to the American Academy of Dermatology in 1961 that in his experiments with seventeen patients suffering from discoid lupus erythematosis, which results in an inflamed and scaly skin, the patients were "allergic to one or more of their own body components. These people may be allergic to their own white or red blood cells, blood coagulation factors or their own kidney tissue."[54]

After this report, *any* old shoe sounds good.

Nursery Rimes Are Innocent Doggerel?

One of the first books a child is given is traditionally a collection of nursery rimes; and even before the book there was the oral tradition—the toe counting ("This little pig went to market");

53. Epstein, *JAMA*, p. 1491.
54. Boston *Traveler*, 5 December 1961.

various charades such as breaking eggs in the mouth by punching both cheeks at once; "This is the church and this is the steeple"; and the various gallopings to and from market, along with "Jack and Jill" and "Mary, Mary." From their long association with the cradle and the nursery, it is probably inevitable that most of us think of these jingles as near nonsense whose words hardly matter, but which do have rhyme and meter, strike up a beat to which one can keep time, and are emotionally satisfactory for recreational purposes with the very young. We accept the myth of their innocuous origins and purposes, and if we think we discern a brief reflection of some ancient cruelty, we dismiss it in joyful rough-and-tumble with a tousled baby displaying his delighted, if toothless, grin.

That myth of tender harmlessness may not be entirely watertight if one wishes to follow the roots back to the seed. The road back may not be a short one, however, since some of the rimes have origins in dark antiquity: back to the dim forests and the druids and human sacrifice; possibly back beyond biblical days when Queen Balqîs of Sheba went to King Solomon's court for a riddle contest, such as was very much *au fait* in Babylonian days.[55]

It has been noted by many students of the subject that stories and rimes for children often seem to have a horror content scarcely consistent with the nursery—involving cruel treatment of children, cannibal witches, jealous half-brothers and sisters, malevolent stepmothers, and cutthroats of various degrees. Regardless of this characteristic, nursery rimes "have become the best known in the world," and "examination shows that not all are the doggerel they are popularly taken to be."[56] Anthony Burgess strongly agrees. "Nursery rhymes are crude-seeming, but they're not doggerel." In Jack Sprat, for instance (1639), "the literary economy is considerable; there is a fine personification of the complementary

55. Charles Francis Potter, "Riddles," *Funk & Wagnalls Standard Dictionary of Folklore*, 2:943.

56. Iona and Peter Opie, *The Oxford Dictionary of Nursery Rhymes* (London: Oxford University Press, The Clarendon Press, 1952), p. 1. Incidentally, Fowler prefers "rhyme" for all uses; Evans allows either, merely remarking that "rime" is older and derives a certain status from Coleridge.

principle. . . ."[57] Perhaps it is a little safer to say they're not *all*
doggerel. Actually, "doggerel" is an orphan word without credentials or ancestry and has no richness in it. Webster III gives it four
lines to explain that it means "trivial" or "bad" when applied to
poetry. It has a better odor when applied to burlesque verse, where
it merely indicates carelessness or irregularity.

But it is the *innocence* of nursery rime that concerns us basically.
In the Goosy Gander poem, we read:

> There I met an old man
> Who wouldn't say his prayers.
> I took him by his left leg
> And threw him down the stairs.

Even if this does not have the symbolic meaning, attributed to it
by Shaw (in *Back to Methuselah*), of a descent into hell, it is still
a senseless violence to throw an old man downstairs for refusal to
perform a religious ritual. Even a very *short* flight of stairs would
be highly painful. But there is a coloring in this quatrain thought
to have come from the schoolboy's somewhat heartless tetrastich,
addressed to the crane fly and repeated as the long legs are pulled
off the insect:

> Old Father Longlegs
> Won't say his prayers.
> Pull him by the left leg
> And throw him down the stairs.

The only possible answer to the cruelty charge seems to be that in
the nursery where these lines are recited, it is the rhythm that
counts, and the meaning is scarcely given a thought. Especially
when the words are given to the accompaniment of the usual smiles
and laughter associated with nursery fun.

More sinister is the story behind "Cock a Doodle Doo." The
legend goes back to Elizabethan days and appears in one of the
popular pamphlets of the time, entitled "The Most Crvell and
Bloody Mvrther committed by an Innkeeper's Wife, called Annis

57. Anthony Burgess, "Don't Cook Mother Goose," *New York Times Book Review*,
5 November 1967.

Dell, and her Sonne George Dell, Foure yeeres since." Annis and George killed a three-year-old boy by the name of Anthony James. This was in Hertfordshire, at Bishop's Hatfield. A hidden witness to the foul deed was the boy's young sister, "not much aboue foure," and when she screamed, the two villains seized her and cut the tongue out of her head. . . . Three years later the miracle occurred: tongueless though she was, the sister, now seven, was suddenly able to imitate a rooster crowing, and being encouraged by a playmate's example, cried out, "Cocka doodle doo,/ Peggy hath lost her shoe." So they took her to Sir Henry Butler, the justice, and she told about the murder of her brother. Such is the bloody tale behind "Cock a Doodle Doo."[58]

One of the most widely known nursery rimes is "Humpty Dumpty," known in France as "Boule, boule," in Sweden as "Thille Lille," in Finland as "Hillerin-Lillerin," and in various parts of Germany as "Hümpelken-Pümpelken" or even "Rüntzelken-Püntzelken"—all apparently derived from the English in one way or another. The youngsters in Saxony, for example, chant:

> *Hümpelken-Pümpelken sat op de Bank,*
> *Hümpelken-Pümpelken fêl von de Bank,*
> *Do is kên Doktor in Engelland*
> *De Hümpelken-Pümpelken kuräre kann?*

It is easy to see why this rime should be so successful: its meter is simple and heavily accented, and the drama, as so graphically shown in the Tenniel drawing in *Through the Looking Glass,* is incomparably satisfactory for the release of tension into laughter. As anyone knows who has dropped an egg, the action is swift and the devastation utter; there is no suggestion of a hope of making amends in any way. The thing is absolute. And the only possible answer is laughter.

But is this song the simple and innocent nonsense that it seems? Some say that it mocks Cardinal Wolsey, who was made cardinal through the influence of Henry VIII and who controlled English foreign and domestic policy for a long period. He was also respon-

58. Opie, *Nursery Rhymes,* pp. 128–29.

sible for heavy taxes to support Henry's expensive government, and had enemies on all sides, all of whom—Anne Boleyn among them —would have been delighted to see him tumble and disintegrate; and they had their will in November of 1530 when the great man was arrested for treason. He died on the way to trial. But it would not have done to revile the cardinal in scurrilous verse or in any other way while he was at the peak of his power. We often find the pamphleteers and poets portraying the disaster of a hated enemy through some fiction. Who can prove it means Wolsey?

A New World parallel is seen on a plaque attached to a street wall in Quebec, showing a dog of gold and below him this quatrain:

> *Je suis un chien qui ronge l'os.*
> *En le rongeant, je prends mon repos.*
> *Un temps viendra qui n'est pas venu,*
> *Quand je morderai qui m'aura mordu.*

This supposedly represents a young man done out of his inheritance by foul means and forced to flee his native France. He says, through the golden dog (whose significance is lost): "I am a dog who gnaws a bone. I gnaw away leisurely, but the time will come when I will destroy him who would have ruined me."

Anthony Burgess points out that James Joyce thought Humpty Dumpty was a symbol for the downfall accompanying human hubris, the deadly sin of pride. Seeking to build too high, man falls with the brittle smack of an eggshell "from the tower of his own creation." And also, "Coarser minds find in the story an allegory of detumescence."[59]

Some of the nursery rimes are riddles—often quite complicated but by no means innocent nonsense. Some are sugar-coated injunctions to good behavior—no wool goes to the crybaby. Others represent simple games like jump rope (not *always* innocent once one realizes that "jumping Joan" was underworld cant for a female of tarnished repute); and still others were counting-out verses to select a victim (and here, too, the ancestry is suspected of some savagery). But most of them, certainly as they are in use today,

59. "Don't Cook Mother Goose."

do fulfill the myth of harmless fantasy and innocence, and one of the best is surely the one with which we began, "This little pig went to market," where the mother gently pinches one toe after the other, building up to the truly explosive climax, " 'Wee, wee, wee' all the way home." Of this there is a variant from California so attractive that we must share it, with thanks to that tireless enthusiast the late Charles Francis Potter. Here the mother begins with the littlest toe and works up:

Little Pee;
Penny Jew;
Judy Whistle;
Mary Gristle; and
Old Big Gobble Gobble.[60]

Each His Own Santa

There were two important ingredients of salvation in the Christianity of the last four or five hundred years: faith and good works. One's faith had to be pure and strong; but faith alone was not enough—God demanded a demonstration in terms of practical altruism. What the proper proportion was, in the mind of God, was a subject very hotly disputed among those who could not possibly know the mind of God.

At any rate, an echo of those old Puritan ethics appears today in the satisfaction shown by persons who join a Christmas Club. They feel that they are doing good works by joining the club and paying the dues weekly. There seems to be something about living in obedience to this sort of voluntary discipline that people find good for the soul. We will not deny that psychological rewards may be present. But it certainly makes no sense financially, and it doesn't seem worthy of the sharp old God-fearing Yankee—the slave trader with the Bible at his bedside—to lend his money without recompense, which is what most Christmas Club members do. (According to Jack Frenaye, president of Christmas Club, only 13 percent of the ten thousand member banks pay any interest, and most of

60. *Dictionary of Folklore*, 2: 804.

those are on the West Coast, where the competition appears to be greater.)[61] When one considers that the clubs held $2.2 *billion* in 1968, the amount of potential earnings is a matter of real interest, if you will excuse us.

But most people don't think about that. They tell themselves that they are saving for a purpose—this is ethically admirable—and that there will be no guilt attached to the spending of this money when the time comes, because that was the whole point of the game. Nobody has a right to say, "Think of the starving children," because they deliberately put away their two to ten dollars every week (that is the average of the clubs) for the specific purpose of spending the money madly when fifty weeks have run their course. Mr. Frenaye points out that members are "goal-oriented, and they don't feel guilty when they spend Christmas Club money, but they do if they take it out of a savings account."

Many people believe that it is the innocent poor who patronize the Christmas Clubs—people with very little money to spend, who want to make sure they'll be able to celebrate at Christmas. This is another fallacy. In 1969 the average deposit came to a total of $139 and the income of the average depositor's family was $12,000. People who join a club one year are likely to continue—a whopping 90 percent do, being urged perhaps by free gifts from the promotion department.

Substantiating the good-works motif is the strong belief in thrift, a feeling that runs through our literature from the earliest days. Even as recently as 1944, E. W. Howe was stating in the *Saturday Review*, "Thrift is to a man what chastity is to a woman."[62] That still has *some* force, even in the 1970s. . . . Kant didn't think much of thrift, though. He said, "Thrift is care and scruple in the spending of one's means. It is not a virtue, and it requires neither skill nor talent" (Königsberg lecture, 25 April 1775). But in general thrift is approved and is as American as Ben Franklin. In theological terms, "Wele thryuethe that God loveth," as some forgotten

61. "Season Pulls Many to Christmas Clubs," *New York Times,* 11 December 1969.
62. "Aphorism," 13 May 1944.

writer put it in a little drama in 1450: if we thrive, it shows we have God's love.

Whatever we believe in these matters, it is not difficult to prove that there is truth in the myth that Christmas Clubs are beneficial, even if we never collect a cent of interest: because the *bank* profits. And surely nobody will say *that's* bad.

City Mouse and Country Mouse

When the city mouse spent a few days with his cousin the country mouse, he found the bucolic life pretty dull, if one recalls. There was good food and fresh air and all that, but everything was so *plain*. Life was too primitive. Variety was lacking.

The country mouse, returning the visit, found the life of his city cousin highly exciting. He had all kinds of delicacies to eat and there was always something interesting going on. But there were also cats and traps; on every side was danger.

The moral was no less obvious than salutary, and the poets have been telling us for a long time that rural living is to be equated with good and urban dwelling with bad. Country girls are sweet and clean and innocent and their milk pails are brimming with white foam. But city girls are likely to be flirts or worse. Depravity lives at the courts of princes, but in the country with the shepherds and the flutes is to be found the quiet mind and the untarnished spirit. Sang Geoffrey Chaucer: "Flee fro the prees, and dwelle with sothfastnesse . . . And trouthe shal delivere, hit is no drede" ("Balade de Bon Conseyl"). It has become part of our heritage. "God made the country, and man made the town," wrote William Cowper in "The Task." To which Cowley echoes, "God the first garden made, and the first city Cain." It seems rather plain on the face of things that we need a close association with nature. Poets, painters, writers, scientists, all "have avowed an intimate need of nature. In some of them the thirst for natural things, for the full sky, landscapes, trees, flowers, wild animals, the tang of the autumn wind, the tumbling seas and tranquil lakes, has been an obsession. The implication is clear that severed from nature man's imagination and inquiring mind would diminish, perhaps wither utterly."[63]

The exalted character of country living received a fillip when the poets and critics began reacting to "the dark satanic mills of industrial England" as compared with "the idyl (real or imagined) of rural life hedged in tradition"[64]—particularly such geniuses as William Morris, who aimed to restore craftsmanship and beauty to lives deprived by the factory and the slum. Eighteenth-century novels were full of this spirit—*Moll Flanders, Clarissa Harlowe,* Dickens, Jane Austen.[65]

In extreme cases fear and hatred of the city can lead to complete misanthropy, as it did with the Desert Saints in the early history of Christianity. In the same spirit, W. L. Call, seventy-five, of Gateway, Arkansas, not long ago left town to live in a cavern in the Ozarks. From a lookout point near his cave, Mr. Call can watch the traffic on faraway U.S. 62. "Day after day I see high-powered cars speeding up and down this old highway, with people in them rushing along, and I don't actually believe half of them realize the real purpose of life, or even where they're going or where they're likely to stop. . . . Too many folks are speed-crazy," he said.[66]

With great regularity—that is to say, in a steady stream—we see books, magazine articles, Sunday features, and interviews with learned or famous persons adding their bricks to the edifice: there is less insanity in rural areas than in urban communities because the pressures in the country are fewer and less intense, we are told by a psychology professor who lives in a university city. And we all nod our heads and write, "How true!" in the margin. J. A. Clausen gives us a thoughtful article, "Sociology of Mental Illness," and cites abundant evidence to indicate that it's not true—in proportion to population, there is more mental illness in the country.

63. Edgar Ansel Mowrer, "Sawdust, Seaweed and Synthetics: The Hazards of Crowding," *Saturday Review,* 8 December 1956.
64. Review of *William Morris: His Life, Work and Friends* by Philip Henderson, *Time,* 8 December 1967.
65. Angus Wilson, "Evil in the English Novel," *Kenyon Review,* March 1967.
66. "Hermit in Arkansas Feels Cars Deprive People of Real Life," *New York Times,* 21 May 1967.

Think of those endless winter nights, snow-blocked roads, large families living under the same roof for days on end—and forget the phony allure of "Snowbound" for a moment, with the cider and doughnuts, apples and nuts, and the storyteller by the great hearth. Read the diurnal hibernal murder stories from the sticks, and you may feel yourself faintly tempted to doubt the myth.[67] Popular exposers have made the same point, such as Leo Rosten in his column in *Look* (26 July 1966 and 16 April 1968).

Then we see discourses undertaking to prove that the noise of the city is bad for health; that crowding is bad; that New York City has two million too many people (this is the urban authority Lewis Mumford, speaking from his "plain but cozy frame house in Leddsville Road," Amenia, New York, at the ripe age of seventy-one, and he adds that the new skyscrapers "are just glass-and-metal filing cabinets," and the new high-rise apartments—"All they contain are filing-card people.").[68]

Of course a great deal of this cannot be denied. Dr. Samuel Rosen, associate clinical professor at the College of Physicians and Surgeons of Columbia University, who has several citations for his research on ear ailments, told New York's first conference on the control of noise in 1967 that the town is so loud that the noise can do "real damage to hearing, affect blood pressure and the heart, and eventually disturb every bodily function."[69] The same opinion was given a year later by Dr. Albert M. Schwartz, newly elected president of the New York County Medical Society. He said, "Much publicity and attention have been given lately to water and air pollution but not to noise pollution. The manifold adverse reactions and deleterious physical changes produced by noise are just beginning to be realized and studied."[70]

And not in New York alone. The Federal Council for Science and Technology issued a report late in 1968 which stated that noise

67. J. A. Clausen, "Sociology of Mental Illness," in *Sociology Today*, ed. R. K. Merton (New York: Harper Torchbooks, 1965).
68. "Mumford Finds City Strangled by Excess of Cars and People," *New York Times*, 22 March 1967.
69. "City Noise Called Harmful to Body," *New York Times*, 19 March 1967.
70. *New York Times*, 30 October 1968.

is "a major health hazard in American industry and an increasingly serious nuisance throughout the nation."[71]

The American fantasy showing an arcadia of good living in the country as opposed to an "apocalypse of robotism" in the cities— what Harold Rosenberg calls a "fantasy of a nation of immigrants and wanderers, the dream small town"[72]—has not lost its grip on our social imagination. The movement toward the bucolic hills continues on the part of thousands of idealists seeking peace, health, a slower pace. But *has* it reached the point where the city is about to be rejected, abandoned to continue its polluted, noisy, high-pressure, dirty, slum-blackened progress to hell? If the city of New York is any criterion, such a picture is false, according to Irving Kristol.[73] First of all, he shows, with statistics, that what "everyone" knows—that we have an urban crisis—is not the whole truth. He makes eight important points:

1. "We have *not* become a nation of big cities—only 10 percent of Americans live in cities of over 1,000,000, not significantly more than in 1910. . . ."

2. Substandard units are on the decline, not on the increase. "In 1960, according to the Census Bureau, less than 3 percent of dwelling units in cities of 50,000 or more were substandard."

3. Estimates indicate that the proportion of urban dwellers living below the poverty line has been cut in half since World War II.

4. Gallup polls show that only 22 percent of Americans want to live in cities; more than half prefer towns and rural areas.

5. Negroes and Puerto Ricans on New York's upper West Side state in overwhelming majority that they like the area better than their previous homes.

6. City homes are not necessarily owned by absentee and careless landlords. In Philadelphia (population two million) 70 percent of the homes are owner occupied. "That particular 'behavioral sink' contains three trees per inhabitant."

7. Here's a bombshell: the traffic in our largest cities may be

71. "U.S. Noise Called a Health Hazard," *New York Times*, 10 November 1968.
72. "Roadside Arcadia," *Partisan Review*, Fall 1958, p. 568.
73. "It's Not a Bad Crisis to Live In," *New York Times Magazine*, 22 January 1967.

worse than it was in 1940, but "such evidence as we have suggests strongly that it is no worse than in 1900, or perhaps even 1850. (There were fewer people and vehicles then, of course; but there were also fewer thoroughfares and traffic was slower-moving.)" He might have added something about horses. In the Years of the Horse there were some very pretty tie-ups when accidents occurred, animals and harnesses and broken wheels and people rolling in the street. Automobiles at least don't get hysterical; and they are set close to the ground. Kristol adds that it's no fair judging other cities by New York in terms of clogged traffic.

8. "By any objective, statistical index, our slum areas today appear positively benign in comparison with the teeming, filthy slums of yesteryear. They certainly are less densely populated than they used to be."

Kristol then points out a dilemma: in the old days, under corrupt and dishonest machine rule and boss politics, things got done. For instance, the machine and the boss expelled thousands of squatters in order to create Central Park. Today's more honest, more democratic city government couldn't do this. If Mayor Lindsay wanted to relocate several thousand people from rural Staten Island for a park, "the real-estate developers, the merchants, the construction unions, and CORE would all rise up in wrath and indignation." Thus it is a disaster that the political boss and the machine have declined. . . .

We'll get off the bus at this point, because city politics is not our problem. Our subject is the consideration of the proposition which most of the poets have supported, that living in the country is practically all good, and living in the city is practically all bad. Not for everyone, it isn't. Michelangelo Antonioni, the film maker, said in *Life:* "I have never felt salvation in nature. I love cities above all. A landscape with its crowds of trees, flowers and grass that repeats itself indefinitely . . . makes me dizzy." Even for the sacrosanct *tree* he has no reverence, this man: "Look at it: it goes on aging for centuries without ever having lived, without ever changing." He finds the Empire State Building much more satisfying.[74]

74. *Life;* 27 January 1967.

Perhaps the whole thing boils down to the human trait of finding the grass greener in the pasture where one is not. Said Horace: "At Rome, you long for the country; when you are in the country, fickle, you extol the absent city to the skies."[75]

The most enormous folly, of course, would be to attempt to arbitrate the truth of the myth that equates good with rural and evil with urban. Nothing was funnier to the London Elizabethan than the countryman, the hayseed. In fact, hayseed jokes appear to be popular in all centuries. Some people would rather die than be removed to the country. Health is not proportionately better in the country—indeed, people come in from the country to consult medical specialists. Old age is not a factor of rural living. Sanity is not a matter of meadows versus paved streets. The kingdom of God, it would seem, is within you. Charles B. Fairbanks was of the opinion that nine-tenths of the great nature passages in our literature were actually written "within the crowded city's smokestained walls."

75. *Satires* 2: 7: 28.

VII
CHAPTER

Myths from Magicians and Other Specialists

The Fable of the Indian Rope Trick

In the case of the famous Indian rope trick, we are dealing with matters that are in pretty murky territory where the lighting is extremely deceptive and the viscera are powerfully involved. There are many Orientalists ready to risk their reputations on the statement that the whole thing is a fake. If it can be performed—and we are making the critical but dangerous assumption that it can be and has been—then it is surely the Koh-i-noor of magical feats, in India or anywhere else. Our purpose in this book is to show supposed folly that is in fact sound truth. Probably almost everybody our readers have ever talked to would assert the rope trick is nonsense. We think not.

First of all for the trick itself. Nothing in jadu art approaches this performance, and an entire mystique has grown up around it. In fact, the Indian rope trick has brought more publicity to that part of the world, it has been asserted, than all its legitimate wonders combined.[1]

The magician, or jaduwallah, according to the most dramatic version of the demonstration, takes up about forty feet of rope and flings one end into the air. With his loose robes flapping in the firelight—for the trick is never performed except at dusk and is

1. John Nicholls Booth, *Fabulous Destinations* (New York: Macmillan Co., 1950), pp. 160–61.

always accompanied by the lighting of bonfires that flicker in the faintest breeze—the magician begins to look unreal, impossible: some sort of exaggeration.

Let us affirm immediately that we are not leading up to a suggestion of mass hypnotism or anything of the sort. We follow the opinion of the experts as resumed in the statement of the reporter and raconteur John Godwin, that "it has been proved absolutely impossible to hypnotize a single individual against his will, and certainly not a gabbling, jostling street crowd."[2]

The jaduwallah's rope end flops back to earth twice, three times, maybe half a dozen times; but eventually it appears to be grabbed by someone up there—someone or something out of sight in the gathering gloom. Then it hangs rigid—or itself reaches rigidly upward—while the incantations of the jaduwallah increase in volume and pitch, along with an increase of the violence of his gesturing.

When he is satisfied that the rope has made up its mind—if that trope can be employed temporarily—and intends to stay put, the magician calls in his bony, knobby-kneed little helper, and the boy, upon command, or after threats, leaps for the rope and climbs up. From his altitude, the boy screams curses and choice insults at the man, and refuses to return when ordered to do so.

The jaduwallah, in a foaming rage, pulls a huge dagger from the folds of his robe, clamps it between his teeth, and swarms up the rope after the boy. There is a confused struggling as he lays hands on the lad—nothing can be seen too clearly by this time—and then the blood-curdling screams of the boy fracture the evening, and a bloody arm, child-size, hurtles down, followed by a leg and an arm and a leg and finally the small head, severed at the neck. Unprepared Occidentals have been known to vomit at this point in the procedures; but of course this only adds conviction to the already screaming tension, leaving no doubt in the audience that it is getting its money's worth.

Now the magician slides down his rope and makes gestures with his blood-dripping blade; whereupon his disciples or assistants, with much weeping and wailing, gather the dismembered anatomical

2. *This Baffling World* (New York: Hart Publishing Co., 1968), p. 150.

sections together in a little heap, which is then examined carefully by the maestro. It is a high spot in the action, and the jaduwallah usually makes the most of it. "Where is his right arm?" he shouts; or perhaps, "The left foot is missing, you dogs!" And they find it where it bounced in the dropping and bring it to him. Then all the parts are dumped into a large box or basket and the lid is closed.

The jaduwallah, now thoroughly aroused, utters a long incantation over the basket; and at the end, he gives it a formal ritual kick and pulls off the lid. The knobby-kneed youngster jumps out, hale and hearty, with a grin from ear to ear. He goes through the audience with his baksheesh bowl. People suddenly released from tension are ready for laughter and a gesture of generosity, and he knows when to pass the hat.

Of course there are variations. The *Memoirs* of the Emperor Jahangir report a performance of seven Bengal jugglers at his court in which a man is cut up into pieces, covered with a cloth, and upon a signal, tosses off the cloth and arises smiling.[3] Sir Henry Yule describes an act put on by "a company of male and female jugglers, armed with bags and boxes and musical instruments, and all the mysterious paraphernalia of the peripatetic *Jadugar*," in which they threw a fifty-cubit chain into the air instead of a rope. We find this a little hard to visualize, but the report is that the jugglers put a dog on this chain and the animal ran up and disappeared; and then they did the same with a hog, a panther, a lion, a tiger—every one of which ran up the chain and disappeared. Later the chain was pulled down, but the animals never were seen again.[4]

The Moorish traveler Ibn Batuta saw the rope trick, essentially as we have described it, performed at the court of the viceroy of Khansa, in China, about 1348; but even as they were plying Ibn Batuta with restoratives at the conclusion of the trick, the Kazi Afkharuddin, sitting next to him, hid a yawn and said, "Wallah! 'Tis my opinion there has been neither going up nor coming down, neither marring nor mending; 'tis all hocus pocus!"[5] There, at any

3. Sir Henry Yule, ed., *The Book of Ser Marco Polo*, 2 vols. (New York: Charles Scribner's Sons, 1903), 1: 318.
4. Ibid.
5. Ibid., 1: 316.

rate, we have reports from two eyewitnesses seeing the very same show.

In the version witnessed in Bavaria about 1670 by the Anglo-Dutch traveler Edward Melton, a rope was used—but it went up out of sight the first time and stuck there. The juggler climbed up out of sight also. The pieces of human body were swept topsy turvy into a pile, and Melton *saw* them gradually move closer together—he used the word "crept"—and finally join into a whole man. Thousands witnessed this event, he reports.[6] We have already said we are ready to defend the validity of the rope trick, but we wish promptly to dissociate ourselves from any crawling dismembered parts. Dismembered once, dismembered for all time, we always say. That part has to be the fevered imagination of Edward Melton, and as far as we are concerned, he's stuck with it.

A correspondent of the *Times* of India, Siddeshur Mitter by name, in his story picked up by the *Weekly Dispatch* of 15 September 1889, described the version of the trick he had himself seen "in the broad clear light of the afternoon" in one of the villages of the Hooghly district. In this version, an assistant held a bamboo stick rigidly upright and the magician climbed it. He said he was going to search for his friend who had suddenly disappeared from a box on the ground. "He has gone to battle with Indra," the jadugar said. "Maybe he needs my help." He disappears at the end of the stick, and the assistant puts the bamboo on the ground. Then the dismembered pieces fall, all bloody—the head always last. At this, the assistant puts the pole up again and the magician descends, mourning. "Too bad. Indra slew him before I could get there." He kicks the box from which his friend had disappeared; the top flies up; and of course the friend, in excellent health, jumps out. Said the *Times,* editorially: "Is not this rather a severe strain on one's credulity, even for an Indian juggling story?" And the answer to *that* is: It depends. . . .

The rope trick is very old and very famous. According to John Godwin, who has considerable experience as a newspaperman and researcher, "the first European to mention the rope trick was Marco

6. Ibid., 1: 316–17.

Polo, who reported that he witnessed a performance of it at the court of the Mongol ruler Kublai Khan in 1289."[7] That king of travelers saw all kinds of magic in the mysterious East; indeed, he can be considered one of the founding fathers of the Mysterious East Syndrome, which John Nicholls Booth believes has been inflated beyond reason. (Booth is an accomplished American magician, former president of the Chicago Assembly of the Society of American Magicians, and the author of many books on magic. His book, *Fabulous Destinations,* already cited, was written after he took a trip to the East partly to learn all that could be discovered of the rope trick and partly to pick up new magic from its natural habitat. He came home convinced that the Orient is as far behind Europe and America in its magic as it is in its science, clinging to the same old stuff that was ancient centuries ago.)

But Marco found magicians in "Keshimur" (Kashmir) who could make idols speak, cause goblets of wine to move from the middle of the room to the speaker's table, and "also by their sorceries bring on changes of weather and produce darkness, and do a number of things so extraordinary that no one without seeing them would believe them."[8] At the emperor's palace in Chandu (Coleridge's Xanadu), the enchanters, so Marco Polo reported, if they could not prevent bad weather, at least kept it from "passing over the spot where the Emperor's palace stands."

Those who take a positive, adamant position that the rope trick is a hoax appear to rely chiefly on the failure of practically *any* reward to lure a practitioner out to perform it. Booth talked to magicians, newspapermen, public officials, religious leaders, and famous jugglers in Bombay, Calcutta, Peking, and Shanghai—and none of them even knew the name of a jadugar who might be asked to perform it. He took expensive advertising space in the *Star of India* offering 25,000 rupees (about $8,000 in 1949) to any conjurer or holy man who would do the trick. The Prince of Wales (later George V) had already tried bribing the magicians—he offered in 1902 to pay $50,000 to see the trick. Years later the famous

7. *This Baffling World*, p. 147.
8. Yule, *Marco Polo*, 1: 166.

American magician Howard Thurston offered $1,000. But neither to fellow magician nor to potentate will the conjurors attempt to show the trick. Shall we concede, then, that the trick cannot be done and has not been done?

As we have said, we think not. For the key word is "trick." At the very beginning it is admitted that the performer is making the attempt to deceive the viewer. Nobody can trick a dismembered body into reassembling. But it is possible to trick an audience, under proper conditions of lighting and with the necessary stage properties available, into thinking, believing that they have seen the dismembered limbs of a child or a man thrown down from a height. . . .

John Godwin has a terse, and to us completely satisfactory, explanation of what happens—and even with the trickery it requires an enormous amount of skill.

Those who made the money offers demanded certain conditions. Booth stipulated that the trick be performed successfully, in the open air, away from any stage set or foliage.

Obviously no jaduwallah anywhere is going to apply under those conditions, since they make the trick impossible. After all, it *is* a trick.

Godwin[9] explains that a prepared setting is necessary, a small and well-trained boy helper, at least four able assistants, and of course a very skillful chief manipulator. There has to be a thin wire of enormous tensile strength overhead between two points— rooftops, trees, post, hilltops, or whatever can be arranged. No wire, no trick. The lighting must be somewhat dusky, and as we have said, bonfires help because they flicker and change, and they attract attention to the ground. In uneven light, the high wire is entirely invisible.

The rope or chain that is thrown up has hooks attached to the end that is thrown. When the hooks catch the wire, the rope stands up—to all appearances—and its presence also helps to focus attention away from the wire.

Under the magician's voluminous cloak are hidden the dismem-

9. *This Baffling World*, pp. 150–51.

bered arms, legs, and body of a freshly killed monkey whose hair has been shaved off. The conjurer has a leather harness strapped to his back underneath the cloak. When he catches the boy, there is a flurry of activity only uncertainly seen on the ground forty feet below; the boy's screams and the dropping members are so awful that nobody sees the youngster crawl into the harness on the magician's back: people are staring at the bloody witnesses on the ground. Thus the boy comes down with the master; and when the magician is checking to make sure all the pieces are in the box or the basket—of which the lid is raised so that it temporarily shields the actions of the man and boy—the lad climbs out of the harness and jumps into the basket. The maestro kicks the basket, the boy leaps out grinning, the magician gestures and an assistant clips the high wire—and the rope is down. Nothing to it.

Of course, if one is going to enjoy the rope trick thoroughly, it must be taken as a gestalt—a *whole* situation involving a religious mendicant, a Bakhshi (Marco Polo called them Bacsis), who through his study of the tantras, or holy books, has learned how to exercise strange powers by means of dharani, mystic Indian charms. It must involve the setting—and remember the traditions of this strange and different world where the unusual, in Mr. Cabell's notable phrase, is rather more than likely to happen. We offer the analysis of John Godwin only because we think it indicates that the trick has been and can be done; but we forget that analysis just as fast as we can in order to feel the gooseflesh rise as the scene ripens.

But we don't want to *see* it done. We go along with Schweitzer: the monkey has his right to live, too; and we have reverence for that life also.

The Ordinary Taxpayer Can Neither Read nor Write

THE MAXIM: Most people graduate from high school illiterate and without being able to say what they mean in their native tongue.

WHO SAYS SO? This is a standard war cry of all freshman-English teachers and of most high school English teachers to whom the students have come from the lower grades. Joining in the chorus are many employers, whose complaints are printed in the newspapers from time to time.

IS THE MAXIM REGARDED AS A MYTH—AS NOT TRUE? Yes. Except for the persons making the complaint, everybody knows that he can say what he means in his native tongue and knows that others can, too. The maxim is just a saying. However, we put up with it because it's a good whip with which to spur students to greater endeavor.

And the truth is:

THE MAXIM IS CORRECT. If one is to judge from correspondence between the general public and almost any government agency—and the surge of mail here is a flood tide—most people cannot say what they mean. In other words, samples of language from the *folk themselves* prove the maxim. Choosing wildly at random, we offer a selection from an Office of Public Welfare in a large Arizona city (it must be understood that none of these instances has been selected for its humorous content alone, and that not one is spurious or fictitious):

"Please send me my elopement as I have a four months old baby and he is my only support and I need all I can get everyday to buy food and keep him close."

"Both sides of my parents is poor and I can't expect nothing from them as my mother has been in bed for a year with the same doctor and won't change."

"Please send my wife's form to fill out."

"I am forwarding my marriage certificate and my children. One is a mistake as you can see."

"Please find out for certain if my husband is dead as the man I am living with won't eat nothing or do nothing until he knows for sure."

"I am writing to tell you that my baby was born two years ago and he is two years old. When do I get relief?"

"In accordance with your instructions, I have given birth to twins in the enclosed envelope."

"My husband had his project cut off two weeks ago, and I haven't had any relief since."

Only the tightest grip on the reins prevents the horses from running free: the material is endless and continues to prove the truth
of the by no means mythical maxim. Most of the mail is distinctly
unclear.

The Fantasy of the Voodoo Death Curse

Being the heirs of the ages and members of a tribe which has not
only mastered control of its environment on the sun's third planet,
but has proudly tramped upon the Moon itself, 250,000 miles away,
and curiously planted the national emblem of the tribe upon that
distant juiceless surface, we are perhaps overquick to greet with a
superior smile the various superstitions of a former age of night.
For we have largely conquered the primal darkness, and in our
manmade light the demons find the atmosphere infelicitous and
inhospitable. One flick of our finger against a wall switch or the
circuit maker of a powerful flashlight and the terror and mystery
of the night are gone.

But take away our manufactured light even for a short time and
we are back in the haunted night, as those who lived through the
East Coast blackout in the early sixties will remember.

To the nonliterate native, however, who *knows* there are malig-
nant powers abroad capable of doing him mischief—especially in
the dark—and whose imagination (as shown in part by his masks)
is by no means inferior to ours, a curse can be a sentence of death.
Of a death which will meet the strictest tests of medical reality,
moreover.

If a reader should learn that his worst enemy had paid a scientist
(or other substitute for a witch doctor) to put a curse upon him,
would he wilt and lie down to die, or would he laugh until his
sides ached? Would he be terror-stricken—or amused? The answer probably is that he would be somewhat disturbed (nobody
likes threatening letters or hate calls on the telephone) but otherwise unconcerned. We don't believe in the effectiveness of such a
curse. We don't make wax dolls and torture them with pins, either.
The whole thing's a hoax, a myth. It has to be, because our entire

intellectual organization revolves around the proposition that every effect has a cause—and we cannot discern any cause in even the most complicated curse sufficient to bring physical death to a victim.

The cause is there, nevertheless; and there have been many witnesses who have observed it at work. We have known something about psychosomatic medicine for some time, and this knowledge should have prepared us for the truth in the voodoo myth—or at least the possible truth. Romantic fiction and verse have long presented us with a picture of a beautiful young—and presumably healthy—girl dying because her lover never returns. One of "the best-loved operas in the repertory"[10] is Puccini's *Madama Butterfly* (1904), in which the crisis is the death of Cio-cio-san as the result of a broken heart.

If our folklore could be host to the belief that one may die of a broken heart, why is voodoo death so hard to accept? Incidentally, a nine-year study of the relationship of emotional stress to longevity reported recently that data developed by the Tavistock Institute of Human Relations in London indicates that grief can, indeed, kill. Within six months of the decease of their wives, a significant enough number of widowers died *over* the number of death expectancies to permit Dr. C. Murray Parkes to say: "It is possible that emotional stress acts by altering the consumption of fats, sugars, coffee or tobacco, all of which have been shown to be statistically related to mortality from coronary artery disease." The death rate among these widowers was 40 percent higher than expected without the grief factor.[11]

The late Professor Walter B. Cannon of Harvard, after a close study of the reports of eyewitnesses and other evidence, became convinced of the reality of voodoo death. He began his study as a skeptic, expecting to find signs of secret poisoning or other natural causes of death. They did not appear. He found that "the implicit faith which a native cherishes in the magical powers of his tribal magician" can also "result in cures which exceed anything recorded

10. David Ewen, *The Complete Book of 20th Century Music,* 2d ed. (Englewood Cliffs, N.J.: Prentice-Hall, Inc., 1959), p. 299.
11. Boston *Herald Traveler,* 6 July 1969.

by the faith-healing disciples of more cultured communities."[12] First is the deep faith.

Second, as soon as it is known that a man is under a curse from the tribal magician, he becomes taboo in some tribes. "All people who stand in kinship relation with him withdraw their sustaining support. This means everyone he knows—all his fellows. . . ."[13] He sees them preparing for his death—and death is his only escape. It sometimes follows very rapidly—in twenty-four hours.

Cannon pointed out that this phenomenon occurs among "human beings so primitive, so superstitious, so ignorant that they are bewildered strangers in a hostile world. Instead of knowledge they have a fertile and unrestricted imagination. . . ." Added to this is a fixed assurance that death *will* intervene if magic is practiced against an individual or if he has inadvertently violated some taboo; and, third, the victim knows that all his fellow tribesmen believe the same thing. As a result, he refuses all food and drink in his terror; he pines away; his strength and his will to live flow out of him; and he dies within a matter of days or weeks.

Cannon himself had investigated the action of the autonomic nervous system, "the so-called sympathetic or sympathico-adrenal division," whose target organs are the viscera and cardiovascular system, serving to "maintain a relatively constant state in the flowing blood and lymph," and which acts without our will being involved at all. When the organism faces a threat, sugar is liberated from the liver, "accelerating the heart, contracting certain blood vessels, discharging adrenaline and dilating the bronchioles." And if the condition of fear continues, "dire results may ensue." The overworked sympathetico-adrenal system becomes responsible for a reduction in the volume of the circulating blood, and thus there is a gradual fall of blood pressure. (He observed parallel conditions in wounded soldiers under shock in World War I.) Deterioration then occurs in the heart "and also in the nerve centers which hold the blood vessels in moderate contraction." Continuation of the emotional stress

---

12. " 'Voodoo' Death," *American Anthropologist* 44, no. 2 (April–June 1942), pp. 169–70.

13. Ibid., p. 173.

ends by killing, and "death can be explained as due to a failure of essential organs to receive a sufficient supply of blood or, specifically, a sufficient supply of oxygen, to maintain their functions."[14]

Again and again Cannon found parallels medically between the condition induced by prolonged fear, and wound shock in human beings. If another factor is added—prolonged lack of food or water —the situation is exacerbated, among both the wounded and the cursed. Thus, according to Cannon, death from "voodoo curse" is death from a true state of shock.

Among the reports he examines—and they run from a voodoo death among the South American Tupinambas Indians observed by Soares de Souza in 1587 to a vivid description of an Australian aborigine who discovers that he is being cursed, which was witnessed by Dr. Herbert Basedow in 1925—the most dramatic seems to us to be the case of a young black on a journey in the Congo who stayed overnight with a friend. In this tribe, a wild hen is taboo for all immature members of the group. This is a ban which must be inviolably observed. At breakfast the host served wild hen; but he told his young visitor that it was something else, and the young man ate heartily and went away with gratitude in his heart. The wild hen, far from poisoning him, sustained him on his journey until late in the day. It was some years later that the two men met again. The former host, apparently not only a confirmed skeptic but a dedicated practical joker as well, asked the young man if he would come and join him in a feast of wild hen. The young black, horrified, said he had been enjoined against that food by a wizard; wild hen was taboo for him. Whereupon the older man, with great laughter, asked why he observed the rules so strictly *now*, when he had enjoyed the wild hen a few years ago on his journey? When the younger man became convinced that this was the truth, he began to shake like a halyard in the wind; the fear truly gripped him; and he was dead within twenty-four hours—from shock.

Voodoo death is no myth![15]

14. Ibid., p. 178.
15. For further material on this subject see "Critique and Cavil," *Journal of the American Medical Association*, 195 (1966): 143; J. C. Baker, "Scared to Death," *Journal of the American Medical Association*, 198, no. 12 (1966): 176.

Murder by voodoo magic is not just a legend, but is the truth. Having said this, we emphasize that it is the truth only in very special cases: only in instances where the persuasion is strong enough to overcome the desperate grasp on life which all organisms have. In short, the victim's mind must surrender wholly to the suggestion; otherwise, it wouldn't work. Until we are convinced that voodoo curses can and may kill us, they are powerless against us.

In an oblique way this brings up the whole field of the psychology of martyrs and of suicides and of those who *wish* to die—really wish, not merely say hysterically, "I wish I were dead." The acceptance of destruction by the mind willing to believe in the curse is not confined to Haiti or some nonliterate savage tribe: it can happen much closer to home, as was illustrated a few months ago by Mrs. Sheila Shearer of Pangbourne, England, who apparently died of shock from a nightmare. She was healthy and young (thirty-one), the mother of a young son, Andrew. But she used to have terrible dreams about her son, and told her husband, Hugh, about them from time to time, shuddering at the recollection. Then came the November night when the nightmare became reality for her, and she was shouting and fighting in her sleep as Hugh tried to awaken her—and she died of shock before he could succeed. Such, at least, was the judgment of the coroner.[16]

The Compulsion to Speak

There has been a great deal of learned speculation recently over the question of communication between animals and men. Do animals speak to other animals of the same species? Do they converse with animals of different species? In particular, are they able to give and receive messages to and from humans? Can we learn to understand what they are saying to each other and to us?

To many sober and intelligent people—possibly to most of those who make up the sturdy, no-nonsense, matter-of-fact yeomanry of our society—any such communication is pure myth. Beyond such language as a whistle, meaning "heel" or "come to me," along with

16. *New York Times* (from Reuters), 7 November 1969.

purrs and growls and a few primitive, nonliterate signals and perhaps half a dozen words used as syllables of command, we are
likely to doubt any breaking down of the language barriers.

Yet our legends, folk tales, fables, and myths are full of examples
in which the communication is precise and exact—not some general
feeling of welcome or danger being exchanged, but explicit directions, very likely given by a friendly fox to a prince on a quest telling him, in orderly detail, the steps he must take to break a magic
spell. . . . Or there is a magic cloak or hat, or something one eats—
and suddenly one understands the language of bird and beast. Our
own beloved Hiawatha "Learned of every bird its language,/
Learned their names and all their secrets,/ Talked with them
whene'er he met them. . . ." In some versions of the story of Solomon, whose "wisdom surpassed the wisdom of all the people of the
east, and all the wisdom of Egypt" (I Kings 4: 30), the great king
spoke, not "of" beasts and fowl, but "to" them; and Konrad Lorenz says, "I feel inclined to accept it as a truth. . . . I can do it
myself, and without the aid of magic, black or otherwise."[17] Lorenz
does not mean that he has had conversations with his jackdaws and
other friends of the animal world; he means that if it is conceded
that certain animals have a signal-code response typical of their
species, one can understand their language if one is able to learn
the vocabulary. This is not too hard to concede: a dog scratching at
the kitchen door is saying as plainly as anyone could, "Please let me
in." The mystery of the deeper myth, which science is presently engaged in attempting to solve—especially with dolphins because of
their large and complicated brains—is still seen through a glass,
darkly, and the skeptics still smile, as did Modell in a *New Yorker*
cartoon (22 March 1969): he showed a man holding a drink in his
hand, ensconced in his easy chair, feet on a hassock, glaring angrily
at the family dog, who is sitting on the floor facing him and glaring
right back. The caption: "Well, what's eating you? I got your chair
or something?"

An inkling of what lies within the unexplored area of language

17. Konrad Z. Lorenz, *King Solomon's Ring* (New York: Thomas Y. Crowell Co.,
1952), p. xiii.

between men and animals is hinted at when our language usage to an animal friend of long standing is changed radically. At the Hawthornden State Hospital in Akron, Ohio, there was a horse which for years pulled a cart around the grounds while his master, a mental patient who gave his orders in Polish, cleaned up trash and rubbish. Toward the end of 1960, the patient was transferred—and the horse became practically useless. The animal, not understanding orders in English, and hearing nothing that made any sense to him, had to be led around by the bridle for a while, like a beginner.[18]

More dramatic was the case of the dog Nurmi. When he was about a year old, Nurmi was purchased from a Finnish farmer near Fitchburg, Massachusetts, by a Russian immigrant from the Carpathian Mountains, a man named Kobotchnik. Mrs. Kobotchnik, fearful that her daughters would never find husbands if they bore such a name, pressured her husband into getting his name legally changed to Cabot. And the dog fared no better. "Who ever heard of a dog named Nurmi? . . . This ain't Finland, this is America. . . . So she and the girls started to call the dog Buster."[19]

Apparently the dog thought they were scolding, and being a friendly dog, he found it very hard to take. His spirit sagged, he stopped running, and squeaked instead of barking. Finally he ran away—back to the farm at Fitchburg, where he fully recovered; but he would not permit his former master to approach him or touch him.

This is still not complex speech, of course; it is communication on the signal-code level. Dr. Lilly is fairly sure that beyond this point, "no interspecies communication has been achieved with primates having smaller brains than man's," and that "complex speech acquisition seems related to brain weights of 800 to 1000 grams, but no smaller."[20]

18. Boston *Traveler*, 1 December 1960.

19. Louis Adamic, *What's Your Name?* (New York: Harper & Brothers, 1942), p. 4.

20. John C. Lilly, *Man and Dolphin* (Garden City, N.Y.: Doubleday & Co., 1961), p. 20; and Ashley Montagu and John C. Lilly, *The Dolphin in History* (Los Angeles: Clark Memorial Library, University of California, 1963), p. 49.

For this reason "the Parret of Indie," although he "will counter-faite redily a mans speach: what wordes they heare, those commonly they pronounce,"[21] nevertheless is not communicating anything more significant than a cheerful spirit, such as one would like to assume is behind any bird's utterance.

Moreover, communication does not necessarily require *speech*. Two psychologists at the University of Nevada recently reported a possible breakthrough toward communication between man and monkeys by using the gestural sign language of the deaf. They managed to teach a baby chimpanzee a repertoire of thirty of these signs in a little less than a year.[22] Communication with fish—particularly with sharks—has been repeatedly demonstrated by Arthur Myrberg, a marine biologist attached to the University of Miami and recently at work on North Bimini in the Bahamas. He placed a sound projector on the floor of the ocean in sixty feet of water; and when he pressed the button, a signal was given out that seemed to any carnivorous fish within hearing like the sounds made by fish feeding or being attacked. This sound is full of the promise of action to the shark. "Within half a minute, the TV screen came alive with thrashing sharks, groupers, snappers and other large inhabitants of the deep."[23]

One can even have a language without *sound,* as various sign languages and the screen acting of Charlie Chaplin demonstrate. One of the best-known books on this phenomenon is *The Silent Language* by Edward T. Hall (Doubleday, 1959). Here an example is given of the American farmer who was part of a team to bring new technological knowledge to Egyptian producers. At one point he asked the Arab what sort of yield he expected of a certain planting, and the Arab, insulted, refused to speak further to him. The silent language at work here is that an Arab thinks only God can foretell the future, and any man who tries to is insane. The

21. John Marplet's *Naturall Historie* (*1567*), quoted in *Shakespeare's England* (Oxford: The Clarendon Press, 1926), 1: 477.

22. R. Allen Gardner and Beatrice T. Gardner, "Teaching Sign Language to a Chimpanzee." *Science* 165 (15 August 1969): 664–672.

23. *Time*, 20 June 1969.

American was calling the sanity of the Arab into question, quite gratuitously.

We all know, of course, that it is not merely verbal expression, but also tone of voice, attitude of body, the look in the eyes, and so forth that makes for communication. As Ulysses said of the Lady Cressida when she was brought to the Grecian camp and strangely disturbed that warrior: "There's language in her eye, her cheek, her lip,/ Nay, her foot speaks. . . ." (*Troilus and Cressida,* IV. v. 38) Sometimes the facial expression is even more important than the words. It was so in that famous frontier incident at the card table when Trampas, having lost heavily to the Virginian, threw in his cards and called his opponent a son of a bitch. Owen Wister did not use that term, any more than did anyone else writing in 1902, when Dr. Bowdler's influence was still strong and decent novels were written for persons of sensibility; but it is the only possible epithet for the occasion. The answer of the Virginian, his hand quivering over his gun, is an all-time classic: "When you call me that, smile!"

Freud, indeed, held that with or without spoken language, man is revealing himself ceaselessly, whether he intends doing so or not. None of us can keep our secrets, he held: if our lips are silent, then we are chattering with our fingers or in some other way betraying ourselves.

Viewing language in its broadest sense—gesture, signal, and verbal—the statement is now being made that communication between men and animals is no longer a myth; but that does not mean that man's vocal language sounds will ever be identical with those of other species. Dolphins, for instance, communicate mostly "in the band of frequencies from about eight kilocycles to 20 kilocycles by means of whistles and sonic clicks. . . . We have reliable evidence that they can hear at least to 200 kilocycles."[24] But "the language of animals is being decoded and understood . . . by the most rigorous scientific methods, and animals—apes and dolphins—are being taught to speak with human voices."[25] Apparently the progress is

24. Montagu and Lilly, *Dolphin in History,* p. 43.
25. Elisabeth Mann Borgese, *The Language Barrier: Beasts and Men* (New York: Holt, Rinehart & Winston, 1968), p. 3.

beyond doubt: "The question is settled: there can be, in the mind of an animal, a certain association between human language on the one hand and objects or actions on the other."[26]

It is to be hoped that as mankind makes progress in its deeper communication with other species—even if it never reaches the level of sparkling after-dinner conversation over the cigars—progress will also be made in communicating honestly and candidly with our own species. "Of the nearly four thousand languages spoken by mankind on this planet today, only a dozen have international or cultural significance," according to Lincoln Barnett;[27] and English has attained the leadership position among *those*. But in terms of real communication, we still have a long road to travel. Not long ago an American woman in London wanted to find a hardware store where she could buy a dishpan—but nobody could help her. It finally developed that she wanted an ironmonger's shop, where she could get a washing-up basin. And when she wanted garters, she had to learn to ask for suspenders. . . .

Language Is to Tell?

Since human beings have the minds of men, it follows that their thought is, as the phrase goes, anthropomorphic. It is difficult to understand why the term should carry a derogatory undertone or a suggestion of ingenuousness: if we had the minds of fish, we would think in a fishlike manner and one could call our thinking piscatorial. But there should be nothing umbrageous about it. No apologies required. Thus to the intended canard "Now you're falling into anthropomorphic thinking," one replies quite reasonably, "Could anything be more natural?"

Part of the business of anthropomorphic thinking is that we tend to see purposes in things and actions. Here is an ax. It was made to chop with. Here is the wing of a bird. It was made to fly with. Here is an alphabet. It was created to spell words with. Here is a

---

26. Jacques Graven, *Non-Human Thought: The Mysteries of the Animal Psyche* (New York: Stein & Day, 1967), p. 180.

27. *The Treasure of Our Tongue* (New York: Alfred A. Knopf, 1964), p. 5.

language. It was made to tell things with—to narrate, to explain, to communicate, to clarify.

All those things are partly true, but none of them made its appearance with a *fiat lux* instantaneousness: I want to chop; I'll make an ax. Let us make a bird; he must have wings. These things came about gradually. With language we can communicate; but language was not invented Tuesday morning after a frustrating Monday. Men have tried to explain the origins of language with various theories, known as the bow-wow, the ding-dong, the yo-heave-ho, the pooh-pooh, the tally-ho and the wig-wag hypotheses among others,[28] and each one has some truth in it. The human purpose holds: to teach, to instruct, to record more and more effectively—and gradually our signals become simpler and clearer. . . .

But the purpose of this section is to challenge the myth that language exists to explain and record. That is in part true; but language is also used to conceal, to hide, to obscure, and to protect. It is used to mislead and obfuscate (as in politics). It is used to soothe and pacify, to arouse and irritate, to feed the ego of the speaker whose pleasure in the sound of his own voice has hypnotized him. . . . And it is used to gain time, and for many purposes other than sheer communication.

The evidence is on every hand. What is to be said of a paragraph like the following, which appears in a book by a distinguished psychologist seeking to explain to teachers how to motivate children who have reading problems, and by this motivation overcome some of the problems?

Perhaps the task of developing proper motivation is best seen, at least in a nutshell form, as limiting the manipulation of extrinsic factors to that of keeping homeostatic need and exteroceptive drive low, in favor of facilitating basic information processing to minimize accurate anticipation of reality.[29]

28. Noah Jonathan Jacobs, *Naming Day in Eden* (New York: Macmillan Co., 1959); Ashley Montagu, *Man: His First Two Million Years* (New York: Columbia University Press, 1969), pp. 126–29.

29. Joseph McVicker Hunt, *Children with Reading Problems* (New York: Basic Books, 1969), quoted by Jerome Beatty in *Saturday Review*, 19 July 1969.

This is *communicating?* The editor must have been taking his coffee break. Goodness, what could Professor Hunt have been thinking of? For certainly it could not have been at the top of his mind to clarify and explain. . . .

We like better the frank acknowledgment of the group chairman who, after several years of periodic meetings, finally concluded the report of the collective conclusions of the group, as follows:

> We have not succeeded in solving all our problems; indeed, we sometimes feel we have not completely solved any of them. The answers we have found have only served to raise a whole set of new questions. In some ways we feel we are as confused as ever, but we think we are confused on a higher level and about more important things.

Occasionally an excellent burlesque exposes infirmities which conventional usage demands should be obscured or hidden completely. Especially vulnerable to such parody is the corporation annual report in an unfortunate year. The stockholders must be told embarrassing news with the delicacy with which a poet describes a pimple on a lady's face. Readers must be left with bad news couched in language usually reserved for those viewing the procedures through rose-colored spectacles. An effective travesty of the formal annual report—after an unhappy fiscal year—was published, with simulated photographs, maps, graphs, tables, and portraits of important personnel, in November 1969, under the title *Annual Reprot.*[30] The letters of the title were cut out to form a stencil plate, and the first words the stockholders received inside were these: "ERRATUM. The words 'Annual Reprot' on the cover should read as follows: 'Annual Report.' The error, regrettably, was not detected until the conclusion of the press run. Your management felt that the sizable cost of reprinting the cover in this expensive process was not warranted. The saving, of course, will be passed along to you, the stockholder." Thus we are given a hint of the catastrophe to come, since no company still solvent would issue such a misprint on the cover of the Annual Report. Now come some fan-

---

30. William Zinsser (text) and James Stevenson (drawings), *Annual Report of the National Refractory & Brake Company* (New York: Harper & Row, 1969).

tastic drawings of enormously impressive shapes and shadows, with such captions as "The heart of the process is the reactor," "To defend our freedom," and "One of our largest industrial customers." The Company then addresses the Stockholder:

1968 was a year of adjustment for your company.

The general slowdown in the American economy resulted in a softening of demand for the products of the National Refractory & Brake Company and a consequent reduction in worldwide unit sales. Unexpectedly high start-up costs were also incurred—notably, in the prototype development of sophisticated capacitors—which contributed to a marked reversal of anticipated gain in 1968.

On balance, however, it was a year of progress. Strong product line in several of your company's new divisions—i.e., anhydrous petrochemicals—found public acceptance indicating significant movement toward profitability. Nor should we minimize the generally healthy performance of the Wholesale Price Index and the decreasing scarcity of Euro-Dollars.

Nevertheless your management concerted its efforts during 1968 on a realignment of production facilities to increase peak-day delivery capacity and to optimize negative factors occurring in the inventory accumulation program. Earnings for the year were $68,412,677, or $1.5 per share, down approximately 31% from $98,612,409, or $2.17 per share, in 1967.

This is language to inform; but it is also language to hide behind; and the thing that makes it so excruciatingly perfect is that the parody sounds precisely like a formal, serious report, such as we have all seen from time to time.

When the shoemaker goes to the ball, he looks at the shoes, according to the old saw. Each occupation and profession, by the same token, has its special jargon which can be used for increased precision, as when one diagnostician confers with another in the face of a medical analysis; or to keep a secret, as when a member of the guild confers with another in cant terms (thieves' slang being one of the most famous). Actually the prescription of a doctor, even in our own day, informing the pharmacist as to the mixture he wants the patient to have, is written usually in the secret code where the Rx is an invocation to Jupiter Rex to make the prescription effective, and "three" is written "iij," and so on. Instances of language to hide behind can be found in medicine, religion, and particularly law, where the language, in its attempt to be all-inclusive and inescapably precise, becomes, to the lay understanding, an incomprehensible babble.

The military mind produces a similar patois, as does "Federal Prose," used in government circles. Thus we find in straightforward English the statement "Too many cooks spoil the broth," which in Federal Prose might become: "Undue single function involves deterioration of quality in the resultant product as compared with the product of the labor of an exact sufficiency of personnel."[31] "Primitive groping," our authorities assure us, "is here replaced by scientific method" and the new version gives the producer "the quiet glow of an inner consummation."

We can expect this process to continue in any living language, especially one which, like English, must take into account so many new "things" like antiballistic missiles and capsules to the moon, along with so many new attitudes, such as the Resistance to war, poverty, and things caused by the generation gap. The word "rap" for "discuss" is a sample of the type of neologism which at first has its own cant meaning and status and later becomes familiar as an accepted part of the language.

In what has been called the fungoid growth of jargon, the official language of the governing classes, otherwise known to philologists as Democratic Gobbledygook and Hieratic Federalese, threatens to displace not alone meaning but also the English language.[32] Federal prose has been defined as "that form of non-metrical composition, apparently English, which can be invariably interpreted as meaning and/or not meaning and/or less than, rather than what, it seems to mean."[33]

31. James R. Masterson and Wendell Brooks Phillips, *Federal Prose: How to Write in and/or for Washington* (Chapel Hill: University of North Carolina Press, 1948), p. 10.

32. For a delightful discussion of this subject see the editorial "Anti-Disincentivism," Washington *Post*, 15 October 1951. Also, Eric Partridge's excellent introduction to "Vigilans," *Chamber of Horrors: A Glossary of Official Jargon Both English and American* (London: André Deutsch, 1952).

33. Masterson and Phillips, *Federal Prose*.

Bureaucrats in all governments seem to fall victim to the same disorder of gobbledygook, becoming infected with the virus of self-importance and pomposity. This is what Maury Maverick thinks he may have had in mind when he coined the word in 1944. "People ask me where I got gobbledygook. I do not know. It must have come in a vision. Perhaps I was thinking of the old bearded turkey gobbler back in Texas, who was always gobbledy-gobbling and strutting with ludicrous pomposity. At the end of this gobble there was a sort of gook."[34]

Consider this extract from an interim report issued by a South African commission:

Legal opinion has been taken in regard to whether, in the event of such amendments being made, there would be any possibility of a successful claim being lodged against superannuation benefits by any party other than the Administration in respect of any amount that might be outstanding at the time of a servant's retirement or death, or of his leaving the service for any reason, in respect of properties purchased from monies obtained from some source other than the Administration, or on any other account. The opinion is to the effect that no difficulty should be experienced in drafting the proposed amendments to cover the phases mentioned and in such a way as to limit the right to reimbursement from benefits accruing under the Act, to the Administration only, and solely for the purpose contemplated."[35]

Of this passage, Professor Greig wryly remarks, "All my attempts to translate this into English have failed." As, indeed, they might.

In the case of legal language, we realize that it is necessary to avoid any possible technical fault in any written instrument and hence the drafts of these documents may strike the layman as considerably more labyrinthine than necessary—sometimes ludicrously so; but the legally trained mind understands that it is necessary to eliminate any and all ambiguity and at the same time cover every eventuality occurring or likely to occur under the rubric at issue. So here we have an authentic instance in which language is deliberately

34. *New York Times*, 21 May 1944.
35. Quoted in J. Y. T. Greig, *Keep Up the Fight for English* (Johannesburg, 1946).

used to communicate from expert to expert, regardless of where it leaves the ordinary citizen. "When appellate courts were reversing convictions because of some technical fault in the indictment those who drafted those documents were careful to omit no detail, in utter disregard of redundancy or syntax."[36] Thus the indictment of James H. Costley, charging that "with malice aforethought" he intentionally shot and killed Julia Hawkes (118 Mass. 1, 1875) took 324 words. And the coroner's inquest (2 August 1804) in the Hamilton-Burr "interview" was equally sedulous. These good and lawful men

. . . charged to enquire for the people of the State of New York, when, where, how and by what means the said Alexander Hamilton came to his death, do upon their oath say that Aaron Burr, late of the Eighth Ward of the said city in the said county, Esquire and Vice President of the United States, not having the fear of God before his eyes, but being moved and seduced by the instigation of the Devil, on the eleventh of July in the year last aforesaid, with force and arms, in the County of Bergen and State of New Jersey in and upon the said Alexander Hamilton in the peace of God and of the people, the said State of New Jersey, then and there being, feloniously wilfully and of his malice aforethought, did make an assault, and that the said Aaron Burr, a certain pistol of the value of one dollar charged and loaded with gun powder and a leaden bullet which he the said Aaron Burr, then and there had and held in his right hand, to, at, and against the right-side of the belly of the said Alexander Hamilton did then and there shoot off and discharge, by means whereof he, the said Aaron Burr, feloniously, wilfully and of his malice aforethought, did then and there give unto him the said Alexander Hamilton, with the leaden bullet aforesaid so as beforesaid shot off and discharged out of the pistol aforesaid by force of the gun powder aforesaid upon the right side of the belly of him the said Alexander Hamilton a little above the hip, one mortal wound, penetrating the belly of him the said Alexander Hamilton of which said mortal wound he the said Alexander Hamilton, from the said eleventh day of July in the year aforesaid, until the twelfth day of July in the same year,

36. Edwin Powers, *Crime and Punishment in Early Massachusetts, 1620–1692* (Boston: Beacon Press, 1966), p. 560.

as well in the County of Bergen in the State of New Jersey, aforesaid, as also at the Eighth Ward of the City of New York in the County of New York aforesaid did languish and languishing did live; on which 12th day of July . . . of the mortal wound aforesaid died. . . .[37]

It is fairly certain that legalese is not written with the intention of obscuring meaning, but of identifying, defining, specifying, and enclosing meaning; yet to the layman, confusion results, and therefore we include it in the classification of language that hides, as any ritual speech conceals, meaning.

Euphemisms form another class of language which, while its primary intention may not be to hide or deceive, tends to make the hard lines of reality considerably softer and more amorphous. The occupation of garbage collector, for example, refers to an entirely respectable and necessary service without which large communities could not live in health. But swill collecting is associated with discarded and rotting—hence stinking—waste food, filth, and foulness. Hence, by popular leveling, we find the word "garbician" coming into the language—at least as a humorous suggestion in a *New Yorker* cartoon; the word is not listed in the new American Heritage Dictionary or any of Eric Partridge's books on slang nor in Webster III. It is of record, however, that Daniel Griskus, offered the job of supervisor of garbage disposal in Waterbury, Connecticut, said he would accept if the city changed the title to "Superintendent of Used Food Collection," and the city agreed.[38] In the same field, a garage mechanic calls himself "an automotive internist,"[39] napalm becomes "incinder-jell,"[40] rat catcher becomes "exterminating engineer,"[41] the river where a factory dumps its waste is called the "receiving waters," a term which is supposed to

---

37. Harold C. Syrett and Jean G. Cooke, eds., *Interview in Weehawken: The Burr-Hamilton Duel as Told in the Original Documents* (Middletown, Conn.: Wesleyan University Press, 1960), p. 156.
38. *Time*, 8 March 1948.
39. *Newsweek*, 6 May 1968.
40. *New York Review*, 3 May 1967.
41. H. L. Mencken, *The American Language* (New York: Alfred A. Knopf, 1936), p. 284.

obscure the horror of pollution and dead fish,[42] and in a campus riot, the capture and occupation of a college building is called "liberating" it. Perhaps the ultimate was the Nazi phrase *endgültige Lösung,* "final solution," meaning the obliteration of the Jews.

Clearly one could continue indefinitely pointing out the use of language for purposes other than to inform or to relate or narrate. Printed advertising is a rich field, to say nothing of TV; but here we would find a sharp difference between the lay mind and the professional. Granville Hicks, layman, said: "Advertising men use language not to tell the truth but to make lies palatable."[43] That statement is surely debatable. We don't mean by this that ads tell the truth; what we mean is that when advertising men talk shop among themselves—as they do in their own trade magazines—they emphasize the necessity of "credibility," not palatability: if the ad will be *believed,* it will be effective, or stands a chance of being effective. John Betjeman in a satirical mood once compiled a glossary of publishers' blurb phrases—not that publishers are the worst offenders in deceptive advertising; surely they are far from it. Betjeman, however, was ready to believe that it is standard among blurb writers to use certain phrases automatically, while they are thinking something quite different. For example, "Has long been known as an authority" really means "Has written one other book on this subject." And "The world-famous authority" means "Has written two books on this subject." "Fully illustrated" means "More than one picture." "This best-selling writer is well up to her usual form" means "This silly book is just like her last one."[44]

To Confucius, "The whole aim of speech is to be understood" (*Analects* 15:40), and we are inclined to adopt that ideal. In any event it's a great advance over dactylology (the art of communicating ideas by signs made with the fingers). In the long run, the myth that language has the end and purpose of clarifying and explaining has truth in it—but that is not the whole truth.

42. "Waterways, Waste and Words," *New York Times,* 20 October 1969.
43. *Saturday Review,* 5 November 1966.
44. "Blurbs," *Time and Tide* (London), 21 October 1950.

Black and White, Simple and Orderly

When we were born, our language was waiting here for us; and so of course we took it for granted. It seemed a handy tool, a likely utility, and as we grew more familiar with it we saw clearly that every word has a definite and nondebatable meaning, a certain pronunciation, and an established spelling. Our formal education gave further proof of these obvious facts, and we grew up perfectly certain that every word has one meaning, one spelling, one pronunciation—and whenever there is a dispute as to what the correct rendition is, one has recourse to a dictionary and the argument is at an end. It took us some time to see the rips and tears in this garment of belief; indeed, we resisted the vision because life is more certain, more comfortable, and more predictable when things are black and white, simple and orderly, and no argument.

But, alas, our language had been in use for some years and had already reached a stage of sophistication where the simple formula "one thing, one name" had been superseded by a system where often enough one word meant several things depending on the context. And our language—English, that is—had proved itself so admirable a tool to deal with the universe that "300 million people—nearly one in ten—employ English as their primary language" and twice that number can be reached by it to some extent.[45] Our speech was dealing with an infinity of things and doing it with a limited number of words. To select at random, "pair" can mean two things of a kind; a couple or brace; in politics, two opponents agreeing not to vote; it can mean to join in couples or, transitively, to form a pair. In the spoken language, the same sound gives "pare," to cut away the skin of a fruit or vegetable; and "pear," the fruit.

There are enough of these words to constitute a certain amount of confusion; but upon careful reflection we begin to see that the ideal language in which one thing has one name and each word

45. Lincoln Barnett, *The Treasure of Our Tongue* (New York: Alfred A. Knopf, 1964), p. 3.

a *perfectly* fixed meaning would be impossible as an aid in communication. The price of fixity would be unintelligibility, as F. C. S. Schiller has indicated. "For if a word has a perfectly fixed meaning, it could be used only once and never again. . . ."[46] If he used "Nero" to refer to the Emperor, then he could not later use it to refer to his dog. "It is evident that the intellectual strain of continuously inventing new words would be intolerable, and that the chances of being understood would be very small."

The confusion mounts somewhat, of course, when one finds the very same word meaning different things, like "fast." A swift hound is fast. But a horse tied to a hitching post is also fast. If the color in one's socks is fast, it will not run. To go without food is to fast. It used to be that a woman with makeup and smoking a cigarette was fast. Yet one could get lost in the fastness of the desert. Ripley in one of his "Believe It or Not" features gave ten meanings for the letter X: Roman ten; cross of an illiterate signature; a deposed ruler; an unknown quantity; the gas xenon; the X ray used in medicine; Christmas; a kiss at the end of a letter; the monarch Xerxes; and the spot where the body was discovered.

But perhaps we ought not to demand an increase in the number of words available until we have used up what's already here. And that we will never do. Webster II (1934) unabridged "has but a total of six hundred thousand words."[47] Webster III (1961) was cut down to 450,000, with the removal from the general vocabulary of many items previously included—such as a gazetteer and biographical material.[48] The Random House unabridged reduced the total again, and finally, as the sixth decade of our century began to come to a close, we seemed ready to settle for a working desk dictionary of about 155,000 entries—the number selected both by the *Random House College Dictionary* and the *American Heritage Dictionary*. (*Webster's Collegiate* carried 130,000.)

What kind of job can one accomplish with only 155,000 words? When there is an infinite universe to deal with, especially! Have

46. *Logic for Use* (New York: Harcourt, Brace, 1930), p. 57.
47. Irving J. Lee, *Language Habits in Human Affairs* (New York: Harper & Brothers, 1941), p. 32.
48. "From the Bookshelf," *Christian Science Monitor*, 9 April 1963.

we not deliberately impoverished ourselves? Have simplification
and sophistication gone too far? We could work out some arm-
bands and start a revolt. . . .

An examination of Shakespeare, who was language master to
the gods by general agreement, shows that he "used less than twenty
thousand different words in his plays."[49] Would he have been more
eloquent if he had used twice as many? As it stands, there are several words on every page of Shakespeare that today's educated
reader cannot understand—at least, the man on the street can't.
Largely that is because the expressions have gone out of use, have
become archaic, and we have replaced them with words needed in
our own culture which Shakespeare could not even guess at. He
would have no idea at all of what a ufologist is, for example. Or
what branch of science is called olfatronics. Any more than we
have any idea what a tucket is, or a fancy-monger. Not to keep the
reader in suspense, a ufologist is a flying saucer buff—"ufo" meaning, as most everyone knows, "unidentified flying object." As far
as we can tell, ufologist was first used in *The New Yorker,* 9 April
1966. Olfatronics is chemical surveillance: *smelling* out the presence
of the enemy in warfare. The technique was used in Vietnam and
was described in the *New York Times* of 16 May 1967. A tucket is
a flourish on the trumpets, often used in Shakespeare to announce
an important entrance. A fancy-monger was a love merchant, a
procurer. Individual word changes of this kind are completely fascinating to the enthusiast and probably equally boring to many
others; so we will content ourselves at this point by reminding our
readers that in Old Testament times, *stoned* meant executed, probably for blasphemy, by having rocks thrown at one; in Elizabethan
English it meant castrated; and in today's slang it means dead
drunk—or did until very recently.

We have three vocabularies: speaking, writing, and reading. It
is easy to see why the speaking vocabulary is smallest: in ordinary
speech, one is isolated from such aids as counsel with a friend or
adviser, a dictionary or thesaurus, a reference work giving facts
and figures, or anything else—in talk, one stands on one's own and

49. Lee, *Language Habits,* p. 32.

uses only the resources which have been stored up and can be called to memory. And if the talk is at all controversial or involves emotional concomitants, memory is likely to falter and one ends up by stuttering what few inane words one can reach for. The writing vocabulary has been estimated at something like seven times as effective; and the reading vocabulary at twice that—which makes sense, because even if one does not know all the words on a page, the context helps us fill in and we can report on the meaning of the page with a little guesswork. For example, if the only meaning in my experience for "tumbler" were "drinking glass" and I came to the sentence "The tumbler accomplished four backward somersaults blindfolded and won great applause for his dexterity," I could not conceivably apply my former understanding of the word; but surely one could fill in from the context and conclude that a tumbler is also a human being and probably an acrobat.

It has been estimated that the average person—that dim and shapeless character—has a speaking vocabulary of about seven hundred words; a writing vocabulary of something like five thousand words; and a reading vocabulary of about ten thousand words. And it has been estimated that a knowledge of forty-three words would cover half of the variety used in any ordinary conversation.[50] These figures may seem ridiculous to the reader meeting them for the first time; but if he will merely note them and watch for opportunities to check them against his own findings, their folly may seem less.

In the beautiful new *American Heritage Dictionary* there is an introductory article which reports from a computer analysis conducted at Brown University that of the more than a million words comprising the "corpus of present-day edited American English"— five hundred samples of fifteen types of prose writing—exactly 50,406 *different* words were used.[51] If all these authors, writing in their own way on so many different subjects for a million words, utilized only one-twentieth of the total that were different, then they must have repeated nineteen-twentieths of the words they used. From this it seems possible to assume that none of us is going

50. *Christian Science Monitor,* 20 March 1945.
51. *American Heritage Dictionary* (Boston: Houghton Mifflin Co., 1969), p. xxxix.

to need more than, say, fifty thousand different words for anything we are likely to compose in our lifetime. In that case, most dictionaries have three or four times as many words as we could possibly need, except for research or clarification. In the computer study, ten words were most frequently used, in this order: the, of, and, to, a, in, that, is, was, and he; and the count ran from 69,971 times for "the" down to 9,543 times for "he."

Professor I. A. Richards, the well-known exponent of Basic English, held that there are one hundred most important words—important either because they are most used or because they explain other words.[52] Perhaps, when all is said and done, we don't really need more than one hundred words. (But we are hesitant to accept the Richards list, since neither "eat" nor "food" have a place in it.)

Professor Henry Kučera, who worked with Professor W. Nelson Francis in the Brown computer analysis, told columnist Charlie Rice: "The total vocabulary of the English language is very large, but the bulk of what we say or write is made up of very few words that occur over and over again. In fact, if you know the 135 commonest words, you can recognize half of the million words we computerized."[53]

So we come back to the myth, where Irving Lee states the problem precisely: "In spite of the ease of demonstrating that a relatively few words are used to represent a vastly greater number of life facts, there persists, rather widely spread among those eager to philosophize, the curious notion that it is possible to discover the one 'real and proper' meaning of any word."[54] And of course this ties into Humpty Dumpty's classic assertion that when he used a word, it meant what he wanted it to mean, and nothing else. In that case, he ran the risk of talking only to himself; because it is the contract we make with other literate people agreeing that twelve inches equals one foot which gives "inch" and "foot" specific significance; and yet it is the context which tells which meaning we have in mind. If I say, "I have six toes on my right foot," my

52. *How to Read a Page* (New York: W. W. Norton, 1942), p. 22.
53. "Charlie Rice's Punch Bowl," *This Week Magazine,* 31 March 1968.
54. *Language Habits,* p. 35.

listener stops thinking in terms of measurement and considers matters of anatomy. He may also offer me a Barnum & Bailey employee application blank.

Certainly there are precise words to give exact meanings. For instance, "floccinaucinihilipilifaction" means precisely the action of estimating things as worthless,[55] but there are other ways of saying it, and we strongly recommend any one of them. But we can utter what is literally nonsense and still communicate intelligibly: "This is the best salad I ever put in my whole mouth," spoken to the hostess in a tone of deep appreciation will still convey the message intended.

---

55. Review of *Language on Vacation*, *Time*, 17 September 1965.

Index

72 73 74 10 9 8 7 6 5 4 3 2